200 YEARS AT
ST. JOHN'S YORK MILLS

THE OLDEST CHURCH IN TORONTO

St John's

YORK MILLS ■ ANGLICAN

To Know Christ and Make Him Known

200 YEARS AT ST. JOHN'S YORK MILLS

THE OLDEST CHURCH IN TORONTO

BY SCOTT KENNEDY
WITH ADDITIONAL MATERIAL BY JEANNE HOPKINS

EDITED BY SYLVIA McCONNELL

DUNDURN
TORONTO

Editor: Sylvia McConnell
Design: Jennifer Gallinger
Cover design: Sarah Beaudin
Printer: Marquis

Library and Archives Canada Cataloguing in Publication

Kennedy, Scott, 1952 February 22-, author
        200 years at St. John's York Mills : the oldest church in Toronto / by Scott Kennedy ; with additional material by Jeanne Hopkins ; edited by Sylvia McConnell.

Includes bibliographical references and index.
Issued in print and electronic formats.
ISBN 978-1-4597-3758-7 (paperback).--ISBN 978-1-4597-3759-4 (pdf).--ISBN 978-1-4597-3760-0 (epub)

        1. St. John's York Mills Anglican Church--History. 2. Toronto (Ont.)--Church history. I. Hopkins, Jeanne, 1939-, author II. McConnell, Sylvia, editor III. Title. IV. Title: Two hundred years at St. John's York Mills.

BX5617 T6 K46 2016   283'.71354   C2016-904368-1
                                                 C2016-904369-X

1   2   3   4   5   20   19   18   17   16

We acknowledge the support of the **Canada Council for the Arts** and the **Ontario Arts Council** for our publishing program. We also acknowledge the financial support of the **Government of Canada** through the **Canada Book Fund** and **Livres Canada Books**, and the **Government of Ontario** through the **Ontario Book Publishing Tax Credit** and the **Ontario Media Development Corporation**.

Care has been taken to trace the ownership of copyright material used in this book. The author and the publisher welcome any information enabling them to rectify any references or credits in subsequent editions.

— *J. Kirk Howard, President*

The publisher is not responsible for websites or their content unless they are owned by the publisher.

Printed and bound in Canada.

VISIT US AT
Dundurn.com | @dundurnpress | Facebook.com/dundurnpress | Pinterest.com/dundurnpress

Dundurn
3 Church Street, Suite 500
Toronto, Ontario, Canada
M5E 1M2

SCOTT KENNEDY

To my Dad and Mom,
Pete and Barbara Kennedy
(1925–2014)

Through love and hard work, they blessed me with the best
childhood imaginable, in this peaceful and beautiful corner of the
world. They supported me in everything I ever did.

AUTHOR NOTE

The artwork used on the cover of this book is the work of Alfred Joseph Casson (1898–1992), the last and youngest member of the Group of Seven. This painting of St. John's York Mills, executed by Casson in 1925, was purchased by several parishioners at auction and donated to the church in 1992. The story behind this painting is that he was inspired to paint the church while standing in the garden of the artist C.W. Jefferys, a friend of the members of the Group of Seven, who lived just down the hill from the church. This is the work of a young man who was to become one of the most iconic painters in the history of Canadian art. He was invited to join the Group of Seven in 1926 and later co-founded the Canadian Group of Painters in 1933.

A.J. Casson is buried on the grounds of the gallery of the McMichael Canadian Art Collection in Kleinburg, Ontario, which displays many of his works. The painting is held in the archives of St. John's York Mills and brought out for display on special occasions such as the church's 200th anniversary or Doors Open Toronto 2016.

TABLE OF CONTENTS

Letter to the People of St. John's from Bishop Patrick Yu   13

Letter from the Reverend Drew MacDonald   15

A Note from the Editor   17

A Letter of Congratulations from the Governor General   21

PART ONE: FROM 1966 INTO THE THIRD CENTURY   23

Introduction   25

    The Rectors and Clergy in Charge of St. John's York Mills, 1827 to 2016   27

Chapter One: Lewis Samuel Garnsworthy, Rector from 1960 to 1968   30

Chapter Two: James Francis O'Neil, Rector from 1969 to 1989   37

    The Wartime Adventures of Able Seaman James Francis O'Neil   57

    A Boat in the Churchyard   59

    The Reverend Margery Pezzack: Pioneer   60

    David Flint and the Aurora Weekends   65

Chapter Three: Hollis Hiscock, Rector from 1990 to 2007   69

    The Old Rectory   104

    Nora Marsh van Nostrand Wedd   110

    Drama at St. John's York Mills   113

Chapter Four: Dr. Drew MacDonald, Rector from 2007   117

    Anne Crosthwait, Associate Priest   143

    The   Reverend Harry Robinson   147

    The Deacons of St. John's   154

        Dr. Bruce Williams   154

        The Reverend Dr. Catherine Keating   157

Chapter Five: The Verger, Bill Dennis   162

Chapter Six: Music at St. John's   174

    Maurice White   175

    Robin Davis   176

    Boni Strang   178

    Monique Ingalls   180

    Infinitely More   181

    Patrick Dewell   184

    Rob Ellis   190

    Handbells, Chimers, and Ringers   194

        Joanne Flint   195

        Carolyn Martin   199

    In Conclusion   205

Chapter Seven: The Women of St. John's   208

Chapter Eight: Walter Seymour Allward   216

Chapter Nine: C.W. Jefferys House   227

Chapter Ten: The Generosity of Connie Comer   233

Chapter Eleven: The Renovations of 2014   236

    The Story of St. John's Grand Piano   248

Chapter Twelve: Beginning the Third Century   250

PART TWO: HIGHLIGHTS OF HISTORY PAST   257

Introduction   259

Chapter Thirteen: Early History of York Mills   261

Chapter Fourteen: Early History of the Church of England in York   265

Chapter Fifteen: St. John's York Mills Church 1816   268

Chapter Sixteen: The Second St. John's York Mills   272

Chapter Seventeen: The Men and Women of St. John's   278

Chapter Eighteen: The Artists of St. John's   289

    C.W. Jefferys   289

    Bruce Napier Simpson Jr.   293

    E.B. Cox   294

Chapter Nineteen: Historical Street Names in the St. John's Neighbourhood   297

Chapter Twenty: Early Neighbours   301

    Seneca Ketchum   302

    Joseph Shepard   303

    John Willson   304

    Thomas Mercer   304

    Christopher Harrison   305

    Thomas Humberstone   307

    Cornelius van Nostrand   309

    Lieutenant-Colonel Duncan Cameron   310

Love and Marriage   312
The Vallieres   313
The Pennocks   313
The Marsh Family   314
The McKenzie Family   315
The Final Word   317

PART THREE: PHOTO GALLERY 2016   319

Appendix   327
Wardens 1960–2016: Churchwardens   327
Assistants in Ministry Through the Decades   329
Organists and Choirmasters Through the Years   330
Some Hymns in the Barrel Organ   331

Bibliographies   333
Bibliography for Part One   333
Bibliography for Part Two   334

Photo Credits   337

Index   340

About the Authors   353

LETTER TO THE PEOPLE OF ST. JOHN'S

from Bishop Patrick Yu

I am pleased to congratulate the people of St. John's on the occasion of your 200th anniversary.

Much has happened over two hundred years. When St. John's was established, Canada had just emerged from the War of 1812, and York had just recovered from its occupation. The community of York Mills grew up around the mills along the Don River. Yonge Street, a military road, connected York Mills to other cities and towns. Over the years, York Mills became a prosperous neighbourhood, connected by the radial railway, which in turn was superseded by buses and the subway. In the age of the automobile, Yonge Street and the 401 make York Mills a major nexus in and out of Toronto.

The Lord Jesus said, "You are the light of the world. A city built on a hill cannot be hid." (Matthew 5:14) This takes on an added significance for the location of St. John's, "The Church on the Hill." It is also a description of your ministry over the years. When men and women live into their baptism and have the light of Christ shine in their lives, people are blessed and drawn to that light. When you gather in worship and service, and take that light into your homes, your work, and your neighbourhood, the community is enriched.

The words of Jesus also serve as an invitation and a challenge. Being the church on a hill is not simply a matter of location, it is also a matter of intention. As previous generations bore witness to the Good News in ways appropriate to their circumstance, we also must continue to listen to our context and find ever more effective ways to be salt and light. The Gospel does not change, but the means to share it does, and must, change. To continue the transportation theme, as horses gave rise to rail and then cars, what is the most effective means of communicating the Good News in an era of social media?

As the whole diocese renews its turn toward God's mission, a mission that includes building communities of hope and compassion, I am delighted to note that St. John's plays an important role in this. Your recent renovations opened up both the worship space and places for gathering. I was delighted to see the Garnsworthy Room arranged for your ESL gathering when I passed through it to another meeting. Your central location and good facilities make it a preferred meeting place for diocesan events, including Diocesan Council. Thank you for your hospitality.

I am all too aware that a Church is both a faith community and an organization with buildings, and managing all of that takes a lot of energy. I am grateful for the leadership of the Reverend Canon Dr. Drew MacDonald and the clergy and layfolks in the leadership team. In the most recent study of statistics of every church in the diocese from 2001 to 2014, St. John's occupied a unique place and was often cited as an example of revival. My prayer is that during your anniversary year, you will draw strength from your history and be given renewed vision to be the church on a hill for mission today and in the years to come.

Yours faithfully,

The Right Reverend Patrick Yu, B.A., M.Div., D.Min., D.D.
Area Bishop of York Scarborough
Bishop Suffragan of Toronto

LETTER FROM THE
REVEREND DREW MACDONALD

For many of us, it is hard to believe that it was fifty years ago, in 1966, that Lewis S. Garnsworthy, Rector of St. John's York Mills and later to become Archbishop of the Diocese of Toronto, penned the foreword to M. Audrey Graham's book, *150 Years at St. John's, York Mills*. It is now my privilege to add my few words and appreciation to those who created this important addition to that significant work of history.

So much has happened in these last five decades that it is only fitting that the chronicling continue. As the present rector of this parish, I am about to enter my tenth year of service and am pleased to say that the community of faith is as vibrant and faithful as ever. This is actually a testimony to the people who regularly worship at St. John's, as the times have significantly changed. No longer do we live in a "Christian culture," as in the days of Garnsworthy or any of his predecessors. Canadian culture has shifted dramatically to what many now call a post-modern, secular society. Being a community of faith in the midst of such clear obstacles is the challenge of the twenty-first century. Yet, the community continues to grow in the midst of such complexity.

Interestingly, the Church is no longer the centre of community life as it once was. On Sunday mornings, people are as likely to be off skiing or attending their children's scheduled hockey game or dance class. This has demanded that the modern Church be clearly focused on its primary business of worshipping and proclaiming the Good News of Jesus Christ. The tough reality is that many churches in Toronto and across Canada have been unable to overcome this cultural shift away from the sacred, and have had to close. Yet, the community of faith of St. John's continues to endure. In any given week there are Bible studies, discussion groups, and speakers — whether it be the premier of the province discussing social justice issues or theologians from Wycliffe College leading the people in theological reflection. Indeed, times have changed. It may be helpful for you, the reader, to be deeply aware of this underlying culture shift as you read the stories of the people and lives written about in this wonderful new book.

In this review of the fifty years of history since the publication of Audrey Graham's work, you will gain an insightful snapshot of how the people of St. John's have journeyed these last, often turbulent, years. To Scott Kennedy for collecting so much information on our parish and making it comprehensible, and to Jeanne Hopkins for providing highlights of the first 150 years, we are most appreciative. Thanks are due as well to parishioner Sylvia McConnell, for without her skill in organizing this monumental task of editing and encouraging so many to gather their thoughts and reflections, this book simply would not exist.

It is my hope that you may find this reading more than informative but inspirational, and that it will encourage you to live full of faith and joy. To the people of St. John's York Mills, I thank you all for allowing me and my family to be a part of your illustrious history.

The Reverend Canon Dr. Drew Vaughan MacDonald,
B.A., M.Div., D.Min. (Princeton),
Rector of St. John's York Mills

A NOTE FROM THE EDITOR

Sylvia McConnell

From the very beginning, this was a labour of love. When I first became aware of Audrey Graham's book, *150 Years at St. John's, York Mills,* a few years after becoming a member in 2003, I thought someone should write a new book, updating the history of the church. When I realized there was a 200th anniversary coming up in 2016, I thought I might have to write this history myself.

A decade later, in 2014, and serving as a warden, I spoke to my fellow wardens and the clergy about the idea of producing such a book about our church, the second Anglican church to be established in York and the first parish church in what was to become Toronto. With my many years of publishing experience, I was the obvious candidate to take on this project. With the blessing of the leadership, we approached the Diocese, which gave us seed money in the form of a grant to kickstart the project. When I met Scott Kennedy at a Christmas party hosted by Dundurn Press, the publishing company we both worked with, the pieces started to fall into place. Scott had written a wonderful history of Willowdale from pioneer times, and I greatly admired his research and writing skills. I asked him to come on board and be the author of our 200th anniversary book.

A few months later, I discovered that we had another local historian in our midst, Jeanne Hopkins, who was already at work on a book about St. John's. And so it was decided: Scott would work on the last fifty years, pulling together the threads of that narrative, and Jeanne would give us highlights from the first 150 years. We would have a full historical picture.

But, how do we approach a church history in the twenty-first century? The history of St. John's is no longer the history of this area of Toronto — York Mills, Lawrence Park, and Willowdale — as was the period about which Audrey Graham wrote. Instead, I could clearly see that the last fifty years of our parish life was the story of our people. And that's how Scott and Jeanne and I approached the writing of this book — as the stories of the people of St. John's York Mills.

The main narrative is collected loosely around the biographies of the rectors who have served us since 1966, the curates and deacons who have influenced us, the musicians who have led us in musical worship, the vergers who have kept our historical building and beautiful property in shape, and, of course, the amazing people of this parish. Collecting these stories has been a wonderful experience. Once started, it seemed we could have continued forever to search out fascinating stories, but at a certain point we had to stop and pull everything together in order to publish this book in time for the anniversary celebration in fall 2016.

I have so many people to thank, and I can't name everyone who helped, but a few names must be mentioned. First and foremost, thanks to Scott Kennedy, who worked so tirelessly on collecting and crafting the stories of the people of our church; to Jeanne Hopkins, who gathered so many interesting highlights from our early years; thank you to all the rectors, past and present, who put so much time and thought into their interviews with the author: the Reverends Jim O'Neil, Hollis Hiscock, and Drew MacDonald; to Bishop Yu for his support and to the Diocese for their grant that helped us get on our way; to Brian Hull, upon whom I called, once again, to develop a cover concept for this book, and who also provided so many photographs; to Yasmina Shamji at Toronto Heritage

Preservation Services for technical assistance; to Linda Grasley for her advice and to Bill Dennis for his encyclopedic knowledge of church and people; to Laura Peetoom for her editorial help, and to Catherine Bryant, who had all the answers; and to our ever-helpful archivist Lynn Austin, who dug into church archives for photos. The author, Scott Kennedy, would like to thank, particularly, previous churchwarden Bill Saynor for his memoirs, which shed light on so many corners of church life. To so many others who shared their stories and their photos, I thank you all. A big thank you as well to Dundurn Press and all the remarkable people who worked on this book to make sure it was as beautiful as possible.

During the course of collecting information for this book, I have been impressed with the accomplishments of the people of St. John's over the years. Their talent and the hard work they put into their church life are truly inspirational. Life at St. John's has changed so much over the years and yet, the one thing that has remained constant is the contribution that these parishioners of the past made — and the people of today's congregation are still making — to their church and to their community. I am happy to have been involved in this project.

If your story isn't included, I regret that, but I am hopeful we will not wait another fifty years to update our history again.

Sylvia McConnell, B.A., M.A. M.Ed.
Editor

I am pleased to extend my best wishes to all those celebrating the 200th anniversary of St. John's York Mills Anglican Church.

Year after year, through their unshakable bedrock of faith, the clergy and the congregation of St. John's have demonstrated that this church is much more than just a building. It is a community centre that welcomes all people; it is a place to rejoice in life's gifts and to take comfort during difficult times; and it provides a contemplative space for reflection when seeking spiritual guidance.

Through all of life's major milestones and events, this church has remained strong and its members unified. The people of this congregation hold a warm hand out to those in need of companionship and reinforce the importance of community. For this, you should all be proud.

I wish you many more years of healthy, vibrant, spiritual life.

David Johnston

September 2016

PART ONE

FROM 1966 INTO THE THIRD CENTURY

BY SCOTT KENNEDY

INTRODUCTION

The last fifty years have proven to be perilous times for the churches of Canada. Great cultural changes in North America, following the Second World War, combined to diminish the central role that churches once played in their local communities. Where once the churches were virtually the sole source of social interaction, they now found themselves competing with all sorts of new activities that offered equal or greater opportunities for socializing. The rise of teenage culture, beginning with the big band era and progressing through the rock-and-roll 1950s and the so-called "swingin' sixties," tore a hole in the fabric of family unity while creating a very tangible generation gap. Young people increasingly looked to their peers and cultural icons for inspiration, while looking away from their parents' values and traditions.

The churches did what they could, engaging the teenagers in their parishes in ways that seem unimaginable today — events such as Friday night dances and weekday drop-in centres — but they were unable to compete with the onslaught of popular culture and the influence of television and radio. The rise of the automotive age also presented a challenge as new and enticing destinations came within easy reach of any family who could afford a car. Rural parishes fared a little better, owing to their relative isolation, but the urban churches soon found themselves fighting a losing battle with movie theatres, coffee houses, sporting events, television, golf courses, summer cottages, and Sunday drives. New immigrants to Canada were more likely to create their own places of worship than to join existing congregations, and the formerly unthinkable notion that "God is dead" became a common theme in public debate.

As the 1970s gave way to the 1980s, the two-income family became a reality and both Mom and Dad began using precious weekend days to complete tasks that had formerly been taken care of during the week, while the introduction of Sunday shopping turned the Lord's Day into just another day. By the turn of the century, home computers, email, and video games conspired to keep families tethered to their devices, a situation that continues to complicate matters today. Add to this mix the inevitable aging of parishioners, whose homes were sold to newcomers who claimed the parishioners' addresses but not their seats in the congregation, and a troublesome scene began to emerge.

Many churches didn't survive. Some congregations merged with neighbouring congregations, selling one edifice to pay for the maintenance of the other. Some churches became mosques, temples, or other places of worship; some were converted to condominiums; some simply soldiered on into oblivion, with dwindling congregations and crumbling infrastructures; some were demolished or simply abandoned. Some, such as St. John's York Mills (SJYM), survived — and thrived.

Things We Didn't Have in 1966

calculators	Sunday shopping	video cameras
bar codes	credit cards (except	digital cameras
bank machines	perhaps Diners Club	VCRs
banks that stayed open	and gasoline company	CDs
after 3:00 p.m. on Friday	cards)	DVDs

cellphones

iPhones

iPads

the internet

home computers

email

microwave ovens

condominiums

video games

more than six teams in
   the NHL

The Blue Jays

The Raptors

grief counsellors

school lockdowns

casinos

self-serve gas stations

food banks

GPS

multiculturalism

voice mail

"mega" anything

home staging

karaoke

lotteries

graffiti

recycling

RRSPs

dumpsters

smoke detectors

tattoos on anyone but
   sailors or bikers

jet skis

SUVs

cars that honk when you
   lock them

trucks and cars that
   beep when you put
   them into reverse

rearview cameras

cars that can park
   themselves

Add to this list some of the things that were just starting to appear in common usage, such as cable television, FM radio, organ transplants, automotive air-conditioning, colour television, and front-wheel drive, and the world of fifty years ago begins to look very different from the world of today. St. John's looks a little different as well, but its heart beats as strongly as ever.

THE RECTORS AND CLERGY IN CHARGE OF ST. JOHN'S YORK MILLS, 1827 TO 2016

During the years 1816 to 1827, the church was served by temporary or travelling ministers and missionaries.

The Reverend Allan Macaulay, missionary, 1827–1829

First Rector Charles Stephens Mathews, missionary, 1830–1836, rector 1836–1841

Second Rector Thomas Henry Marsh Bartlett, 1841–1842

Third Rector Alexander Laing Sanson, in charge 1842–1844, rector 1844–1852

Fourth Rector Richard Mitchele, 1852–1867

Clergy in charge from June 1863–1867

> The Reverend Richard Sandars, 1863–1864
>
> The Reverend Thomas Tempest Robarts, 1864–1865
>
> The Reverend John Langtry, 1865–1866
>
> The Reverend Henry Capelthwaite Webbe, June to November 1866

Fifth Rector Thomas Peter Hodge, 1866–1873

Clergy in charge

> The Reverend Archibald Lister George Trew, 1873–1874

Sixth Rector Henry Bath Osler, 1874–1900

Seventh Rector Richard Ashcroft, 1900–1926

Eighth Rector Arthur Clendenning McCollum, vicar 1926–1947, rector 1947–1960

Ninth Rector Lewis Samuel Garnsworthy, February 24, 1960, to December 31, 1968

Tenth Rector James Francis O'Neil, March 17, 1969, to October 31, 1989

Eleventh Rector Hollis Hiscock, September 23, 1990, to January 31, 2007

Twelfth Rector Drew MacDonald, September 4, 2007, to the present

Sketch of the church by John Snell

CHAPTER ONE

Lewis Samuel Garnsworthy
Rector from 1960 to 1968

Archbishop Lewis Garnsworthy

W hen the Reverend Lewis Garnsworthy was inducted as the ninth rector in St. John's history on the evening of Wednesday, February 24, 1960, many felt that he had big shoes to fill. After all, he was succeeding the longest serving incumbent in the parish's history, Arthur Clendenning McCollum, who had served for thirty-four years. However, Archdeacon McCollum himself put that notion to rest when he noted dryly that "The Good Lord did not give him *my* shoes to fill: he must fill his own."

The new incumbent inherited a healthy, growing parish in an area of Toronto that was still in the middle of a post-war building boom. Arthur McCollum had presided over a time that saw new housing developments built on much of the former farmland in the area. He had tried to visit every one of the new households and invite the residents to join his parish, demonstrating a long-standing Anglican notion that the rector was responsible for everyone in his parish, not just the Anglicans. By the time Lewis Garnsworthy arrived, the nearby St. Andrew's Golf Club had been sold for a new housing development that by 1964 would stretch from Old Yonge Street to Bayview Avenue. Other subdivisions — such as Silver Hills, near the southwest corner of Leslie Street and Highway 401 — were

The Reverend Garnsworthy (left) officiated at the wedding of Maurice Bent and Pat Weller in 1963. Maurice was later to become a warden at St. John's.

popping up all over the area at the same time, providing even more potential parishioners. The new rector, along with his wife Jean, son Peter, and daughter Kathy, settled into the rectory at 174 Old Yonge Street and got down to business.

Lewis Garnsworthy brought with him a reputation as a "preacher of some note," as Jim O'Neil once remarked, and before long his sermons were attracting Anglicans from all over the city. In 1963, a nine-thirty service was added to the eight o'clock and eleven o'clock Sunday morning services to handle the overflow. In April 1963, Lewis wrote and delivered a series of talks for a CBL (CBC) radio program called *Plain Talk*. His six-talk series included one on Prayer, the Clergy, Hymns, the Bible, Going to Church, and the Family Unit. Throughout the rest of 1963, there was so much traffic in the parking lot on Sunday mornings that sidesmen were pressed into service as traffic police.

In 1964 Lewis Garnsworthy was appointed canon of the Cathedral of St. James in downtown Toronto. In 1966 he presided over the 150th anniversary services at St. John's York Mills. Planning for the anniversary began in 1964. The addition to the church that came to be known as the Arthur C. McCollum Wing was constructed as the centrepiece of the celebrations. One of the more interesting stories concerning the fundraising for the project involved well-known parishioner and wealthy businessman E.P. Taylor. At that time, Mr. Taylor lived nearby on Bayview Avenue at Windfields Farm, where he bred race horses. It seems that when E.P. was first approached, he was told that the construction would cost $225,000. After doing a quick calculation in his head, he concluded that the actual cost would be closer to $250,000, and since he never contributed more than 10 percent of any given project, he wrote St. John's a cheque for $25,000.

Above: *An open house and historical tour was held to mark the 150th anniversary. Mrs. E.G. Thompson and Mrs. D. Pankhurst, in the styles of 1816, examine the pulpit in the sanctuary.*

Right: *The menu of the 150th anniversary dinner held at the Inn on the Park in 1966*

MENU

Celery Sticks, Radishes, Mixed Olives

* * *

Fresh Fruit Cocktail

* * *

Roast Half Spring Chicken Chasseur
Parmentier Potatoes
Peas Paysanne

* * *

Tossed Green Salad — French Dressing

* * *

Bombe Praline

* * *

Demi Tasse

Blessing
THE REV. CANON L. S. GARNSWORTHY

Thanksgiving
'Praise God from whom all blessings flow;
Praise Him, all creatures here below:
Praise Him above, ye heavenly host;
Praise Father, Son, and Holy Ghost'.

National Anthem

Toast to Her Majesty The Queen

Dinner

Chairman
MR. W. R. WILSON

Greetings
The Rector — THE REV. CANON L. S. GARNSWORTHY
THE RT. REV. G. B. SNELL, Bishop of Toronto

Introduction of Guest Speaker
MR. A. C. TULLY

Address
THE HONOURABLE CHIEF JUSTICE G. A. GALE
Chief Justice of the High Court of
The Supreme Court of Ontario

Presentations
THE CHAIRMAN

Benediction
THE VEN. ARCHDEACON A. C. McCOLLUM

The 150th Anniversary Parish Dinner was held in the Centennial Ballroom of the Inn on the Park, the much-loved, mid-century modernist hotel that once graced the northeast corner of Leslie Street and Eglinton Avenue East. Sadly, the main parts of the hotel were demolished in 2006. By 2015, the ballrooms and the tower built in the 1970s to accommodate additional guests were also gone.

On Thursday, November 21, 1968, the new wing of St. John's York Mills was dedicated. Lewis Garnsworthy had named the Arthur C. McCollum Wing in honour of Archdeacon McCollum, who had died on February 18, 1967.

Left: *The original cornerstone of the church is removed so it can be placed in the entranceway of the church's new addition.*

Right: *Archdeacon Arthur McCollum on May 18, 1961, taking part in a dramatic production of* The Mad Hatter's Tea Party.

Lewis Garnsworthy had been elected Suffragan Bishop of the Diocese of Toronto on October 8, 1968. He was consecrated on Saturday, November 30, 1968, and granted permission to remain at St. John's until the end of the year.

Lewis Garnsworthy was born in Edmonton in 1922. He received his early schooling in his home province and graduated from the University of Alberta with a B.A. in 1943. He then journeyed to Toronto, where he enrolled in Wycliffe College at the University of Toronto. He was ordained a deacon in 1945 and graduated the following year. It was here that he met Jim O'Neil, who would become a lifelong friend. Jim was a junior at Wycliffe when Lewis was a senior. Their paths would cross many times over the years, but while Jim completed his studies, Lewis was sent to St. Paul's Anglican Church in Halifax, where he served his first curacy. After Halifax he returned to Toronto where he served as curate at St. John's Norway Anglican Church, at the corner of Kingston Road and Woodbine Avenue, where Jim O'Neil was also serving. The two men lived in the same boarding house while serving at St. John's Norway, and travelled to England together in the early 1950s to study at St. Augustine's College in Canterbury.

Lewis served as Jim's best man at Jim's wedding at St. John's Norway on July 21, 1954. Jim returned the favour when Lewis married shortly after. Jim O'Neil also preached when Lewis was inducted as rector of St. John's York Mills on February 24, 1960 — the first time Jim ever preached here. Deacon Margery Pezzack also served at St. John's Norway with Lewis and Jim, proving that it can be a very small world indeed. It was Lewis Garnsworthy who, while bishop of Toronto, ordained Margery Pezzack on March 22, 1977, as the first woman priest in the Diocese of Toronto. The ordination was not without incident however, as many were opposed to the ordination of a woman and one group actually rose during the ceremony to voice their displeasure. The tall, bespectacled bishop, though

The ordination of Margery Pezzack, the first woman priest in the diocese

somewhat shy and reserved "off stage," was not to be trifled with while in control of the proceedings. The ordination went ahead as planned and a new chapter was written in the history of both St. John's York Mills and the diocese itself.

After his time at St. John's Norway, Lewis was inducted as the rector of St. Nicholas Anglican Church on Kingston Road in Birchcliff. In 1956 he was posted to the Church of the Transfiguration on Manor Road East, just east of Yonge Street. His next stop would be St. John's York Mills, where he served until December 31, 1968.

He was appointed the ninth bishop of Toronto in 1972 and returned to SJYM as celebrant and guest preacher on Christmas Eve 1973, when the midnight Eucharist was broadcast live on television station CFTO. In 1979 Lewis Samuel Garnsworthy was elected Metropolitan Archbishop of the Ecclesiastical Province of Ontario, the highest position in the Church ever achieved by a rector at St. John's. He died on January 26, 1990. He was cremated and his ashes were interred at St. James Cathedral. He was the first St. John's rector not to be buried in the St. John's churchyard in more than ninety years.

Left: The interior of the church during the Rev. Garnsworthy's time, showing the blond wood of the chancel

Right: The exterior of St. John's York Mills as it was when the Rev. Garnsworthy arrived

CHAPTER TWO

James Francis O'Neil
Rector from 1969 to 1989

The Reverend Jim O'Neil greets his parishioners after a service.

Canon James Francis O'Neil celebrated his ninetieth birthday in Toronto on Tuesday, September 23, 2014. It was a long way from his birthplace in the mining town of Coleman, Alberta, and an equally long way down his personal road of spiritual development. His mother was Anglican. His Roman Catholic father worked in the dry goods business, serving the mining towns of the west. The family made a couple of moves when Jim was young, first to Michel-Natal in British Columbia's Crow's Nest Pass and finally to Victoria, B.C., by which time Jim was a young teenager. The family weathered the Great Depression better than many, owing to his father's ability to find employment, although they would often be humbled by the sight of railroad cars full of homeless men, riding the rails in search of work.

Jim graduated from high school in Victoria and, not long after, made the decision that would ultimately change his life. Like many young men of his time, Jim felt compelled to join the Allied forces and fight for victory in the Second World War. Although he had previously felt drawn to his mother's religion, it wouldn't be until Jim joined the Royal Canadian Navy that he would truly feel himself drawn to dedicate his life to the service of God and humankind. It was there, on the waves of the war-torn North Atlantic Ocean, that he would feel the hand of God reach out to comfort his wounded shipmates and realize that here was a power he could not ignore. He assisted the ship's chaplain, Padre William Hills, who would later encourage Jim to become a priest. Some of Jim's wartime exploits are detailed later in this chapter. His civilian exploits, while somewhat less dangerous, are no less impressive.

After the war, James followed Padre Hill's advice and journeyed to Toronto to enroll first at the University of Toronto and then at Wycliffe College, where Padre Hills had graduated in 1936. He was ready to prepare himself for a life in the church. His parents were not all that enthusiastic about what they saw as a lengthy and expensive undertaking or, as Jim recalled, "They were not cheering for me to be ordained." With the assistance of his veteran's benefits however, Jim was able to succeed. After graduating from the U of T, he spent three years at Wycliffe before graduating in 1951. He was ordained a deacon that same year by Bishop Alton Ray Beverly at St. James Cathedral. It was the largest post-war ordination ceremony ever held. He was ordained to the priesthood on Sunday, June 8, 1952, at his home church St. John's Anglican in Victoria, by the Most Reverend Harold Sexton, Archbishop of the Diocese of British Columbia. While at Wycliffe College, James had become friends with fellow students Fred Pierce and Lewis Garnsworthy. Both men would forever be a part of James's life, but it was his friendship with Fred that would yield the most immediate rewards.

Shortly after he was ordained a priest, the Rev. O'Neil accompanied Fred Pierce to Petrolia, Ontario — where Canada's first oil well had been erected in 1859 — to be best man at Fred's wedding to Beth MacCallum. While there, James met and began to fall for Beth's sister, Jean. Jean had just graduated from medical school at the University of Toronto and was interning at Toronto's St. Joseph's Hospital in the city's west end. James soon found himself appointed assistant curate at St. John's Norway, in the *east* end. Their respective situations at opposite ends of the city meant that they became extremely familiar with the Queen

Street streetcar. They met in the middle for many of their early dates before the chivalrous assistant curate escorted Jean all the way back to the west-end hospital before turning around and making the lonely journey back to the east end. His long trips back and forth were not in vain, however, as Jean and Jim were soon engaged. The wedding was put on hold for a year while Jim and Lewis Garnsworthy took advantage of an opportunity to study at St. Augustine College in Canterbury, England.

Jim's time at St. John's Norway was a satisfying period in his life. The new curate was especially impressed by the size and age of the churchyard where, he says, "I used to walk along and preach my sermons to the tombstones."

The O'Neils finally tied the knot at St. John's Norway on July 21, 1954. Jim's best man was, not surprisingly, Lewis Garnsworthy. Shortly after, Jim would return the favour when he was best man at Lewis's wedding. The new Mrs. Garnsworthy was also named Jean.

The O'Neils took some time off for a brief honeymoon to Cape Cod, followed by the Reverend James Francis O'Neil's induction as the rector of St. George's Anglican Church in the parish of Haliburton. Lewis Garnsworthy preached at the service of induction. The three-point parish served the bustling resort community of Haliburton, as well as Maple Lake and West Guilford. Jim described it as an excellent place to learn the ropes of the ministry. His wife Jean became a welcome addition to the local medical community, and the O'Neils' first child Peter was born in the eight-bed Red Cross Hospital in June 1957. Later that year, the family moved to Richmond Hill, where Jim was inducted as rector of St. Mary's Anglican Church on the northwest corner of Yonge Street and Major Mackenzie Drive. One of the new rector's main tasks was to oversee the construction of the beautiful church building, which serves the congregation to this day, as well as the construction of a new rectory. Thankfully, the old church was preserved and now provides the parish with meeting and event space. The O'Neils' daughter Mary was born in Richmond Hill. After Mary's birth Jean decided that being a rector's wife and raising two children was quite enough to keep her occupied and, aside from assisting in vaccination campaigns and continuing her studies in psychiatry, she put her medical career on hold.

The Reverend O'Neil first preached at St. John's York Mills in February 1960, at the induction of Lewis Garnsworthy as St. John's ninth rector. Nine years later on St. Patrick's Day 1969, Jim was inducted as St. John's tenth rector by the Venerable Terence Crosthwait, Archdeacon of Toronto, after Canon Garnsworthy had been elected Suffragan Bishop of the Diocese of Toronto. Though he had suddenly gone from a parish of about four hundred souls to one more than three times that size, the new rector wasted no time and personally got to know the members of his new congregation. It is believed that he visited at least one parishioner every day during his time at St. John's. Parishioner Bill Saynor

Left: The Rev. O'Neil catches a water balloon at a parish picnic in 1983.

Right: Picnics were a popular summer event with the many children attending Sunday school at St. John's.

Facing right: As rector of St. John's, the Rev. O'Neil was constantly with his "flock."

described him as follows: "Jim's jovial, friendly, outgoing, caring, and genuine personality endeared him to everyone with whom he came in contact. He was indeed a true parish priest!" The new rector, in turn, felt at home almost immediately.

"They were very happy days here because it was a big parish." he recalled in 2014. "I wasn't sure it was my piece of cake — you know, from a four-hundred-person parish to thirteen-hundred, but the people welcomed me very well and in many ways I was kind of a good bridge between what McCollum had been for thirty-three years and Garnsworthy for eight years. They were very different sorts of people. St. John's really venerated the rector. Whatever I said, you know, they did. Now that was because they trusted me and so on, but I was lucky that I had a happy time. It could have been different, you know, with all the wealthy people. There was a lot of wealth here, but no one really tried to run my show. I guess they saw the Irish look in my eyes."

Jim and his wife Jean endeared themselves to everyone they met, as both were deeply involved in parish life. Jean took a special interest in restoring and redecorating their new home in the Old Rectory at 174 Old Yonge Street in a historically accurate fashion. She had always loved old houses. When she assisted in the design of the new church and rectory at St. Mary's in Richmond Hill, she found she also had a natural flair for the design process.. She was always willing to open the doors of the rectory to host events that would benefit the church.

When asked in autumn 2014 if he felt he had presided over the "glory years" of St. John's, Canon O'Neil was quick to share that glory, recalling, "I inherited a good parish to start with. Garnsworthy was a preacher of some note and he built a good congregation, so I inherited all of that. He and I were good friends. He was curate in the east end, and I followed him there and lived in the same boarding house as he did, so until we were married, we were pals. The Bobbsey Twins, they called us."

Canon O'Neil and Jean O'Neil in 1984

He also extended his gratitude to the Reverend Arthur C. McCollum, who preceded Lewis Garnsworthy as the rector of St. John's. "McCollum came in and really built it up from a little village church to the suburban thing it is today." The Reverend Arthur C. McCollum's time as rector of St. John's — December 1947 to January 1960 — coincided with a post-war building boom in the area that saw the surrounding woods and farmland claimed by tracts of suburban housing.

It should be mentioned here that from 1926 to 1947, Arthur McCollum was the "Vicar of St. John's" — a position that differed only in name from his later stint as rector. Richard Ashcroft, who served as the rector of St. John's from 1900 to 1926, retained the title of rector after his retirement. Upon his death in 1947, the title of rector was transferred to Arthur McCollum. The Reverend Richard Ashcroft was the

The Reverend Jim O'Neil at the opening of the Kaye Gate in 1985 with Archbishop Garnsworthy and members of the Kaye family

last clergyman in the Diocese of Toronto to be allowed to retain the office of rector after his retirement. After his death the office of vicar was never used again.

The Reverend McCollum had taken full advantage of the building boom, appearing personally on each freshly built doorstep to invite the new residents to worship at St. John's. His efforts were a tremendous success and the parish list grew and grew. Many of the new parishioners weren't even Anglicans before Reverend McCollum's invitation — a situation that marked a major change in Toronto's religious life, where traditionally "Anglicans were Anglicans." Arthur McCollum, however, felt that anyone within the boundaries of his parish was his responsibility. As Canon O'Neil recalled, "It was a new adventure for some of those people."

One of the Reverend O'Neil's first initiatives was the introduction of a parish newsletter. Introduced in 1969 *The Link* was printed by one of Jim's old parishioners at St. Mary's: Sam Cook of *The Richmond Hill Liberal.* Another of the new rector's early changes was the introduction of the "Visitation and Response Program," which was a way of replacing pledge cards with a "kinder, gentler" approach. Jim devised the program after watching the way professional fundraisers went about raising money for their clients' projects. He decided to adapt the basic concept, using St. John's volunteers instead of paid specialists. Under the new program, a pamphlet was produced every two years to outline the goals and needs of St. John's. It also included a tentative budget and provided parishioners with other pertinent information of the day. The pamphlet was paired with a response card, asking each parishioner to decide on a reasonable, personal contribution they might consider making to help meet the needs of the church over the following two years. The rector appointed more than one hundred "visitors" by personal letter, asking each one to commit to visiting five to ten parishioners to deliver the pamphlet. Visitors who had already made their pledges were only required to *deliver* the package. If they were invited in for a visit, that was fine, but parishioners were under no obligation to do so. Even if the visitors were invited in, they were instructed not to discuss church finances, but to direct parishioners to the phone numbers of the churchwardens involved in such matters. With a parish list of more than 1,300 names, it was easy to see why so many visitors were needed, and why the church was in constant need of funds to meet the needs of new parishioners.

The first Visitation and Response Program began on October 31, 1971, and was chaired by Bill Englebright. That same year the Reverend O'Neil would gain a new title when he was appointed a Canon of St. James Cathedral — an honourary title that didn't interfere with his duties at St. John's. His friend Lewis Garnsworthy was appointed the ninth Bishop of the Diocese of Toronto the following year. Bishop Garnsworthy would go on to be elected Archbishop of the Ecclesiastical Province of Ontario in 1979.

Canon O'Neil was quite content in his position as a parish priest. "People approached me with the bishop thing because this was the kind of parish where

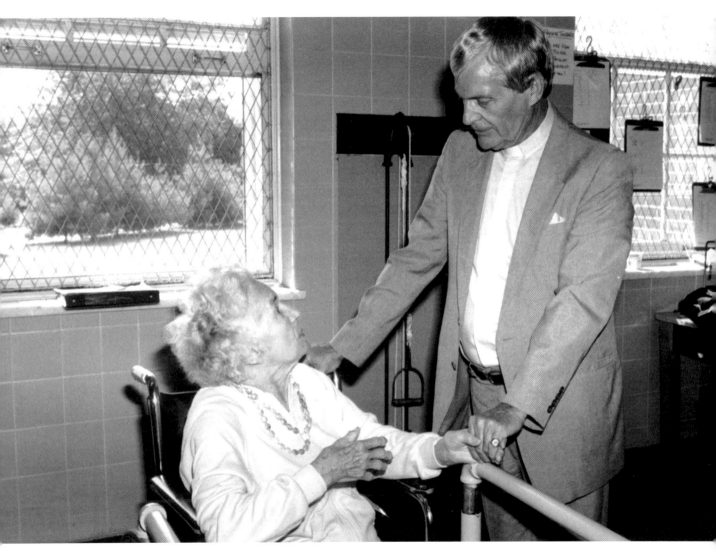

*Even after retirement
Canon O'Neil continued
as a chaplain at St. John's
Rehabilitation Hospital.*

they got them from. My wife said, 'If you become a bishop, I'm going to leave you.' Actually, I never saw myself as bishop material; you know, the things a bishop has to do I wouldn't be good at. I felt St. John's is where I should be, as a parish priest, and I stayed there."

It is interesting to note that, since he was first ordained, Canon O'Neil has worked closely with another St. John's. "For many years, indeed since ordination," he recalls, "I was associated with the Sisters of St. John the Divine as an associate priest, beginning with my curacy days and continuing as a regular celebrant from my Richmond Hill days and again from the York Mills days." He has continued this relationship with the sisters, serving as part-time chaplain in the chapel of their rehabilitation hospital on Cummer Avenue in North York after his retirement from SJYM. He later served as a volunteer celebrant at Wednesday morning patient services and special services such as Easter and Remembrance Day.

The mid-1970s marked a very busy time for St. John's. The world was changing at what seemed to be an ever-increasing pace and the church was changing as well. In 1973, the Midnight Eucharist at St. John's was broadcast on television station CFTO on Christmas Eve. The celebrant and guest preacher was Bishop Garnsworthy. In 1974 Canon O'Neil dedicated the Cambridge Cremation Plot, a gift from Don and Martha Cambridge.

It was also in 1974 — Sunday, November 17, to be precise — that Her Royal Highness Princess Anne and her husband Captain Mark Phillips attended the 9:30 a.m. service, under the watchful eyes of the Metropolitan Toronto and Royal Canadian Mounted Police. The event was supposed to be kept quiet but someone leaked the news to the social editor of the *Globe and Mail* and the crush of photographers and reporters made for an exhilarating morning. The couple specifically asked to attend the early service as they needed to get to the Royal Winter Fair

in time for an equestrian event later that day. While in Toronto they stayed with Bud McDougald and his wife Maude at Green Meadows, the McDougalds' spectacular farm on Leslie Street, just south of Finch Avenue East.

Although Bud McDougald was not on the parish list of St. John's, his more famous partner in the mighty Argus Corporation, E.P. Taylor, *was* on the list. He was friends with Arthur McCollum and preferred to attend the early Sunday service. E.P. was often there with his cheque book when the church's need was greatest. In fact, he shared a much more intimate bond with Canon O'Neil, although it's doubtful that either man knew the connection existed. During the Second World War, E.P. Taylor was appointed Director General of Supply and Munitions by Federal Minister of Supply and Munitions, C.D. Howe. The position paid one dollar per year. The two men were very much hands-on, to the point of actually travelling with supply convoys to Europe. On one such trip their ship was sunk

Left: *In 2016 the Cambridge Cremation Garden underwent a beautiful upgrade, designed by parishioner Judith Adam.*

Right: *Princess Anne at St. John's York Mills, November 17, 1974, receiving a copy of Audrey Graham's* 150 Years at St. John's, York Mills *from Canon O'Neil.*

by a German torpedo, and they spent nine hours in a lifeboat on the frigid North Atlantic before being rescued.

St. John's celebrated its 160th anniversary in 1976, a landmark that was celebrated in part by the realization of Canon O'Neil's long-held desire to publish the stories of the church's stained glass windows. The brochure that made this dream come true featured the photography of Krena Laing and the stories of the individual windows. It was written by parishioner and university student Kevin Flynn, who would later become the Reverend Kevin Flynn and who currently serves as the dean of the Anglican College at the University of Ottawa. The brochure was published through the generosity of Bill Saynor and made available to all parishioners. Canon O'Neil wrote the introduction. It was also around this time that the canon expressed a desire to change the transept into an area dedicated to baptisms. While he would get his wish in fairly short order, the impetus behind the change would prove very unconventional indeed.

It seems that, one day, long-time parishioner and evangelical Christian Isabelle Bailey was startled by the sight of a number of scantily clad women practising yoga in the church auditorium. She was so upset by this perceived violation of church decorum that she threatened to withdraw her financial support. Bill Saynor — a fellow parishioner and friend of Isabelle's — volunteered to visit her at home to see what could be done to address her concerns. After a discussion that lasted several hours, the yoga issue had been resolved and Isabelle told Bill that one day she would make a sizeable donation to St. John's. Bill told her about Jim's plans for the transept and Isabelle, much impressed by the idea, wrote a cheque for $5,000 on the spot and gave it to Bill for the project. After further discussions between Jim O'Neil and Isabelle, the changes were made.

First, the baptismal font was moved from the Memorial Garden to the transept. Pews were replaced by wooden chairs that could be moved to accommodate different seating arrangements, and a tapestry was added to the east wall. This was also the time when plans were made to add a number of stone carvings of baptismal symbols to the south wall of the baptismal font.

Stone carver E.B. Cox — whose main stipulation was that the project should involve "no committees" — then completed the carvings depicting a fish, a shell, water, and a Celtic cross, and mounted them on wooden frames on the wall. Since the renovations of 2014, the carvings have been moved and now hang in the Memorial Chapel on the north side, closer to the new location of the baptismal niche.

Elford Bradley Cox, whose story is told in another chapter, was an internationally renowned Canadian sculptor. He was born in 1914 and died in 2003. Other examples of his work can be found at McMaster University in Hamilton, the University of Toronto, Duke of Connaught Public School, the MacDonald Block at 900 Bay Street, and on the CNE grounds near the Dufferin Gates in his *Garden of the Greek Gods* — a massive, twenty-piece sculpture. He also made smaller sculptures and even jewellery, which the O'Neils would often purchase to give as gifts. One of his statues, titled *Seated Bear*, stands in the garden near St. John's front door.

When completed, the new baptistry envisaged by Jim O'Neil had been reconfigured so that family members and godparents were seated near the baptismal font, with additional friends seated to the right front of the nave. Parishioners loved the new baptismal area. Isabelle watched over it like a mother hen, going so far as to personally remove poinsettias that had been placed in the font one Christmas, as she felt this to be a desecration.

In September 1976 Canon O'Neil — never one to shy away from an interesting conversation — invited Bishop John Robertson, the former Bishop of Woolwich, England, to St. John's. The bishop was a New Testament Scholar and author of several books including *Honest to God*, which was considered extremely controversial for questioning a number of the Anglican Church's core theological beliefs. The bishop preached at St. John's one Sunday morning and it seems that even the more conservative members of the congregation found nothing controversial in the text of his sermon. The bishop dined on the Saturday night before his sermon with the O'Neils, the Saynors, the Crosthwaits, and Margery Pezzack. He stayed at the home of parishioner Shirley Ingram while in town, and invited Shirley to visit him at his home in England as a way of returning the favour. The trip would, sadly, prove to be her last. While walking along a sidewalk in the seaside town of Hastings, she was struck by a car that mounted the curb and killed her instantly. Her family and estate ensured that her memory would live on at St. John's by making donations to establish the Churchyard Sustaining Fund to help with maintenance of headstones, and a donation for the purchase of the handbells that would mark the beginning of the Ingram Bell Choir.

On May 22, 1977, Jim's old friend and colleague, Margery Pezzack, became the first woman to be ordained to the priesthood of the Anglican Church in Toronto. On Sunday, June 7, 1977, Margery assisted at celebrations held at St. John's to mark the twenty-fifth anniversary of Canon O'Neil's ordination as a priest. Margery had been ordained a deacon in 1949 and had served with Jim O'Neil and Lewis Garnsworthy at St. John's Norway in the early 1950s. She was the first of the trio to come to St. John's York Mills when she was appointed director of religious education in 1955.

June 1978 marked the 100th anniversary of the Old Rectory at 174 Old Yonge Street. A Strawberry Festival, organized by Penny Potter, Shirley Robinson, Anne Bawden, Evie Ogden, and others, was held on the rectory grounds on Saturday,

June 24, to mark the occasion. All parishioners and neighbours of the rectory were invited. Six hundred people gathered to enjoy strawberries and cream with sugar cookies and sparkling white wine. The rectory itself was opened for tours and everyone was impressed by Jean O'Neil's skilled and accomplished historic restoration and redecoration. A commemorative tree was planted on the grounds by churchwardens Bill Coles and Albert Fisher.

Sadly, the celebrations were dampened by the news that parishioner and well-respected architect, Bruce Napier Simpson Jr., had perished the day before in a plane crash in Newfoundland. Bruce was the man who had designed the St. John's Lodge in 1958, as well as an archives display in the narthex of the church. He was remembered for his work at Black Creek Pioneer Village and Niagara-on-the-Lake, and for the homes he had designed for St. John's parishioners and other families in the area. In addition, he had been the architect responsible for the reconstruction of the David Gibson House, which is now a much-loved museum in Willowdale. He was on his way to celebrate an early historic settlement near St. Anthony's Bay in northern Newfoundland when he died.

A party at the Old Rectory marked its 100th anniversary in 1978.

By the 1980s, the residents of York Mills — and indeed, the residents of most of North America — had begun to follow a more secular path. Churches were no longer the social centre of the rapidly expanding communities they sought to serve. Young people in particular were now restlessly looking elsewhere for answers that the churches had traditionally provided. Churches did their best to adapt, replacing robed choirs and organ music with new kinds of musical ensembles, instruments, and vocalists. Guitars and folk music began to be heard in the church, and casual home-based Bible study groups were formed to offer an alternative to the usual Sunday services. Handbell choirs were formed to offer young people a new way to stay involved after confirmation. But in spite of these changes, parish lists continued to decline and it seemed as though there was really nothing anyone could do. The churches were fighting a paradigm shift in community values that was propelled by forces beyond their control. St. John's survived, partly by patterning itself as one of the more liberal churches in the Diocese of Toronto.

Margery Pezzack's ordination as a priest in 1977 had served notice that St. John's was more than willing to stand for change in a changing world. By the mid-1980s, St. John's had taken another step into the future when Canon O'Neil married a young couple and baptised their first-born child on the same day — an event that would have raised more than a few eyebrows even at that late date. The parish's survival was also buoyed by the inordinate number of skilled business people in the congregation. "There was tremendous leadership in the parish in those years," Canon O'Neil recalled in 2014. "This was the kind of community where the up-and-coming executives live, so we had Chief Justice Gale, [The Honourable Chief Justice G.A. Gale; Chief Justice of the High Court of Ontario and former churchwarden at St. John's] and people of similar stature, so it wasn't hard to get leaders and churchwardens. They had no trouble raising money in this place." Still, the business of the church didn't always go according to plan.

Parishioner Linda Grasley, in a costume reminiscent of pioneer days, talks with church historian Penny Potter on Heritage Day in 1984.

By 1973, the subway had been extended to York Mills Road. Wilson Avenue was extended down the hill to meet up with a realigned York Mills Road at the same time, and it wasn't long before the unthinkable concept of office buildings in Hogg's Hollow became a reality. By the mid-1980s, the first building of the York Mills Centre was under construction on the north-east corner of Yonge Street and York Mills Road. The complex constructed by York-Trillium and financed by Confederation Life was going to house office space, a new subway station, retail space, underground parking, and a bus terminal for the Toronto Transit Commission. After all of the plans were finalized and approved, however, the developers decided that they also wanted to add a GO Transit bus terminal to the project. The problem was that this additional construction would exceed the density limits of local zoning regulations.

An important part of the business of the church is performing marriages. Martin Block and Jane Walker were married by Canon O'Neil in 1973. In 2016, Martin was the treasurer of St. John's York Mills.

St. John's was approached by York-Trillium who wanted to purchase the air rights over the church's footpath, a legal manoeuvre that would give the developers the density they required for the new bus terminal. A price of $1 million was agreed upon, and St. John's was given a $50,000 deposit. Sadly the remaining $950,000, to be paid upon completion of the project, was never paid. A recession gripped the country from the late 1980s to the early 1990s, creating an oversupply of office space. Much of the brand new York Mills Centre remained unoccupied. York-Trillium was forced to declare bankruptcy, taking Confederation Life down with it. Anyone who has seen the monumentally extravagant office complex built by Confederation Life and now occupied by Rogers Communications, where Mount Pleasant Road turns into Jarvis Street, might argue that what happened in Hogg's Hollow could well have been the least of the insurance company's worries.

St. John's became further involved with its newly minted corporate neighbours when the church signed a ten-year license agreement with the CFIB (Canadian Federation of Independent Business) for an eight-foot strip of land that the church owned, adjacent to the building at 4141 Yonge Street. The strip of land was important because it included Yonge Street frontage that gave St. John's "standing" in any development decisions in the area. The license stipulated that CFIB would maintain the parcel of land in exchange for the first right of refusal should the church ever decide to sell. The agreement was later extended to June 30, 2000, after which it lapsed.

The year 1987 also marked the ninth year of the Visitation and Response Program, started by Canon O'Neil in 1971.

In March 1989 Ann and David Bawden held a party to celebrate the twentieth anniversary of Canon O'Neil's induction as the tenth rector of St. John's. Two months later Jim announced his retirement, effective October 31, 1989. The announcement was greeted with both sadness and surprise. The parishioners all knew that Jim had earned a well-deserved rest, but they also wished that he would never leave. "Well, it wasn't easy," Jim recalls, "because I was still keen and the parish was in good shape. Things were running well, but my wife said, 'You know [you've] reached sixty-five … and we ought to think about this.' She was not anxious for me to be one of those hangers-on. I was ready to retire in the sense that I was tired. I was not unhappy." The O'Neils realized they could have stayed on a year-to-year basis but they felt the time had come to move on and let some new blood into the parish. They never severed their ties completely, however. Jim was invited back to preach on two separate occasions after his retirement, and continues to visit parishioners in times of need, on a non-official basis, until this very day. In a sense then, everyone got their wish. Canon O'Neil was known by all as a man who had the rare gift of being able to communicate complex thoughts with very few words, or in his own few words, "I was not a wordy preacher." His sermons were effective and to the point and the many memorable Festival greeting cards he wrote were valued by all.

Despite the O'Neils' reluctance to be fussed over, a farewell dinner was organized by the churchwardens and generously hosted by Robert Finlayson at the Granite Club on Thursday, October 26. The dinner was attended by all living churchwardens and their spouses, as well as the widows of former churchwardens. The O'Neil children, Peter and Mary, gave spoken tributes to their parents.

Farewell services were held at St. John's on Sunday, October 29. Nearly one thousand people in total attended services at 8:00 a.m., 9:00 a.m., and 11:00 a.m. (The usual 9:30 a.m. service was moved to 9:00 a.m. to accommodate the unusually large crowd.) The associate priest was the Reverend David Flint. Assistants in the ministry were the reverends Bruce Fraser, Margery Pezzack, Phelan Scanlon, as well as Sally Armour Wotton, Catherine Bryant, and Dr. Bruce Williams. Maurice White was the organist and choirmaster.

Canon O'Neil preached the sermon at all three services with his children reading the lessons at the final service. Bill Saynor gave the farewell address. Churchwardens Michael Ogden and Robert Finlayson presented the canon with a generous financial send-off, courtesy of the parishioners, and the Anglican Church Women (ACW) gifted the O'Neils with a round-trip ticket to Florida on Air Canada. After all three services, everyone proceeded through the tower doors onto the lawn

Left: *The Reverend David Flint was both a part-time and full-time associate at St. John's throughout the 1980s and 1990s.*

Right: *The Reverend Jim O'Neil and his wife Jean say goodbye to parishioners after his last service before his retirement in October 1989.*

where, on a lovely sunny day, Jim and Jean had the chance to greet and thank every-one personally. They put the parishioners' gift toward a new home at 107 Ridley Boulevard. The Reverend Donald S. Henderson was appointed priest-in-charge by Bishop Arthur Brown and thoughts slowly turned to finding a new rector.

On November 2, 2014, two days after the twenty-fifth anniversary of his retirement, Canon O'Neil attended the rededication service of the beautifully renovated St. John's York Mills Church. He was moved to see that space had been reserved for a stained-glass window in his honour.

Created by Sue Obata, a practiced artist in the creation and restoration of stained glass, the completed window was dedicated on Sunday, August 23, 2015, with the O'Neils in attendance. The window was a gift from parishioners Heather and Ian Stewart as a tribute to the ministry of the Reverend Canon Jim O'Neil and his wife Dr. Jean O'Neil.

Canon Jim O'Neil returns to St. John's from time to time. Shown here chatting with the Reverend MacDonald at the rededication of the sanctuary on November 2, 2014.

THE WARTIME ADVENTURES OF
ABLE SEAMAN JAMES FRANCIS O'NEIL

When Great Britain declared war on Germany on September 3, 1939, Jim O'Neil was still twenty days shy of his fifteenth birthday. Like most boys of his generation, however, he was soon caught up in the emotion of the times and it wasn't long before he felt the urge to "do his bit."

At the tender age of eighteen, he decided to go to sea with the Royal Canadian Navy, completing his basic training at Winnipeg, Cornwallis, and Halifax. His first posting as a newly minted able seaman was to the HMS *Nabob*, an escort aircraft carrier. Escort aircraft carriers — also known simply as escort carriers — were smaller slower versions of full-sized aircraft carriers, usually only half as long and displacing around one-third as much water as their larger sisters. Escort carriers were much cheaper than their full-sized counterparts and faster to construct — two reasons for their immediate popularity. They were understandably more vulnerable than full-sized carriers, however, owing to the fact that they were not as well-armoured or well-armed and they carried fewer planes. Escort carriers were initially used to protect supply convoys from attacks by enemy submarines and airplanes, although they were later used as part of "hunter-killer" groups that actually sought out and destroyed German submarines and warships.

The *Nabob* had been built in the United States and christened the USS *Edisto* when she was launched on March 22, 1943. But she never saw actual service in the U.S. Navy and was transferred under Lend-Lease to the United Kingdom on September 17, 1943, in Tacoma, Washington. She sailed on her maiden voyage from Vancouver in early 1944, carrying a crew of 750, including 450 men from the Royal Canadian Navy. She was commanded by Captain Nelson-Lay, who was a nephew of then-Prime Minister William Lyon Mackenzie King. Naval combat of the day was so intense that many vessels didn't last long. HMS *Nabob* was sadly among that group, taking part in only two offensive missions: Offspring and Goodwood. Jim O'Neil was on board for both missions.

Jim was assigned to serve as yeoman to the ship's chaplain, Padre William Hills. One of Jim's first responsibilities was the care of a group of refugee children who were being taken to safety in Canada. He also assisted Padre Hills as a server at services and other tasks, including overseeing the ship's library, where he was working when the ship was hit by a German torpedo on August 22, 1944, in the Barents Sea, off the coast of Norway. HMS *Nabob* had been taking part in the Goodwood operation at the time — an operation that included a strike against the *Tirpitz*, the largest battleship in the German Navy. Jim's ship was damaged beyond repair. Twenty-five of his shipmates were killed and many more were injured. Despite being so heavily damaged, HMS *Nabob* managed to limp into the Scapa Flow naval base in Scotland's Orkney Islands. Though many of the sailors had been transferred to other undamaged ships, Jim volunteered to remain on board for the perilous final voyage. He was still a month shy of his twentieth birthday when he was sent home to Canada on a well-deserved leave. He travelled with Padre Hills and many others on board the ocean liner *Queen Elizabeth I*, which had been reconfigured as a troop carrier. He never returned to active service. Though the HMS *Nabob* was never refurbished as a fighting ship, she did supply parts for other ships until the end of the war. She was then sold for scrap to a shipyard in the Netherlands in 1947, and was eventually rebuilt and relaunched as a commercial merchant ship. She finally met her end at a scrapyard in Taiwan in 1977.

Though he would express some chagrin in later years that he hadn't been involved in more aggressive duty when the torpedo hit, Jim was also quick to point out that this was the turning point in his life that would ultimately lead him to the priesthood. Although Jim had been interested in the Church before enlisting, his connection to the chaplain, and the chaplain's ability to comfort the victims of the explosion, allowed Jim to truly witness the good works of the Lord, even amidst the horror of war on the vast North Atlantic. Jim saw Reverend Hills as a mentor and as someone who was glad to "shepherd a wandering sheep."

This very real and personal brush with mortality at such an early age gave Able Seaman James Francis O'Neil a new appreciation of his life, which he thereafter lived to the fullest. Following the war he moved to Toronto where, after graduating from the University of Toronto and Wycliffe College, he was ordained a deacon in 1951. He was ordained a priest by the Right Reverend Harold Sexton, Archbishop of the Diocese of British Columbia, in Victoria on Sunday, June 8, 1952.

A BOAT IN THE CHURCHYARD

One day in the 1970s, the Reverend James O'Neil was approached by a home-owner, whose Don Ridge Road home abutted St. John's churchyard, with a most unusual request. The neighbour had a boat that he wanted to repair in his backyard, but the layout of his property was such that he was unable to move the boat from his front yard to his backyard, so he asked the reverend's permission to move the boat through the churchyard. O'Neil — a seafaring man himself — readily agreed. The matter was then forgotten, but when moving day finally rolled around, it was immediately apparent to all present why the neighbour had made his request.

The boat in question — *yacht* would be a more accurate term — was so large that it had to be transported on the back of a flat-bed truck, with a massive overhead crane in tow to lift the boat off the truck and through the air into the neighbour's backyard. On hand that day were several parishioners whose loved ones were buried in the churchyard. They were understandably concerned when they saw this yacht hanging in mid-air over the headstones of their family members. Their concern was expressed to church officials, who agreed that a more carefully crafted plan must be devised for the day of the yacht's removal.

The truck and crane returned on the appointed day at the early hour of 5:30 a.m. Churchwardens Bill Saynor and Peter MacPherson agreed to be on-site to supervise the operation. They saw to it that no damage was done by the yacht's removal, and as the big truck slowly pulled away, all concerned heaved a sigh of relief. To the best of anyone's knowledge, this was the last yacht ever to be seen in the churchyard.

THE REVEREND MARGERY PEZZACK: PIONEER

It seems only fitting that a pioneer church would produce some pioneers of its own. With that in mind, one name immediately stands out: that of the Reverend Margery Pezzack, the first woman priest in the Anglican Diocese of Toronto. Her ordination in 1977 not only set the diocese on its ear, it also served notice that St. John's was now a leader in moving forward toward a more liberal outlook as the Anglican Church of Canada faced the future.

The Reverend Margery Pezzack preaching

Margery was born in 1919 and ordained a deacon in 1949. She served at St. John's Norway with Lewis Garnsworthy and James O'Neil before coming to St. John's York Mills as the new director of religious education in 1955. She arrived when York Mills was still a rather rural community, though certainly an educated and affluent one, and not yet completely surrounded by the housing and roadways that would soon claim the former farmland. Highway 401 was still under construction and St. Andrew's Golf Club still offered green space and fresh air, from the eastern border of St. John's all the way over to Bayview Avenue.

There were new subdivisions in York Mills at this point, although it would be nearly twenty years before the parish was "built out," as they say in the real estate business. The building boom would actually benefit St. John's church school in the fifteen years following Margery's arrival, providing additional students that would double the school's enrollment from two hundred to four hundred students.

The church school was extremely effective and well organized under Margery's leadership, and it featured different course outlines for each age group. She was ably assisted by Shirley Coles and Penny Potter, among others. Of particular importance to the lessons was an Anglican catechism that emphasized the positive aspects of the Ten Commandments, rather than the threat of hellfire and brimstone. For instance "Thou shalt not steal" was taken to mean that the students should learn to *give* and not take.

Margery Pezzack was an effective and organized Sunday school teacher.

In January 1970 Margery played a major role when one of the largest confirmation classes in St. John's history was presented to Bishop Snell. The class was so large that approximately fifteen separate group leaders were required to teach the catechism to all of the students. During autumn 1969 Margery and Shirley Coles led a weekend training session at the Anglican Training Centre in Aurora, Ontario, to educate and organize all of the team leaders. Some of the leaders of the time were Bill Saynor, Al McFarlane, and Bill Coles.

These were the glory days for St. John's, with more than eight hundred parishioners involved in more than twenty separate church committees. Much of this success must surely be attributed to Margery's ability to capture the interest of the young people of the parish. She famously ended each address to her students by raising her left hand, touching each one of her four fingers and thumb as she repeated the verse from Matthew 28:20: "I am with you always." As the latter part of the 1970s rolled around, however, Margery made a move that would reverberate far beyond the brick walls of St. John's.

On March 22, 1977, Margery Pezzack was ordained to the priesthood by the Right Reverend Lewis Garnsworthy, Bishop of Toronto. She was the first woman priest in the Diocese of Toronto and her ordination caused a tremendous uproar. Several hundred priests in the diocese went so far as to draft and sign a manifesto that stated, in part, "It is impossible, in the divine economy, for a woman to become a priest." One lay group in the diocese described her ordination as "intrinsically schismatic if not heretical." Another group, known as the Council of Faith, went so far as to actually speak out during the ordination service itself to ask the bishop to stay the proceedings, but as St. John's parishioners knew, Lewis Garnsworthy was not a man to be trifled with. The ordination proceeded as planned and the Reverend Margery Pezzack returned to St. John's as an assistant in the ministry of Canon James Francis O'Neil. She assisted at the celebration of Canon O'Neil's twenty-fifth anniversary as a priest on Sunday, June 5, 1977. Margery had been at St. John's for twenty-two years, but now she could celebrate the Holy Communion.

After the Reverend Margery Pezzack's ordination, St. John's parishioners Shirley Coles and Catherine Barley were also welcomed into the priesthood, while the reverends Mary Lewis, Pat Blyth, Anne Crosthwait, and Carol Langley, have served the Church as associate priests. Hundreds of women have been ordained as priests in both the Diocese of Toronto and the broader Anglican Church of Canada since Margery set the precedent. In addition, numerous women have also been consecrated as bishops, including Victoria Matthews, now a bishop in Christchurch, New Zealand; Ann Tottenham, the second woman to be consecrated a bishop in the Toronto area and later to become headmistress of Bishop Strachan School; and Linda Nicolls, the area bishop serving Trent-Durham.

In 1989, Margery hosted a dinner party at the Toronto Cricket Club to celebrate her forty years as a deacon. Among the attendees were members of the church school staff, both past and present. On Sunday, September 23, 1990, Margery assisted as a bishop's chaplain when the Reverend Hollis Hiscock was inducted as the eleventh rector of St. John's.

Hollis once described Margery as the thread that held the parish together. She served with four different rectors, in a parish that has only had a total of twelve rectors in two hundred years. Her presence helped ease the transition between rectors, especially when the time between rectors had been long — as was the case between Jim O'Neil and Hollis Hiscock.

While describing his arrival at St. John's, Hollis gave her full credit when he said, "Here we were lucky because Margery Pezzack was here and Margery knew the congregation better than anyone." Hollis recalls that she was retired by the time he arrived, but "Margery and I met (and we met more than this) every year. We would get together and I would say, 'Margery, what do you want to keep doing?' and she would say, 'I don't want to preach anymore' or 'I'll preach on Thursdays only' or whatever the case might be. So we had a good relationship.

"Once I asked her, 'How come your college never acknowledged you with an honourary doctorate?' and she said, 'Well, I don't know.' So I wrote a letter to the

From left to right, server Scott Lister, Primate Michael Peers, the Rev. Margery Pezzack, and the Rev. Hollis Hiscock present the new parish banner, commissioned for the 175th anniversary of the church in 1991.

college — Wycliffe — and asked the same question. Next convocation she had her honourary degree.... She was very, very helpful, a wonderful woman."

Margery Pezzack died on March 11, 2001, at the age of eighty-one. A Service of Celebration and Thanksgiving was held at St. John's on Sunday, March 14, 2001, to honour Margery's life and memory. The celebrant the Right Reverend Michael Bedford-Jones, Bishop of Toronto, was assisted by Hollis Hiscock and the Reverend Doctor Patrick White. The homily was delivered by the Reverend Canon Dr. James Francis O'Neil. Following the service, the congregation proceeded through the tower doors into the tranquil and historic churchyard, where this remarkable woman — known to all as "our dear Marge" — was laid to rest, forever to be surrounded by friends.

DAVID FLINT AND THE AURORA WEEKENDS

David Flint was an ordained priest as well as a high school teacher. During the 1970s, he was a part-time honorary associate at St. John's York Mills and the head of the history department at A.Y. Jackson Secondary School in North York. His church duties were mostly limited to helping at services on Sunday mornings.

However, he was approached by the leadership of the church in 1982 and asked to come on staff full-time to direct the Christian education program, with the title of associate priest. David took a leave of absence from the school board and ended up staying on full-time at St. John's for almost eight years. His responsibilities to the church school involved recruiting the teachers to help out at church school at both the nine-thirty and eleven o'clock services, planning the curriculum, and conducting worship for the children in the Children's Chapel. The Christian education committee, which he recruited, met monthly and organized at least two major events a year involving the children. He also organized what came to be called the Aurora weekends.

Above: *The Reverend David Flint*

Below: *The Anglican Conference Centre*

The Aurora weekends were family weekends held at the Anglican Conference Centre, at the time a diocesan centre in Aurora.

This property, originally belonging to the Sisters of St. John the Divine, was sold to the Diocese of Toronto in 1956. There was a fine old building and sixty-seven acres of land located on St. John's Sideroad in Aurora. The centre was modernized in 1965, then closed in 1999, the building demolished in 2000, and the property sold in 2002.

The purpose of the Aurora weekends for St. John's Church was to build Christian community, mixing fun for the children, socializing

for the adults, and a time of learning and discussion for everyone. Some of the events were planned to be for all ages, such as the square dancing organized by a professional square dance caller. There might be a hay wagon or sleigh ride where everyone dressed up warmly to take part. Adult parishioners became leaders, caregivers, and teachers. There were always outside specialists brought in, such as Kelly Walker, an ex-Roman Catholic priest who wowed the groups with his musical abilities. Many St. John's parishioners stepped up to the plate in leadership roles, such as Jay Burford, Carolyn Martin, Joanne Flint, and Elizabeth Eckert, who was later to become Mother Superior of the Sisterhood of St. John the Divine. Sally Armour Wotton, the drama leader at the church, brought her special expertise to help the children present liturgical skits. The weekends always had a theme, such as "Dreams," a very Biblical concern.

David organized other special children's events within the church. The Ash Wednesday program involved releasing the children from school for the morning, and returning to school after lunch. Volunteer teachers prepared a program of

Facing left: *Drama director Sally Armour Wotton and Deacon Bruce Williams square dancing*

Top: *There were many activities for the children on the Aurora weekends.*

Bottom left: *Sally Armour Wotton and music leader Carolyn Martin are having some outdoor fun with the children.*

Bottom right: *Catherine Bryant, church administrator at St. John's York Mills in 2016, relaxing on an Aurora weekend*

Christian themes around Lent and a learning service around the imposition of ashes. As many as fifty children would attend, some of them coming from the surrounding community.

With so many children, confirmation played a large role in Christian education, and classes were conducted not only for early teens but also for adults. The teens had to memorize the Lord's Prayer, the Ten Commandments, and the Apostles' Creed. Confirmation itself was preceded by a weekend retreat at the Teen Ranch, south of Orangeville. Many volunteers gave of their time to help run these classes and weekends: Steven Gravely, John Coulman, Phelan Scanlon, and Andy Gordon were just a few of them.

The director also visited the homes of children about to be confirmed to help prepare them for Holy Communion before confirmation. The whole family would be involved and one further session would be held in the church. There the children would learn about taking communion prayerfully and with dignity.

As an integral member of the staff during those years, David remembers the weekly staff meetings with Canon O'Neil and the music director Maurice White, who made sure that everyone listened respectfully to each other and co-operated as they planned the services and church events.

David Flint left the staff to return to teaching a year after Jim O'Neil retired, but he did take on a role in another church as a part-time associate priest. He served at Trinity Church Aurora from 1995 to 2000 with the Reverend Philip Poole, later to become the Right Reverend Philip Poole, Suffragan Bishop of the Diocese of Toronto.

CHAPTER THREE

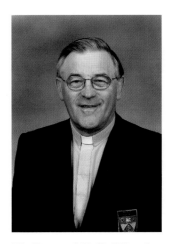

Hollis Hiscock
Rector from 1990 to 2007

The Reverend Hollis Hiscock with the St. John's crest on his blazer

Hollis Robert Nathaniel Hiscock was born on March 4, 1941, in Salvage (pronounced *Salvayge*), Newfoundland. His father was a teacher and, as a result, the family moved every four or five years, which was the custom for teachers in the area at the time. Hollis was therefore schooled in various places throughout Newfoundland before enrolling in Queen's Theological College and Memorial University in St. John's, Newfoundland, in 1959.

Since the day Hollis Hiscock was ordained a deacon in 1964, he has served God in his own unique way. "On September 29, 1964, two days after my ordination," Hollis recalls, "I was playing softball with a group of friends. Our priest came by, beckoned to me, and I raced over expecting to be invited to preach the next Sunday. I was raring to go, ready to save the world in three easy sermons. Instead his first words were 'Why are you not wearing your clerical collar?' I thought he was joking until I looked into his eyes. I said, 'I never wear a collar when I play softball.' He looked at me rather sternly and said, 'I wear my collar all the time. I never take it off.' I knew then that I was becoming a radical priest.

"I was shocked when he said that to me. It wasn't that I saw myself as a rebel. I mean, we all went through university and all that sort of thing in the days when everything was being questioned, and so I guess I really didn't feel that being ordained had changed me that much as a person. I don't think ordination should put me or anybody else up on a pedestal … because Christ was never there, so why should we be there? I guess I never saw myself elevated by ordination. I'm not sure where I learned that, but I would probably attribute it to my father."

Never one to hide behind rigid precepts or dogma, Hollis brought a breath of fresh air to St. John's York Mills when he arrived in the summer of 1990. He had served the church in his native Newfoundland since his ordination. He had built a resumé that was so impressive, he was known far beyond the bounds of his own parish when St. John's sought a new rector following Canon James Francis O'Neil's departure on October 31, 1989. Hollis's stated goal was "to serve God and people by employing my talents in the educational, liturgical, pastoral, counselling, administrative, and other areas of life to which God called me to serve."

The scope and depth of the Reverend Hiscock's accomplishments before he came to St. John's are almost difficult to comprehend, as we will see.

After he was ordained a deacon by John Alfred Meaden, the Bishop of Newfoundland, Hollis was assigned as the assistant in Flower's Cove, on the northwest coast of Newfoundland. It was a parish that embraced thirty-one different communities and stretched out over four hundred kilometres. The area had been settled around one hundred years earlier by pioneers wishing to take advantage of its sheltering harbours and abundant fish stocks. By the time Hollis arrived, the parish was well served by modern roads, although Hollis was initially unaware that he was ushering in a new era of parish travel. It seems that previous incumbents had to be constantly on the move in order to cover the vast territory. Every day was considered a Sunday in one community or another, so that all might be served. The bishop at the time told Hollis, "Don't you worry about getting around. You don't need a car. People will take you around." By the time Hollis arrived, however, the situation had changed, so although every Sunday still found Hollis in a different community, the remaining days of the week were now being used to conduct other parish business in any number of communities.

"I was there about two weeks," Hollis recalls. "In fact, when I arrived, the rector said to me, 'Where's your car?' and I told him the story. He replied, 'Well, stay two weeks, then head back to St. John's and get yourself a car.' So that's what I did."

On June 13, 1965, Hollis was ordained a priest. After his time at Flower's Cove, he was posted to the nearby Cow Head Parish, a smaller parish that served only eighteen communities spread across a mere two hundred kilometres. He would remain there until 1969.

In 1970 and 1971, he taught religious education at Bishops College and Booth Memorial High School in St. John's, as well as organizing and supervising various recreational and extracurricular activities. From 1972 to 1979, he served as an administrator and instructor at the Memorial University of Newfoundland, where he accomplished the following:

- organized a study skills program to encourage students to stay in school;
- developed an "initiation to university" program for seniors;
- initiated a joint media campaign with other educational and recreational institutions;
- developed professional, business, and general interest courses and workshops;
- managed a multimedia department that included film and television;
- taught psychology; and
- organized the transfer of thirty-five faculty members and their families to the new regional campus in Corner Brook, Newfoundland.

By 1979, Hollis once again felt called to be a parish priest. "When St. Thomas' Parish in St. John's, Newfoundland, wanted an associate priest, I spoke to the bishop and said that I would consider taking the position, provided he would also appoint me as editor of the tri-diocesan newspaper, *The Newfoundland Churchman.* I always wanted to be the editor of that newspaper. Bishop Robert Seaborn said, 'Let me see what I can do.' The next day he phoned and offered me both positions."

Later that year, the Reverend Bill Askew, the incumbent at St. Thomas' retired to British Columbia and Hollis applied for the job. Three months went by. Then Bishop Martin Mate called and said, "I am with St. Thomas' search committee, and they want to offer you the job as rector. You may want a day or two to think it over." Hollis replied, "I have been thinking about it all summer. The answer is yes, but tell the committee I will be there until I retire." Years later, he would reflect, "Our plans and God's plans do not always agree."

Hollis Hiscock would serve as rector at St. Thomas' Church in St. John's, Newfoundland, for ten years.

From 1980 to 1990, Hollis served as rector of St. Thomas' Parish, the largest Anglican parish in the country. It included at the time more than 1,200 families and a staff of ten. It is also one of the oldest parishes in the country, dating back to 1836, when it was known as the Old Garrison Church because it stood right next door to the British garrison. Hollis was the first native Newfoundlander to serve as rector of St. Thomas' in nearly sixty years and relished the challenge of overseeing such a large congregation. Once again, he went above and beyond the call of duty in his efforts to ensure the well-being of the parish. While there, as part of a team ministry, he helped prepare and deliver television and radio shows, organized a float in the Santa Claus Parade, initiated drama programs and mystery plays for public schools and the church, and established a tourist program for the church that included guided tours and a museum. In addition, he expanded parish outreach by developing worship programs for national groups, such as the Law Society of Canada, and by organizing teachers, interpreters, and bus drivers for the Provincial School for the Deaf.

From 1979 to 1990, Hollis served as editor-in-chief of the monthly newspaper *The Newfoundland Churchman,* now called *Anglican Life*. During his tenure, the paper won awards for best paper, editorials, humour, and individual columns. Hollis was responsible for all aspects of publishing the paper, including writing articles, taking photographs, editing, copy layout, and more. He organized meetings of editors and the board of directors, as well as supervised advertising and circulation. He extended the paper's reach by developing a parish-based reporter network and initiating programs that allowed children to write for the paper. From 1964 to 1990, he served as chaplain at various elementary, junior high, and high schools, as well as at institutes of higher learning. He also found time to earn the following degrees: Bachelor of Arts (Theology), Licentiate of Theology, Bachelor of Divinity, Bachelor of Education, and Master of Education (Psychology and Counselling).

Hollis Hiscock was indeed well qualified to take over St. John's York Mills in the summer of 1990 — a church with a steadily declining parish list that had been without a permanent rector for more than a year. At first, however, he didn't even want the job.

Following Canon O'Neil's announcement in May 1989 that he would be stepping down as rector of St. John's at the end of the following October, an unusually large Canonical Parish Selection Committee was formed that included Linda Grasley, William Barnett, Bill Saynor, Robert Finlayson, Corrie Fraser, Michael Ogden, William Palm, Dunbar Russel, and Winifred Herington, who was also the first female churchwarden in St. John's first 174 years. The committee met with Bishop Arthur Brown of the Diocese of Toronto to determine his ideas for the search and ask for his assistance in this new endeavour. Many committee meetings followed as candidates were discussed and assessed. Many phone calls were made. Many churches were visited, and when a suitable candidate still could not be found, the committee informed the bishop that they would like to expand their search beyond the borders of the Diocese of Toronto. Hollis discovered much later that a member of the search committee was also on a corporate board of directors. He says, "Wherever this man travelled on business, he would ask people, 'Who are the Anglican priests whose names get mentioned most where you live?' and somebody who was a member of the Presbyterian Church in Newfoundland mentioned my name. I was here at St. John's for two or three years before I knew the story. So when they say, 'God moves in mysterious ways …'"

In the autumn 1989, the Reverend Hollis Hiscock's phone rang in St. John's, Newfoundland. "Bishop Art Brown here. We met at General Synod." (The synod had been held in Newfoundland earlier that year and Hollis had chaired the local planning committee.) "I'm calling because St. John's parish, York Mills, would like to talk to you about becoming their rector."

"Where is it?" the Reverend asked.

The bishop laughed his famous deep laugh and answered, "If you were a priest in the Diocese of Toronto, you would not only know the parish, you would probably give anything to be their rector."

Hollis's wife Helen happened by his office shortly after the bishop's phone call. The Hiscocks discussed the offer and agreed that moving wasn't really in their plans. Nevertheless, Hollis felt he owed it to the bishop to at least consider the offer. Shortly afterward when Hollis found himself in Toronto on synod business, he took a small detour to visit St. John's York Mills and meet with the search committee. He told them that the family would consider the church's offer but, "If we did move, we wouldn't move until the summer. We wouldn't take our daughters out of school." Telephoning Helen rather late the same night he said, "If we're going to think about moving, it's probably a good parish to be in."

Hollis also visited the Old Rectory and when he found that Jim and Jean O'Neil had virtually finished moving out, he reasoned that St. John's would probably not be willing to wait until the following summer for a new rector and put the matter out of his mind. Hollis then returned to Newfoundland, where he soon fielded another call from Bishop Brown. This time, as luck would have it, one of the Hiscocks' daughters was coming to Toronto to attend a convention at the Prince Hotel at the same time that Hollis was returning for another meeting. The whole family made the trip together and Hollis met once more with the St. John's committee, but by now it was close to Christmas and, after returning home, the Hiscocks decided that to be fair to everyone — including their own St. Thomas' Parish — they would have to say no. Hollis called Bishop Brown and said, "It's not the time."

The committee, however, would not take no for an answer. Sometime in January, Bishop Brown called Hollis again, saying that members of the search committee would like to visit Hollis at St. Thomas' Parish in St. John's.

Win Herington and Bill Palm of the St. John's York Mills search committee visited the Hiscocks in St. John's, Newfoundland, in February 1990.

The February weekend they chose to pay their visit was the coldest, windiest, and stormiest weekend in St. John's that year. Representing the committee were Win Herington, Robert Finlayson, and Bill Palm. They dined at the Hiscock house so as not to arouse suspicions. The three visitors attended the Sunday service the following day, arriving and sitting separately. They must have liked what they saw because two days after they returned to Toronto, Bishop Brown called Hollis once more to tell him, "If you want the job, it's yours."

After that, Hollis and Helen decided to reconsider the idea of moving. Years later, Hollis would say, "I think to determine the value of a priest by the sermon or the way they conduct worship is about 20 percent of what a parish priest's work should be."

One Sunday morning, St. Thomas's choir was singing the hymn "Whom Shall We Send," and when they got to the line, "I will go if you lead me," Hollis suddenly got the feeling that he would not be there the following year. "I don't normally work that way," Hollis recalls. "It was almost like an insight."

Sometime before Easter, the bishop called again to say he was going away in a week's time and he would like to settle the matter once and for all. Hollis replied, "Call me in two days. Our conversation will be one word: yes or no."

"So that's when we decided that probably this St. John's was where God wanted us and maybe we should respond.... It wasn't that we had any reason to leave St. Thomas'," Hollis says, "far from it. It was thriving. Parishes go in cycles and at that stage we were up here," (he indicates the top of a wheel), "so that was a good place to be."

On March 21, 1990, churchwardens Robert Finlayson and Michael Ogden informed St. John's York Mills of Hollis's appointment via a letter. The letter also included a reminder that not all members of the congregation had returned their pledge cards for the current fund drive and asked that they please do so, lest the new rector be greeted with an unfavourable first impression.

St. John's York Mills in 1990 was described in an essay by a Trinity College student as being "like a duck in the water; smooth and unruffled on top and paddling like hell underneath." The Chancellor of the Diocese of Toronto described St. John's as a "ship tied to the dock — ready for the voyage — that never left the dock." Hollis responded, "Let's take her out into the middle of the ocean."

Hollis and Helen Hiscock on their arrival at St. John's

The Hiscocks moved into the Old Rectory during the first week of August, 1990. Accompanying Hollis and Helen were their daughters Karen and Allison. "I think when I got here, people were anxiously awaiting my arrival in a way," Hollis remembers. The parish had been too long without a permanent rector, and even though interim priest-in-charge Donald Henderson had done his best to hold things together, there were issues that needed to be addressed. The Hiscocks were guests at a dozen or so get-togethers hosted by search committee members so they could get to know the parishioners. Ranging in size from six to more than thirty people, these open-house events gave everyone, including teenage parishioners, a chance to meet the new rector and his family. Hollis was grateful to have the Reverend Margery Pezzack to help with the transition. "We were lucky," he said, "because Margery Pezzack was here and Margery knew the congregation better than anybody."

Two other members of the clergy — Mark Genge and Matthias Der — joined the staff at St. John's York Mills with Hollis. Hollis explains, "Mark was a bishop in Newfoundland and his wife Maxine was doing her doctorate at OISE (the Ontario Institute for Studies in Education), and I guess he was talking to the bishops here about what they could do, and one of them — it wasn't my idea — had the idea that perhaps he could do a term here for two years, as an assistant." Bishop Brown approached Hollis with the idea and Hollis readily agreed, saying later that "Mark was an excellent pastor, an effective preacher, and obviously, being a bishop, he had other skills as well." When asked what it was like having a bishop working for him, Hollis laughingly replied, "He took orders very well."

Matthias, who was from Hong Kong where his father had been a priest before coming to the Diocese of Toronto, was being ordained a deacon. After being at St. John's, Matthias served as rector in another Toronto parish before returning to Hong Kong to become Dean of the Cathedral. Mark Genge returned to Newfoundland after his wife completed her studies.

Hollis first walked into St. John's as the church's new rector on Wednesday, August 1, 1990. He preached his first sermon the following Sunday, using an analogy that compared the history of the church to Highway 401. He stated that he, and those who had accompanied him, were now entering from the ramp to the collector lanes to join the parishioners on their spiritual journey. In his first sermon, the new rector said, "We have travelled far — geographically, culturally, and hopefully spiritually — to be with you. We believe this is where we should be as we face the challenges confronting us in the last decade of the twentieth century."

There were indeed challenges to be faced and Hollis would face them in his own inimitable way. When he arrived in York Mills, there was at least one letter waiting, already asking him to deal with one of these challenges.

"One letter awaiting my arrival," Hollis recalled on the occasion of the fortieth anniversary of his ordination as a deacon, "came from a woman who lamented the fact that women were not being appointed to important positions at St. John's York Mills. Now, being the only male living in a house with three females, I could easily relate to what she was saying. I checked the parish history and noted that Win Herington was the only female churchwarden since 1816 (in 174 years). When I went to my first nominations committee meeting, all those who were nominated for different positions and different committee heads were male and my question was, 'Well, where are all the females in this parish?'"

This type of exclusion had long been a thing of the past in Hollis's native province and he wasted little time setting St. John's on a more progressive path. By the time he retired in 2007, twenty-two churchwardens had been elected or appointed. Ten of the twenty-two were women. Hollis adds, "To me that was no big deal. That was just the way it should be."

Another surprise confronted Hollis when he realized that St. John's had no copies of the contemporary prayer book, *The Book of Alternative Services,* which had been in use in the Canadian Anglican Church for more than a decade. "There were no copies here," Hollis recalls, "and at one of the first weddings I conducted, I was the only person with a book. The next time the wardens met, I said, 'You know, I can't remember — in the smallest community in Newfoundland — ever conducting a service, or a wedding, where I was the only one holding a book.' Well, it wasn't too long after that we had the books."

Not everyone was pleased by this change, but Hollis did his best to include everyone in the decision on whether to use *The Book of Alternative Services.* "Sometimes in the church, I think we need to take stands for the minorities rather than necessarily for the majority. With the two books, if certain strong people are against the new book, then that might not necessarily be the right decision. So we used the contemporary book at the 9:30 a.m. Sunday service, and we said we would use it for a year and then make a decision. The morning we made the decision was right after one of the services. We had a little quiet time so people could think about it."

Questions were asked and answered, followed by another period of contemplation and a vote by secret ballot. When the votes were tallied, roughly 97 percent were in favour of continuing with the new book. Afterwards, Hollis was approached by a parishioner who said, "You've got to change that. You've got to change that vote!" Hollis replied, "Even if I wanted to, I couldn't."

Hollis always had faith in the ability of lay parishioners to make good decisions. "I think if you give them the information — education is the important thing — let people think about it, and let people vote on it…. It may not necessarily be the thing that I would want, but I think they make wise decisions, and I would rather work that way than me dictating. I believe in team ministry in a church, and we all have our roles to play…. I have always felt that and I've always believed it and I've always practiced it and that's why, when I came here, I was surprised that there weren't more people involved in leading worship, and there weren't more women in leadership positions."

"No one person is the parish," Hollis says. "They used to say at one time, 'When lay people came in the church, they left their common sense and their talents at the door,' and I guess I felt that in any church I was going to be part of, there would be a place for people to employ their talents and their skills and their experiences and we'd all be better off for it…. I believe strongly in people making decisions and moving ahead. I have great faith in lay people in the church and I think it's the lay people who carry it. Clergy come and go." This opinion is based on Hollis's great faith in the importance of sowing the seed of the Gospel, which he has called the "hallmark of my approach to Christian ministry" and "my constant guide."

In his first sermon at St. John's, he said, "St. Paul wrote in one of his letters that one person plants the seed, another takes care of the growing, and the third brings in the harvest." Years later he would say, "I think that's a great thing for clergy because it puts things in perspective … we never become the final product. Very few of us ever see the final product because you don't know what the final product is going to be." In the sermon he preached on the fortieth anniversary of his ordination as a deacon, he stated, "God wants us to 'sow the seeds (message) of the Gospel' and leave the rest to God. We are not to become preoccupied with the 'soil,' with the 'people,' or with the 'conditions of society.' Our job is simply to keep sowing … keep telling God's Good News in Jesus Christ."

Once the vote had settled the issue of the new prayer books, another problem confronted Hollis that was a problem for virtually every other parish in the country: a declining parish list. Numbers had been declining for years and there was no sense trying to ignore it. Hollis and his team decided to tackle the problem head-on. "When I was given the numbers, the current parish council said, 'You know, many of these people never come to church.'"

It had been Hollis's practice in Newfoundland to "refresh" the parish list on a regular basis to get an accurate picture of the parish. "We would gather a group of people, churchwardens and some people who knew the parish well, and we would go through the parish list and identify people, and then we would make contact. Sometimes we would send out a note to people and say, 'You're on the parish list. Do you still want to stay on the parish list?' And, so basically, that's what we did here, and the list dropped substantially because many were only names on the mailing list, not attending members." Some people had died. Some had moved away. Some were in assisted-living facilities. Some had moved to other parishes and some had simply disappeared.

The situation was exacerbated to some extent by the fact that it had become increasingly unrealistic to depend on the Visitation and Response Program initiated by Canon O'Neil to stay in regular touch with parishioners. Not only had it become almost impossible to find enough parishioners to handle the visiting and captaining duties, it was hard to find parishioners at home with enough time on their hands to welcome the visitors. These are only some of the reasons parish lists change. Archbishop Ted Scott — the Primate of the Anglican Church of Canada — used to say that there were two types of people on a parish list:

supporters and adherents. Only the former could be counted on to contribute to the maintenance of a healthy parish. The latter would pop up at Christmas or Easter, or occasionally look to the church to perform a wedding or a funeral. It's important to know the difference when planning for the future. It was also clear that Hollis's outreach skills would soon be coming in very handy.

Hollis Hiscock officially became the eleventh rector of St. John's York Mills when he was inducted by the Right Reverend Arthur Brown, Bishop of York-Scarborough, on September 23, 1990. Archbishop Ted Scott told those gathered that day about the "demanding and glorious challenges of being a rector in a large parish like St. John's York Mills." The archbishop then reminded those who gathered that day that the role of a parish priest is "to comfort the afflicted and afflict the comfortable." Hollis was well prepared, inasmuch as he was one of the few rectors in St. John's history who was actually coming from a larger parish. He has often said that he loves big churches. He also loved the history of St. John's, although his father once warned him not to get "caught up" in history and not to stagnate.

Remarks Hollis made at his induction showed that he considered himself a part of the congregation, not above it; remarks such as "… when we have differences of opinions, as we shall, let us deal with them as Christians should, through open and loving discussions." Hollis later said that, "In my estimation, worship is number one; the second (thing) would be programs, and the third would be property and finances. There is no church that ever survived if the only thing it preached was money. The commitment has got be made, based in Jesus Christ. It's in worship that we bring everything together and the programs are what basically build up the worship, and the property that you use is a vehicle. People are more important than buildings or rules or regulations."

Hollis and his team began their first full year at St. John's on January 1, 1991. On Sunday, January 27, Hollis chaired his first annual vestry meeting. Income for the previous year was reported as $635,121. This total actually represented an increase of 250 percent over the $252,000 income reported in 1976, just fourteen years earlier.

The year 1991 was also a year of celebration, as it was the 175th anniversary of the congregation of St. John's first meeting, held on March 16, 1816. The theme of the anniversary celebration was "Growing Together in Faith" — a theme suggested by parishioner Susan Stanley. The first commemorative service, with guest Bishop Arthur Brown, was held on Sunday, March 17, to celebrate the events of March 16, 1816. On another Sunday Mel Lastman, mayor of what was then the City of North York, presented St. John's with a commemorative plaque to thank the church for its years of service to the community. The words on the plaque read:

Left: *On the occasion of the 175th anniversary of St. John's York Mills in 1991, Mayor Mel Lastman presented the Rev. Hiscock with one of his famous neckties.*

Right: *Councillor Joanne Flint, the Rev. Hiscock, and Deacon Katy Waugh, following the unveiling of the plaque presented by the City of North York*

St. John's York Mills Anglican Church, established 1816
In Honour of 175 Years of worship to God
and service to the community,
City of North York, Sept. 20, 1992
Presented by Mayor Mel Lastman and Members of Council

The plaque hangs on the exterior wall of the entranceway to the church.

On the first Sunday of every month, former members of the St. John's clergy were invited back as guest preachers. Included were the Reverend Canon Dr. James Francis O'Neil, the Reverend David Flint, the Reverend Canon Ronald Davidson, and the Reverend Phelan Scanlon. Also invited to speak were the dean of St. James Cathedral, and the rectors of St. Clement's Eglinton Avenue and St. Paul's Bloor Street — the two mission churches of St. John's. A croquet tournament was held at the Old Rectory in June 1991.

However, perhaps the most poignant service was held later in the year. A Service of Thanksgiving took place on Sunday, September 15. It commemorated the laying of the cornerstone of the first wooden St. John's church building on September 17, 1816. Guest preacher and celebrant was the Right Reverend Terence Finlay, tenth Bishop of the Diocese of Toronto. The service included a candlelight procession, with a candle lit from a flame at the Cathedral Church of St. James. The candle was brought to St. John's to commemorate the original journey of the Reverend Doctor John Strachan, who had travelled from St. James to conduct the first services for the congregation that would become St. John's. The candle which was carried by senior-surviving, past churchwarden John Frewer, was carried in an old farmer's lantern — a metal device with a perforated cover that kept the flame inside while letting the light out. The lantern, purchased by Hollis Hiscock in St. John's, Newfoundland, was a replica of the lanterns used by farmers in Ontario and fishers in Newfoundland in earlier times.

The Old Testament lesson at that service was followed by the Epistle and the Gospel in the form of a drama group presentation. The 175th anniversary hymn was sung for the first time. It was a hymn composed by musical director Maurice White with words by parishioner Olivia Lee.

The service closed with the presentation of the parish banner to Bishop Finlay for dedication. The banner was given in memory of Alice and William Butler by their daughters Barbara Alice Flynn and Beverly Jean Lewis. The banner depicts the parish coat of arms, which incorporates the Rose of York and the Mill Rind with the Lamb of St. John the Baptist and the Eagle of St. John the Evangelist.

A reception was held in the Garnsworthy Room after the service. Later, the churchwardens and deputy churchwardens hosted a luncheon at the Cricket Club for Bishop Finlay and his wife Alice Jean, Hollis and Helen Hiscock, John and Joyce Frewer, and Bill and Marg Wilson.

Now that the church's rich history had been respectfully honoured, it was time to turn to more current affairs.

The Anniversary Year of 1991 had already seen the introduction of some new services, including Tenebrae on Wednesday in Holy Week and the Stripping of the Altar on Maundy Thursday, as well as Advent and Easter carol services. By the time Hollis arrived in York Mills, he was also well aware of how important outreach programs were to the church in the modern era. No longer could a parish rest on its laurels, confident that it was the "only game in town." Now, in fact, the opposite was true, and as the twenty-first century loomed on the horizon, churches all across the world were seeking new ways to attract parishioners. Hollis certainly had an impressive list of outreach successes in his Newfoundland parishes. Now it was time to apply his abilities in the parish of St. John's York Mills. The following are some of the new initiatives taken during Hollis's tenure.

The Real Christmas Story: **A Walk-Through**

A theatrical presentation, written and produced by Hollis Hiscock and his daughter Allison Lynn, was held outdoors during the month of December to tell the real story of why Christmas is celebrated around the world. Up to 125 people participated in various roles. Over its ten-year run, five thousand spectators attended in person and an estimated hundred thousand people watched on television and video.

Verger Bill Dennis and the rector take part in The Real Christmas Story.

Passport to Easter

A holistic Lenten program, in the beginning it featured a small book or journal, written by parishioner Olivia Lee and dealing with a specific Gospel. The studies were based on the lectionary Gospel for the year in which they were used. As the series continued over the following years, the name was changed to Passport to Life, enabling the program to be expanded to include The Acts of the Apostles and to be used year-round. It included discussion topics for groups, worship resources, and its own blog. There were more than one hundred participants in the first year alone.

Music on the Hill

A twelve week lunchtime concert series, Music on the Hill was designed to attract office workers from the buildings down the hill in Hogg's Hollow. The program featured musical groups as well as individual performers. The Music on the Hill committee also produced six concerts of Christmas music that were performed in the York Mills Centre office complex during the two weeks leading up to Christmas.

Remembrance Day

In consultation with the management team responsible for the office complexes on Yonge Street in the North York area for a number of years the staff and clergy conducted a Remembrance Day service on November 11 at eleven o'clock in the York Mills Centre for the workers and visitors. This service continues to this day.

Que and Pew

This mid-week summertime program, initiated by associate priest the Reverend Carol Langley, featured an outdoor barbecue as well as a short evening worship and a dramatic portrayal of a Biblical or Christian figure.

Gospel Vespers

Marketed as "Worship in a Lighter Key," Gospel Vespers was a monthly late afternoon service led by a Gospel choir or singer. Every month it featured a different parable from the Gospels, designed to appeal to young people and non-churchgoers.

Other programs initiated during Hollis's time included MusicFest, featuring the bell ringers led by Carolyn Martin, and Passiontide and Gospel Concerts organized by the music director Robin Davis. Some of these programs were designed as fundraisers, while others were created strictly as part of the church's

Left: *The Remembrance Day service held at the York Mills Centre, November 11, 2003*

Right: *Youth minister Simon Chambers, Allison Lynn Hiscock, Carol Langley, and the Rev. Hollis, presented Bible characters at the weekly summer Que and Pew. Other parishioners also took part in the Biblical portrayals.*

The 200th anniversary of Yonge Street was in 1996 and people of St. John's, dressed in period costume, joined the parade. Hollis Hiscock is dressed as Bishop Strachan, who travelled on horseback from St. James Cathedral to worship services at St. John's.

outreach program to attract new parishioners. When asked about the fate of these programs in 2015, Hollis replied, "Most of these are no longer in existence, which is regretful from a personal point of view, but it's like everything else, they run their course. They had their purpose; they were relevant; they were important. Other things replaced them and the things that replaced them are just as important."

During his time at St. John's, Hollis also served as chair of the Communications Board of the Diocese of Toronto and wrote articles for local and national newspapers.

By 1993 St. John's was changing, little by little. Lay people were now leading the intercessions. Drama and music were becoming more integral to worship. Handbells were heard more frequently at the 9:15 a.m. service — which had been moved back from 9:30 a.m. to allow the parking lot to clear before the 11:00 a.m. service — and the church school was more connected to the regular services. The last decade of the twentieth century was a time of change behind the scenes as well.

The St. John'smen came into being in 1992, largely through the efforts of parishioners Bill Prentice and David Bawden. They were a loosely organized group of men who worked together on fundraisers and held an annual dinner, just for the men, featuring a guest speaker. Although not as active as the many women's groups, the group's activities did allow the men to bond and to work together to prepare for special occasions at the church.

Three years later in 1995 the Advisory Board was replaced by Parish Council. The new Parish Council now had the power to make actual decisions based on meetings, motions, and votes. It was no longer a purely advisory body. This was also the year when changes were made to procedures governing the churchwardens.

It seems that parishioners were increasingly reluctant to commit to the four-year term required of a churchwarden, so changes were made at the annual vestry meeting in January 1995. Under the old system one warden and one deputy were elected by Vestry, and one warden and one deputy were appointed by the rector. They all served for four years and were re-elected or reappointed at each annual vestry meeting. Under the new system, two wardens and one deputy were nominated jointly by the rector and the nominations committee and elected by Vestry. This allowed for a three-year rotation with one warden and one deputy warden being replaced annually — a shorter term for the individuals to serve, and an opportunity to include a new person each year, permitting continuity and newness. As the challenges and workload increased for the Corporation, the number of deputy churchwardens was increased to four, with each person taking on specific responsibilities and duties in the life of the parish. This decision was taken at a special vestry meeting on May 20, 2004, with the proviso to try the new arrangement for one year. The renewed structure worked and the following year Vestry approved that it continue. It should be noted that the Constitution of the Diocese of Toronto restricts the number of churchwardens to two, but there is no such ceiling or limit on the number of deputy churchwardens.

The last year of the century began with a report from the real estate committee, outlining necessary infrastructure repairs that would cost in excess of $250,000. After a special vestry meeting in April 1999, it was clear that parishioners would rather reach into their pockets than sell any church assets. So a new financial appeal was scheduled for the year 2000. Before the appeal got underway, however, a November 2000 letter from the churchwardens showed that repair estimates had skyrocketed and now the urgent and necessary repairs were pegged at $750,000. The following year began with the launch of the "Building for the Future" campaign to raise the $750,000.

The church hired professional fundraiser Michael O'Hurley-Pitts's organization Faith Matters Incorporated to handle the campaign. The March 2001 parish list had 652 names, down from 1,070 names just nine years earlier. Clearly, the fundraisers would have their work cut out for them. But Hollis wasn't about to panic. He recalls, "I think the people who were still on the list were our core supporters." Events would soon prove him right. An amendment was made at a congregational meeting to reduce the target amount from $750,000 to $500,000,

Cutting the ribbon in 2002 to begin the "Building for the Future" campaign. It would make St. John's more accessible, especially after the installation of the lift.

based on the feeling that the initial sum was just too much for people to wrap their heads around. The amendment was defeated and by April 1, 2002, church-wardens Mary Nelles and Randy Smith announced that campaign pledges stood at $970,000, with $422,000 already in the bank. The extra funds wouldn't last long.

On April 9, 2002, a construction estimate from Dalton Engineering pegged the cost of improvements at $1,129,574, broken down as follows:

Barrier-free access, including elevator	$346,699
Building renewal	$524,395
Auditorium and kitchen renewal	$50,000
Exterior security and lighting	$128,480
Engineering and architectural fees	$80,000
Total	$1,129,574

It was then announced at a special vestry meeting on August 7, 2002, that serious and widespread deterioration had now been found in the masonry of the McCollum Wing. Repairs were estimated at $580,000. They were deferred until 2003. By November 12, 2002, pledges and grants totaled $1,094,149.13, including a $100,000 grant from the Diocese of Toronto, with $565,512.63 — not includ-ing the grant — already in the bank.

The campaign received a tremendous boost when parishioner Grace Patterson sold her beloved Bentley sedan and gave the proceeds to the church. "The day I went to see her," Hollis recalls, "she said, 'You know, this is a happy day for me and a sad day,' and I said, 'Why?' and she said, 'Because I just sold my Bentley; but the good news is I'm giving the money to the campaign.'

"We do these church campaigns and ask people for money and people give money, lots of money," Hollis said, "but for somebody to say, 'This is one of my prized possessions and I'm going to take it and get whatever I can for it and that's what I'm going to give to the church to do its work,' to me, that's what stewardship is all about.… And none of us knew … I didn't know anything at all until that day." Contributions would eventually top $1,300,000.

Unfortunately, repair estimates also continued to rise. The revised repair budget now stood at $1,072,722 plus an additional $1,103,054 estimated to complete deferred repairs. Eventually, all the repairs and renovations considered necessary were completed.

On March 11, 2001, parish business seemed suddenly less important when word came that Margery Pezzack had died at the age of eighty-two. Margery had served as a deacon and a priest with four different rectors in her forty-six years at St. John's. Following a service of Celebration and Thanksgiving for her life on Wednesday, March 14, she was laid to rest in the churchyard. Hollis — who once said that "people are more important than buildings" — assisted the celebrant, the Right Reverend Michael Bedford-Jones, at Margery's service. It wasn't surprising to find that many parishioners were encouraged to contribute to the building fund in Margery's memory.

One controversial proposal for a new revenue stream was raised and quickly quashed by strong opposition in spring 2003. An article in the May issue of *The Link* by the chairman of the churchyard committee suggested opening the churchyard to non-parishioners. Then, as now, burial plots in the churchyard at St. John's have been reserved for parishioners, and even then, only at times of need. Traditionally, the only person with the power to allow the interment of a non-parishioner has been the rector. James O'Neil once gave his blessing to the burial of a woman who belonged to the Salvation Army and was the mother of a close friend of one of the canon's children. The burial was granted on compassionate grounds as the woman's family had no other options. Hollis Hiscock also once approved the interment of a non-parishioner. The story shows how St. John's has adapted to changing times.

"A woman here was married to a Muslim," Hollis recalls, "and when I first arrived at St. John's, she came to see me. She had already talked to Jim O'Neil about this — and she wanted to know if her husband could be buried in the churchyard, and I guess she and Jim had agreed that yes, he could. Well, I discovered that he was a sidesperson at worship on Sunday morning, very involved in the church here, but still kept his faith; and when he died, the leader of one of the Muslim groups here came to do the service in the churchyard. But before the day, he contacted me and said, 'I want you to do some of your Christian prayers as well,' so we did it together and to me, that was very touching … and the way it should be."

Another parish activity that falls under the rector's prerogative is the decision to invite a former rector back to preach. This usually takes place at the request of long-time parishioners who may have spent more time with a former rector and feel the need of comfort and familiarity at the time of a life-changing event, such as a wedding or a funeral. Former rectors are also often invited back to preach at special anniversary services to mark a milestone in church history.

The handbells lead a Palm Sunday procession from the rectory through the churchyard.

Some years after Hollis retired from St. John's, he was invited back to preach at the 175th anniversary of his former parish — St. Thomas' in St. John's, Newfoundland. "I started off by asking, 'How many people were here twenty-five years ago?' and a hundred hands went up," he recalled in 2015. "I wasn't naïve enough to think that the church was going to die after I left. I don't believe in that mentality at all," Hollis says laughingly, "and they're thriving, and that's the way it should be — same as here at St. John's York Mills. Things are happening in both parishes that could not have happened when I was there because the church is constantly growing and evolving."

The year after the Hiscocks arrived in York Mills, St. John's would also celebrate its 175th anniversary. Hollis invited former rector Jim O'Neil back to preach, as well as a number of associates who had served over the years. Hollis appreciated the results, saying, "Having different preachers brings different dimensions, which is good for a church." Still, it is commonly understood among the clergy that it isn't always easy for a new rector to wean parishioners off a former incumbent.

In 2004 the young people came to the rectory to sing carols and receive goodies.

Parishioners often phoned the former rector first, putting the current rector in the awkward position of almost having to agree. Though such requests are rarely — if ever — denied, the situation is best served if parishioners go to the current rector first. The current rector, in fact, becomes a buffer for the former rector.

By 2003 the parish list at St. John's was down to 580, a decrease of 46 percent from 1992, although some of this must be attributed to the "refreshing" of the list. Average Sunday attendance was down to 212, compared to six hundred in 1977. By 2004 budget deficits had been run in seven out of the previous eight years. Through it all, the parish kept paddling and kept its head above water.

In 2015 Hollis reflected on some of the reasons he thought the parish was able to thrive. "We weren't tied to one type of worship," he remembered, adding that services at St. John's had evolved to become "a combination of the traditional and the contemporary. We did a lot of special services, like Tenebrae during Holy Week."

Services also featured a variety of music that allowed all — especially parish youth — to feel involved. "I remember one Christmas we started with the old organ that's up in the balcony, the barrel organ. The verger Bill Dennis played one of the Christmas carols, and then we slowly added all the rest of the music until finally the choir came in, and so we had the keyboard, drums, guitars, and the pipe organ.… Often, at special services, the handbells would start to introduce the hymn and they would play certain verses and then the keyboard would play certain verses and then the pipe organ, and then at the end they would all play together."

It was also during this time that the handbells became a regular part of the services. Rather than being heard only twice a year, they were now an integral part of the music program, featured every month except during the summer. They were also heard at special services during Christmas and Easter. In fact, creativity in all artistic disciplines, such as special holiday presentations and various drama programs, is another reason Hollis cited as St. John's ability to attract and hold a congregation, recalling that "Jim (O'Neil) had a big commitment to the drama program … and so do I, because I think what we do is drama in many ways.…" Members of the St. John's drama programs performed "off-campus" as well, especially at the Performing Arts Centre in North York where, under the direction of Sally Armour Wotton, they presented a number of productions over the years.

Hollis also credits the congregation's positive outreach efforts as a reason for the survival of St. John's. "I think we had a strong emphasis on outreach, trying to get the people of the congregation to see that outreach was theirs to take ownership of it." Outreach was now being redefined to include any volunteer efforts done beyond the walls of the church. Whether parishioners were volunteering their time to teach English-as-a-second-language to new immigrants or tutoring children in math, this was now considered just as much a part of their Christian commitment as raising funds for the church or spreading the Gospel. "They were doing it, but not necessarily knowing that they were doing it," Hollis recalled. "I think what we were trying to do here is say to people, 'You don't have to be on the street

corner, preaching and calling out to people, but there are things that you can do.'"

Other forms of outreach involved something as simple as taking a copy of the current bulletin and leaving it where a non-parishioner was likely to pick it up and read it. Speaking in 2015 Hollis also mentioned the importance of more traditional outreach, of spreading the Gospel, citing, "people's responsibility in spreading the word; bringing people in; talking about their faith outside the church — which by the way is not an easy task."

New blood is important to any church, and Hollis said that young people have long been an important part of St. John's. "I think we had a big emphasis on youth, involving young people in more than just the traditional things young people do in churches, and we always tried to have a part-time youth worker, if not full-time … and the youth worker was part of the ministry team, making sure that on Sunday morning at worship they were there with the kids."

During Hollis's time the longest serving youth minister was Simon Chambers, who is working as the communications coordinator at the Primate's World Relief and Development Fund at the present time.

The pattern was set to do a children's talk near the beginning of each Sunday service, so the children would stay in the adult service for a while, before they went off to church school. Hollis made sure that Simon Chambers would preach periodically to the congregation, "because that way you kept the ministry of youth in front of people." As well, children were now being invited to read in church and were included in special programs, such as The Real Christmas Story, where they had roles and costumes.

It was also around this time that the little children's chapel upstairs — once an exact replica of the church itself — was humanized a bit for the children by replacing the rigid pews with more flexible seating. After the changes, the chapel suddenly became a popular place for other activities as well, such as Bible study and meditation.

One particular event early in the new century showed just how important the youth of St. John's had actually become to the church. One week before Remembrance Sunday, the St. John's youth conducted a service based on Jesus' miracle of feeding the five thousand, and challenged the church to provide meals for five thousand needy people at a cost of fifty cents per meal. Hollis mentioned the challenge in his Remembrance Sunday sermon, and that morning alone $1,200 was donated by the congregation. A member of the Gospel choir was toying with the idea of hosting an evening showing silent movies. He decided that the time was ripe to do it, in conjunction with the young people's plan to provide Christmas dinners for the needy. At the first Silent Movie Night, more than a hundred people of all ages attended, from pre-teens to those born before the 1926 movie was made. At the end of the evening, the young people added more than $800 to their fundraising. The Silent Movie Nights became very popular and, until very recently, were held three or four times per year. They are still held today, though less frequently.

One Sunday shortly after Christmas, the St. John's youth attended services at St. Peter's Church on Carlton Street in downtown Toronto and presented them with a cheque for $3,200. Through the efforts of the St. John's youth, 6,400 people were fed a holiday meal.

On Sunday, September 26, 2004, Hollis preached a sermon that celebrated his fortieth year in ordained ministry. In the sermon he noted that he had conducted nearly five thousand worship services, baptised more than five hundred babies, preached more than three thousand sermons, performed approximately eight hundred weddings, and attended more than twenty-five thousand meetings. He concluded by saying, "I am still sane and I have kept my faith."

Archbishop Desmond Tutu attended a service at St. John's during one of his visits to Toronto.

Hollis Hiscock reached his desired retirement age on March 4, 2006. Twenty-two days later, on March 26, 2006, he wrote a letter to the parishioners and church-wardens of St. John's to announce that he had noti-fied the diocesan bishop, the Right Reverend Colin Johnson, of his intention to retire from the priest-hood on January 31, 2007. His last service at St. John's was scheduled for January 17, 2007. Hollis, who once said that "parishes go in cycles," had decided that his seventeen-year cycle as rector of St. John's — indeed his time as an active full-time priest — was coming to a close.

Helen and Hollis Hiscock in 2007, contemplating retirement

When asked years later why he gave such a long notice when Canon Law only requires a two-month notice, Hollis grew thoughtful. "I remember once saying to Michael Bedford-Jones, who was the bishop, just before I retired, 'You know, when I get to the stage of retirement, I will give you at least nine months notice,' and I said the reason why I'm doing that is because I would like to see the things in place to have a new rec-tor, if not appointed, then close to appointment. I've done interims. I think they're helpful in some ways, but in other ways they're not, and if a parish is doing well and they drop down for eighteen months, then it takes another two or three years to build them back up, if you ever do. I always said that I would give a long notice. Another part of me says that it would be great if the outgoing rector could be with the incoming rector for a month, unless there are problems. If there are problems, you don't do it, but there was no problem, as far as I know — with Jim O'Neil, or when I left. I think it would have been a big advantage if Jim O'Neil and I could have sat down and spent a month together."

Hollis's retirement announcement read:

> On March 24, 2006, I informed the Bishop and the Parish
> of my intention to retire on January 31, 2007. In my letter I
> explained my rationale for providing such an extended notifi-
> cation, "In providing the Diocese and Parish with an extended
> notice, I trust that the search process for, and the appointment
> of, my successor can be completed before my retirement. This
> would provide us with an opportunity of consultation to ensure
> a seamless transition, so that the ministry and mission of the
> Parish can continue."

Hollis Hiscock's seventeen years as rector at St. John's represented almost exactly the average amount of time that his ten predecessors had also served. A parish search committee was formed in April 2006 to find a new rector.

Although the year 2006 would then proceed, as all years do, through the unchanging events of the Christian calendar, each celebration would be tinged with some sadness as the story of the Hiscocks at St. John's proceeded to its final chapter. The year was not without its milestones, however. One of those was the introduction of the Anglican Church's latest version of the hymn book *Common Praise*, and the placing of 450 copies of the new book in the church.

Near the end of that year, a musical celebration was held to honour the six hymn writers at St. John's. The church received an award recognizing the parish — out of all two hundred parishes in the Diocese of Toronto — for being the highest financial contributor during the first ten years of Faithworks. This was also the year that parishioner Catherine Keating was ordained a deacon. The Reverend

Bruce Williams was the first deacon ordained at St. John's, in the year 2000. Following that year's Christmas celebrations, which included the tenth anniversary of *The Real Christmas Story,* thoughts turned to the retirement events.

Shortly before his retirement, Hollis was contacted by a parishioner who wanted to make a sizeable contribution to establish a fund to further some of his initiatives at St. John's. Subsequently, the Helen and Hollis Hiscock Initiative Fund was established. Its purpose was two-fold: first, to continue "funding for the creative, spiritual, educational, and other programs" initiated during his incumbency; and second, always looking to the future, "to provide funding for future creative, spiritual, educational, and other programs to fulfill the vision and mission statement adopted by the parish of St. John's York Mills." The fund was to be administered by the parish, with decisions being communicated to the donors, to Helen and Hollis, and to the parish. The interest and up to 10 percent of the capital would be distributed annually to support the purposes of the fund.

A church picnic was always a fun event. This one was in 2005.

On Saturday, January 6, 2007, churchwardens past and present hosted a farewell dinner for Hollis and Helen at the Granite Club. The following Saturday, hundreds of people gathered for an evening of fun, food, and enjoyment at St. John's, to show their appreciation for Hollis's time as incumbent and to give the Hiscocks a proper send-off. Helen Neville supervised the preparation and service of more than two hundred meals in the auditorium. Two seatings were required to accommodate everyone. Dessert was served in the old Garnsworthy Room, and presentations — both serious and humorous — were made in the church proper. Presentations included speeches, songs, and anecdotes, the humour being supplied mostly by their daughters Karen and Allison. A photographic journey through Hollis's life was also included.

The next day, Sunday, January 14, a service of celebration and thanksgiving was held, designed to reflect the richness and diversity of the parish and also to highlight Hollis's "philosophy and theology of ministry and life." The two days of celebration were organized by Deputy Churchwarden Bev McLeod. Hollis showed that the thanksgiving flowed in two directions when he wrote the following words to the congregation:

Thanksgiving

Helen, Karen, Allison, and I thank you for a wonderful weekend of celebrating our ministry in the Church of God, and especially at St. John's York Mills Parish. Thank you for your support, encouragement, and gifts you have provided to our family during our approximately seventeen years at St. John's York Mills Parish.

Thank you to all who made a contribution to our retirement "purse." Your kindness has enabled us to acquire our house in Burlington, which we love. We were so pleased that many of you came to our "open house" in November. Our gratitude goes far beyond what words can truly express.

As we give thanks for and celebrate our years and ministry together, I pray that God will continue to bless and guide us as we move ahead into the future God has prepared for us. Thank you for all that you have done to help me both personally and professionally.

We will keep you in our prayers, both as individuals, as a parish, and as members of the various groups in which you participate. We ask that you remember us in your prayers as we begin a new chapter in our life's journey.

The Future

During my nearly seventeen-year tenure as Rector of St. John's York Mills Parish, our Anglican Church, locally, regionally, and worldwide, has struggled with a multiplicity of questions and challenges. We have not been exempt from, nor tried to avoid, any of those, whether they have affected liturgy, faith questions, equality issues, programs, membership, or any other aspect of our Christian Faith and Practice.

I am very optimistic about this parish and the future of the Anglican Church. When we place our full trust and confidence in our all-loving God, we will be guided and given the power to accomplish what God wants us to do in our mission and ministry. These past years are a glowing example of that, and I hope the Gospel vision will continue to grow in the coming decades.

On January 31, 2007, I terminated my role as your rector, but I continue to be your friend.

May God bless all of us each moment of our earthly lives and into eternity.

In his retirement, Hollis was looking forward to "writing, editing, photography, developing power-point presentations for retreats and missions, and becoming an extra in movies, or another occupation that I have not yet considered."

Unfortunately for St. John's, the parish search committee was unable to find a replacement by the time Hollis retired. It would be another eight months before the congregation welcomed a new rector, the first rector in 128 years who would not call the Old Rectory home.

THE OLD RECTORY

The Hiscocks were the last rector's family to occupy the rectory at 174 Old Yonge Street. Their departure in early 2007 closed the book on nearly 130 years of church history. The sale of the house in 2007, although a sound choice financially and from a maintenance point of view, would divide the congregation and leave a hole in the fabric of York Mills. Although this house, still standing at the same address, was not the first rectory in the St. John's Parish, it may well have been the last.

St. John's involvement with the property dates back to October 20, 1841, when the deed was transferred from settler William Marsh to the Lord Bishop of Toronto, Dr. John Strachan, for the sum of £200. The purchase included two acres of land and the buildings standing on it. One of the buildings was a small, two-storey house covered in rough-cast: a mixture of mortar and small pebbles. The windows were small, the interior ceilings low, and the house proved to be in much worse condition than had been revealed on first inspection. It was in such bad condition, in fact, that incumbents of the day were often forced to live elsewhere. By the time the Honourable and Reverend Thomas P. Hodge was appointed as the new rector of St. John's on December 1, 1866, the rectory had deteriorated so badly that the parish had to rent another house for him where he would stay until his retirement in 1873.

By the time Canon Henry Bath Osler took over at St. John's on May 31, 1874, the rectory had been vacant for more than eight years, used only for storage and by groups preparing decorations for seasonal celebrations. The canon toured the rectory shortly after his arrival, and by July 1874, a committee had been formed to decide whether to repair the old house or build a new one. A solution

The first rectory, purchased in 1841.

became more urgent as the canon had to move three times during his first two years in the parish, sometimes to houses that were so far from the church he was unable to find his way in to preach when bad weather made the roads impassable. By January 1875, a decision had been reached to build a new rectory.

The project was hindered by the fact that the 1870s were depressed times in the area and by a clause in the original purchase agreement from 1841 that prevented a mortgage from being put on the property. On December 14, 1875, a demolition bee was held to dismantle the old rectory and carefully store the stones, planks, and timbers on-site. By the following February, plans, budgets, and contractors had been approved for the new construction, including the relocation and reconstruction of the old barn that would now house a carriage room, a tack room, and three stalls. Dedicated fundraising efforts were required to cover the final cost of $2,042.96, but it was worth it. Completed by 1878, the new rectory soon became the scene of many happy parish

Left: *The new rectory as it looked in the early 20th century*

Right: *The Rev. Hollis Hiscock in the library of what had come to be called the Old Rectory*

activities, including picnics, dinners, teas, fundraisers, and meetings. The new rectory was beautiful. It still is. By the late 1930s, however, it was in need of some serious repairs. The question of demolition was raised, but cooler heads prevailed and, after renovations totaling nearly $7,000 in the early 1940s, the house had a new lease on life. Indoor plumbing had not been added until 1926, at Arthur McCollum's insistence before he moved in.

In 1950 the northern portion of the lot was sold and two new houses built there. Following the retirement of Archdeacon Arthur C. McCollum on January 31, 1960, the Reverend Lewis Samuel Garnsworthy moved into the rectory, followed by the Reverend James Francis O'Neil in 1969, and the Reverend Hollis Hiscock in 1990. By the time the Hiscocks departed in 2007, the rectory was once again in need of major repairs. This time there would be no reprieve.

A parish search committee had been formed in April 2006 to find a replacement for Hollis. It was not until more than one year later, on May 23, 2007, that a notice from churchwardens Chris Prentice and Stephen Bent indicated that the search committee had selected a candidate, but it also indicated that the issue of the rectory should be dealt with first. A special vestry meeting was held on June 6 to deal with the matter. It was estimated that the rectory in its then-current state should be valued at somewhere between $2,000,000 and $2,500,000, and that the repairs necessary to bring it up to diocesan standards would be somewhere in the neighbourhood of $500,000. These repairs would have included new plumbing, new wiring, the lowering of the basement, and the construction of a two-storey addition at the rear of the house.

Various plans were put forward and discussed. One idea was to sell the Comer house and use the proceeds, estimated at $1,250,000, to repair the Old Rectory, with the balance going to fund further maintenance of the church itself. Another idea was to sell the Old Rectory, demolish the Comer house, and build a new rectory on the Comer property. The final plan was to sell the Old Rectory and buy an existing house to serve as the new rectory. Feelings ran high on all sides. Several years earlier, when the sale of church assets was being considered, one parishioner summed up the feelings of many when he wrote the following letter in defense of the Old Rectory:

> This fine heritage building is the right complement to St. John's role as the first mission church of the new settlement of York, and one of the few remaining signs of the old village of York Mills. It has been well cared for, and I may say, loved, over the years. There are many valid reasons for its retention, but one of the most important is its permanence within the community, attesting to the presence of our church in York Mills from early settlement, through rural, to urban community. By its very presence, it "reaches out" to the community.

The Old Rectory in winter

The special vestry meeting ended with a motion to sell the Old Rectory. It passed by a vote of 57 to 22, with the motion recommending that the Old Rectory be sold for "not less than $1,600,000" and a new rectory purchased for no more than that amount. On Sunday, June 10, churchwardens announced that Bishop Yu had appointed the Reverend Dr. Drew Vaughan MacDonald as the twelfth rector of St. John's York Mills, effective September 4, 2007. A new rectory was purchased at 91 Haddington Avenue, just east of Avenue Road, four streets south of Wilson Avenue, and outside of the parish. The cost was $1,450,000.

The Old Rectory was sold for $2,410,000, with a closing date of September 28, 2007, but the deal was cancelled two weeks prior to closing when it was discovered that the potential new owner had applied for a demolition permit. The property was relisted for sale on September 24 at a slightly reduced price of $2,395,000. On October 4, Heritage Preservation Services of the City of Toronto officially opposed the Old Rectory's demolition when it stated in a letter to the rector and churchwardens of St. John's that:

> "The property at 174 Old Yonge Street has been identified as a significant part of Toronto's built heritage. The City of Toronto is interested in designating this property under Part IV of the Ontario Heritage Act. When a property is designated, it gives City Council the legal authority to ensure alterations are appropriate to the property's heritage character. Heritage Preservation Services is responsible to Council, and administers the development review process of Toronto's heritage properties. Its staff is composed of architects, planners, and historians who have expertise in the development process, within the City of Toronto. They work to ensure the valuable legacies of our past are considered during the review process."

The Old Rectory was eventually sold for $2,100,000 on November 30, 2007, with the purchaser intending to restore and inhabit it. At this writing, the Old Rectory is still standing, although the southern portion of the lot was recently sold and a new monster house built there that dwarfs the Old Rectory and diminishes what was once the pride of the community.

The Old Rectory was designated as historically significant under Part IV of the Ontario Heritage Act by Toronto City Council on April 4, 2013. Part IV of the heritage act designates buildings of cultural heritage value for preservation. No alterations or demolitions are allowed if they are likely to affect the property's heritage attributes — unless the changes are specifically debated and approved by city council.

The Old Rectory as it looked in 2016 after its sale and renovation work

NORA MARSH VAN NOSTRAND WEDD

The van Nostrands were there when the cornerstone was laid for the first wooden St. John's Anglican Church, York Mills, on September 17, 1816. Patriarch Cornelius van Nostrand, though eighty-six years old and too ill to attend the ceremony, watched through the rain from his nearby home, comforted by the knowledge that his descendants would now have a proper place to worship. He died on May 24, 1817.

Cornelius was born in 1730, twenty-six years before Mozart and eleven years before the first performance of Handel's *Messiah*. He brought his family to Upper Canada from their home in Oyster Bay, Long Island, in the winter of 1799–1800, settling on five hundred acres of land in Markham Township that had been granted to him by the government of Upper Canada. In 1805 Cornelius bought the two-hundred-acre Lot 13-1E in York Mills from Alexander Gray Jr. The new farm ran from Yonge Street to Bayview Avenue, halfway between York Mills Road and Sheppard Avenue East. The family would farm this land — and additional land they would purchase in the area — until 1929. Although some family members moved to Vandorf, Ontario, to pursue their farming and business interests, the van Nostrands who remained in York Mills continued to be hard-working, respected members of the community.

In 1914 following the outbreak of the First World War, the first local branch of the Canadian Red Cross opened under the leadership of Mrs. Arthur van Nostrand, wife of Lt.-Col. Arthur J. van Nostrand. The branch raised money through concerts, bake sales, and donations. The money they raised was used to supply Canadian troops at the front with bandages, clothing, and parcels from home. Daughter Nora van Nostrand chipped in when she opened the Orchard Tea Garden on Yonge Street, just down the hill from St. John's Anglican Church, to raise money and provide additional meeting space.

Nora was one of the most interesting van Nostrands of all. She had been the captain of her high school's ice-hockey team before opening the tea house, and when her boyfriend Basil Wedd sent her a cable from the trenches during the early days of the First World War saying, "Come and marry me," Nora replied, "Even if I have to swim there."* They married shortly afterward in England, returning to Toronto after the war with an infant son. In 1919 she danced several dances with the Prince of Wales at a ball held at the York Club in downtown Toronto. It was the prince, then just 22, who had taken an interest in Nora, then 26. She liked to joke in later years that he seemed to prefer older women. She also danced with both the Prince of Wales and his brother, the future King George VI, in 1927 at a ball to commemorate the opening of the Princes' Gates. The ball was held at the spectacular Strathrobyn estate, just southwest across the valley from St. John's and still standing as the site of the Canadian Forces College.

After the war the Wedd family moved to France, where Basil had business to attend to. When he found himself trapped with his son in Britain at the outbreak of the Second World War, it was left to Nora to drive their two daughters across Europe, one step ahead of the advancing German army. They made it back to Toronto, as did Basil and son William who had both fought in the war, with Basil returning as a brigadier-general.

Hollis Hiscock remembers Nora fondly. "The first time she remembered coming to church was on the handlebars of her father's bike.… I had a lot of association with her because I visited fairly often. When she was one hundred years old, Tom Kneebone wrote a play about her life, at least a portion of her life, and it was performed in a number of places. One Sunday morning she came here to a service at St. John's. In the afternoon they were doing the play in the seniors' apartment building where she was living, so she came up here in the morning, and she went to the play in the afternoon, and afterward she said to me, 'You know, I really enjoyed the church service more than the play about me.'" Hollis smiles as he says, "You would go to visit her … it was like you were going into the presence

---

* The *Globe and Mail,* January 8, 1997, A14.

Nora van Nostrand Wedd
(left) *and the Rev. Jim O'Neil*

of a queen because, when she felt you were there long enough, she would say, 'Thank you very much for coming' and dismiss you, very graciously."

Nora died in 1996 at the age of 103, outliving both her son and husband by thirty years. Hollis recalls, "She died in winter, but in her will she wanted a party in May or June … and she had it all worked out, and so we did that. We had the service for her when she died and then, in the springtime, there was a big celebration on a Saturday at one of the pubs downtown and then the next day, everybody came back here for the service."

On her 99th birthday, she received a signed photograph from Wayne Gretzky, #99. To mark her 100th birthday, she threw a party for one hundred people in the same ballroom of the York Club where she had danced with the Prince of Wales, three-quarters of a century earlier. Up until the last month of her life she held a weekly party for her friends at a local restaurant, although she stopped offering martinis after she turned one hundred. The wine, however, kept flowing. Parishioner Linda Grasley recalls being invited to lunch at Nora's Manulife Centre home, along with John and Joyce Frewer, where they would be treated to cocktails and appetizers in Nora's living room, made by Nora herself, followed by lunch in the top-floor dining room.

The van Nostrand plot in the churchyard

Hollis believes that Nora was the last van Nostrand to be a parishioner at St. John's. She is buried in the churchyard, in the Wedd plot of her husband's family. "The van Nostrands have a reunion every ten years," Hollis says. "They would invite us out for lunch periodically to their home in Vandorf, so we kept in touch. There was always a connection."

York Mills is left with the family plot and memorial wall in the churchyard at St. John's. The plot contains room for interments, although the name of any North American van Nostrand may be put on the memorial. They don't have to be buried there. Here in the churchyard, where the dates on the headstones span four centuries, six generations of van Nostrands are at rest. The stories told in carved granite and limestone offer vivid proof of this family's remarkable journey.

DRAMA AT ST. JOHN'S YORK MILLS

St. John's stood for many years at the centre of community life and, as such, theatrical productions were often a church-sponsored activity. Re-enactments of Biblical stories were an integral part of the children's ministry, and that tradition continues to this day with the production of special videos at Christmas and Easter and occasional themed presentations to the adult congregation.

Left: *Olive McCollum in the* The Mad Hatter's Tea Party *in 1961*

Right: *Ruth Davis as Isabella in* The Belles of St. John's

At one time the adults of St. John's were also involved in drama productions that were offered even to the community at large. In the mid-twentieth century, one parishioner particularly, Ruth Orr Graydon, fostered a group of thespians at St. John's to present plays that she had written, all in rhyme, and even Canon McCollum and his wife Olive took part. In 1957 with the help of dozens of women of the Anglican Church Women (ACW), Ruth directed and narrated *Your Life, Fifty Years of Fashion*. In 1961 she wrote and produced *The Mad Hatter's Tea Party*, and in 1968 *The Belles of St. John's*. Her final play was presented in 1975, *This Above All – Why Not?* In St. John's archives today, one can still find the text of these plays with photos of St. John's members in full costume. In the 1980s a group of St. John's thespians formed a drama group and called it St. John's Theatre Arts Program. Its mandate was to enrich the worship and the education program at the church. In 1984 Sally Armour Wotton, a workshop leader and performer, joined the staff team along with Henri Audet, a tenor well known for his work with children. A headline in the Anglican diocesan newspaper of the time proclaimed "St. John's York Mills Hires Entertainers." And thus began almost two decades of drama and music at the church under her leadership. Sally also took on working weekly with the church school, alongside Associate Rector David Flint.

Sally began the theatre program working with the adults to present liturgical dramas, and once she had a core group, she began teaching drama skills to the youth. Soon she had two or three groups of young people who began producing, along with the adults, liturgical dramas for Sunday morning services, and eventually major productions at the church on a weeknight or Saturday evening, often preceded by a potluck dinner. The groups often took their dramas to other churches, and by 1995 they were performing at the Ford Centre for the Performing Arts, now called the Toronto Centre for the Performing Arts.

Above: *Sally Armour Wotton working with one of the children*

Left: *Alison Hendrick, Fraser Woodside, and Don Woodside in a production of* The Three Musketeers

Some of the highlights of their programming included a half-hour presentation of Dickens's *A Christmas Carol*, taped at Rogers Television Studio and shown every year for many years. A cast of thirty presented *Robin Hood* at the men's minimum security prison in Brampton, and in 2006 Sally Davis and, music director at the time, Robin Davis, produced Murray Schafer's *Jonah* and toured with the cast to half a dozen other churches.

By 2004 parishioner and drama cast member Stephen Monk had taken over the direction of the evening performers in response to the expansion of the drama program. Some of the productions they staged at the centre were *The Wind in the Willows*, *Charlotte's Web*, *Pinocchio*, and *Beauty and the Beast*. In 2008 *The Lion, the Witch and the Wardrobe*, staged with actors and shadow puppets, was the last play presented at the Toronto Centre for the Performing Arts. School children from the area were bussed in to the performances.

In 2007, *The Real Christmas Story* — an outdoor walk-through written by the rector Hollis Hiscock — but often revised and updated, marked its tenth season in the churchyard. This was the last full season for Sally Armour Wotton, who left the staff of St. John's in 2008 to take up a teaching position at Trinity College.

Left: *In 2008 costumed children prepare to perform in* The Lion, the Witch and the Wardrobe *at the Toronto Centre for the Performing Arts.*

Right: *Stephen Monk and Catherine Bryant face off in* The Family Portrait.

CHAPTER FOUR

Dr. Drew MacDonald
Rector from 2007

The Reverend Dr. Drew MacDonald at the west entrance to the old narthex of St. John's

The Reverend Dr. Drew Vaughan MacDonald took over as the twelfth rector of St. John's York Mills on September 4, 2007. Like his predecessor Hollis Hiscock, Drew inherited a parish that had been eight months without a permanent rector — a long gap, but not quite as long as the gap between Jim O'Neil and Hollis Hiscock. Interim priest-in-charge Douglas Blackwell had maintained the status quo, but Drew inherited a church anxious to greet a new rector.

At the time of Drew's arrival, there were three services on a Sunday morning: a small traditional communion service at 8:00 a.m.; a family service at 9:15 a.m., drawing its liturgy from *The Book of Alternative Services*; and an 11:00 a.m. service that featured a choir with traditional organ accompaniment and used *The Book of Common Prayer*. Drew noted early on that there was little opportunity on Sunday morning for parishioners attending services to get to know one another and build the fellowship that could help counteract cultural and other pressures contributing to declining attendance.

Drew Vaughan MacDonald was born into a "nominally Anglican" family in Vancouver on August 18, 1955. His maternal great-grandfather, an Anglican clergyman, had been the Regional Dean of Wales. Drew says, "I think there's a spiritual pedigree there, but my paternal side was very non-faith." His paternal grandfather had a Ph.D. from Harvard and was the head of the English Department at the University of British Columbia (UBC). As a young adult Drew attended St. John's Anglican Church in Shaughnessy, a suburb of Vancouver where, coincidentally, Harry Robinson of York Mills was the rector. Interestingly, Drew had been baptised as an infant at St. John's and was confirmed at St. Mary's in Kerrisdale, a neighbouring parish.

Growing up he attended elementary and high school in Kerrisdale before studying political philosophy and history for two years at UBC. At that point he interrupted his studies to spend a year working in the pulp mills on the Sunshine Coast. Using the money he saved, Drew ventured off to Europe for just short of a year. He said, "Interestingly, through travel, I got a glimpse of the world I had studied and was struck how my faith gently began to grow." He had been touched by the Gospel through youth ministry while a teenager of fourteen or fifteen. But by the time he left for Europe as a young man in his early twenties, his interests lay elsewhere than in the Church. Faith in God was quite another matter.

Upon returning from Europe, Drew moved to Ottawa to study political history at Carleton University. After earning his B.A., he returned to the West Coast. "When I went to university, I really wanted to understand how the world worked. I studied Aristotle and Plato and Descartes, among others, and I came to the conclusion that for all their brilliance, I found they didn't answer life's core questions. This is where the deep truths of Christianity began to reveal themselves to me. I guess I was just ready for something more and the teachings of Jesus began to resonate deeply within me."

At the same time, he said, he found the world to be confused, if not confusing. "No one I encountered really seemed to be any further along than I was. I was also struck by the world of 'adults' that seemed to be pretty broken. So, in hindsight I can see that what drove me to the Church was not just the teachings and life of Jesus, but what I have come to call 'the poverty of the world' — both intellectually and morally. I was seeking a moral and intellectual compass and was driven almost by default into the arms of the Church. I finally bumped into some church people who had a real humility about them, a real love about them, and I said, 'These people have something I don't have and I want that!'"

And thus began Drew's deeper walk with God. "I made a simple commitment to attend church every week, along with reading and studying my Bible with other Christians. I would leave the rest up to God and see how my life would change from there. In two months my life was so dramatically transformed, I never looked back. My world was blown apart. The Spirit had gotten hold of me, and I had to reread and rethink everything I'd learned. So, unlike many, I had a very serious conversion. I was blind, but now I see — as the famous hymn 'Amazing Grace' says."

Drew had majored in history and, in particular, "The Great Revolutions"— British, French, American, and Russian — at UBC and later at Carleton University. From there he began to study for his Master of Arts in Canadian–American relations at the University of Western Ontario in London. But then in the midst of his work, he received a call to work as a political organizer for the British Columbia New Democratic Party, under the leadership of Dave Barrett. Deciding that it was better to "do" than just to learn, he took the offer and moved back to the West Coast, where he worked in various ridings preparing candidates and volunteers for the coming provincial election. Throughout those years, as his experience and skills grew, he also worked across western Canada, where he says he was touched by the social gospel and the deep influence of people such as the great Tommy Douglas.

After spending this time in the realm of politics — and perhaps because he had rediscovered his faith — Drew was feeling the limitation of politics. He decided to study law, since he felt the power of justice, and both friends and aptitude tests confirmed this direction. He packed up his belongings and with the blessings of his parish priest Harry Robinson, headed east to enroll in law school at Dalhousie University in Halifax.

"I drove across the country, but by the time I got to Halifax I realized that I was pursuing law for everyone but me. Just because I had an aptitude for it didn't mean it was where my heart was." Instead, Drew enrolled at the Atlantic School of Theology (AST). "I started taking some seminary classes," he recalls. "They let me in the door, and I was just poking around, taking a look at what was offered and found I was having the time of my life. Now I was studying theology and my real passion of Church history."

Notwithstanding a real love of academics and a possible future in teaching, Drew was being encouraged by one of the best recruiters the Church has ever produced, the Rev. Dr. Peter Mason, who later become principal of Wycliffe College and then Diocesan Bishop of Ontario. At the time, Mason was the rector of the prestigious St. Paul's Halifax — Drew's newly adopted parish. And so it was that Peter Mason encouraged Drew to study for ordained ministry. As Peter would say, "The church needed more 'type A' personalities in leadership and Drew most definitely fit that description." AST thus became the school where Drew completed his Master of Divinity.

While still a student, Drew got his ministerial groundings working at the Cathedral Church of All Saints in Halifax, under the mentorship of Dean Austin Munroe and the Rev. Fred Hiltz, now the Primate of the Anglican Church of Canada. Drew was ordained a deacon at St. Paul's on June 22, 1986, by Bishop Russell Hatton. (Interestingly, St. Paul's is the oldest building in Halifax and the oldest existing Protestant place of worship in Canada, erected in the summer of 1750. From a historical point of view, it could be considered a foreshadowing of Drew's future time at St. John's York Mills, the oldest parish in the Toronto area.)

After his time at St. Paul's, Drew served as a curate at Christ Church in nearby Dartmouth. On September 29, 1987, Drew was ordained a priest by Bishop Arthur Peters, of Nova Scotia and PEI. Harry Robinson, his former pastor from St. John's Shaughnessy in Vancouver, flew all the way from B.C. to preach at the ordination. Soon after, Drew was assigned to his first parish — Eastern Passage in the Borough of Dartmouth — where he stayed for two years. The parish grew dramatically under Drew's leadership and was a positive early experience.

Drew left Nova Scotia to take a position as chaplain at Ridley College, a first-tier private school for boys in St. Catharines, Ontario. He also taught world history and world religions and helped to coach the school's rugby team. He was well suited for the latter task as he had represented Canadian rugby sides in international competition while still in high school, competing against teams from countries such as Japan, Northern Ireland, and the United States.

Despite his varied roster of activities, Drew became dissatisfied with his situation. "I loved the students and I loved the teaching, but I wasn't comfortable with the culture of the private school," he recalls. "They were old school. I felt they were encouraging religion, and I wanted to develop faith. I didn't care if the students became Anglicans; I just wanted them to get to know God." Drew eventually resigned, feeling that he needed to go back into parish ministry.

Though he had a job offer in Halifax, he decided to stay in Ontario, where he soon took up parish responsibilities in the Diocese of Huron. He served as a parish priest at the Church of the Redeemer in London for several years. While there he also involved himself in fundraising work: helping hospitals, churches, and libraries realize the goals in their capital campaigns. With the extra work, he still was able to take time off in the summer to fulfill residency requirements at Princeton University in New Jersey, completing his Doctorate in Ministry at Princeton Theological Seminary in 1999. Drew was then posted to a church in Windsor. While there, he was asked to take over Trinity Church in Cambridge, Ontario, one of the oldest churches in the province and also — like St. John's — consecrated by Bishop John Strachan. It would be this posting that would ultimately lead Drew to St. John's York Mills.

While in Cambridge, Drew was part of a clergy-led, Wednesday morning study group. One member of the group was a Christian counsellor who interestingly had a relationship with the newly elected Suffragan Bishop of the Diocese of Toronto, Patrick Yu. Bishop Yu had the opportunity to meet with his friend and spiritual director in Cambridge before his consecration. This is where Drew encountered the bishop and, in time, an invitation to interview for St. John's.

Like Hollis Hiscock before him, Drew initially turned the offer down because he was content in Cambridge. He says that he was never much of a networker, but he gave the offer another chance when he realized that Bishop Yu was probably seeking him out to help St. John's with a specific challenge, faced by many churches at the turn of the century: holding on to old parishioners while simultaneously trying to attract new ones. "I'd been blessed with growth in churches that I had pastored before and Bishop Yu said, 'You need to come to Toronto and do this.'"

Drew MacDonald arrived in Toronto with his new bride Carolyn Dobias, and the youngest of their blended family, Chloë. It was during this transition that the parish made the very difficult decision to sell the rectory on Old Yonge Street. It was in need of significant repair and with rising costs it just seemed prohibitive. Thus, with the help of real estate agent and parishioner Connie Hunt Hamson, St. John's purchased the new rectory at 91 Haddington Avenue in the summer of 2007. The new clergy family happily moved into their accommodations on August 18 — Drew's fifty-second birthday.

Carolyn was an interior designer by profession, and was pleased to move into such a comfortable and spacious home. Their daughter took up her studies at Lawrence Park Collegiate, while the four older boys — Conor, Adrian, Benjamin, and Jamie — were all continuing their academic pursuits in universities in Quebec and the Maritimes. Carolyn absolutely loved living in Toronto. She grew up in London, England, where she was educated at South Hampstead and the American School in London. She later majored in psychology and French at the University of Western Ontario and, after a few years of work, completed a further degree in interior design in London, Ontario. She found the cosmopolitan lifestyle of Toronto very much to her liking. "I always feel at home at St. John's York Mills. I think our backgrounds in major urban centres allowed for us to be a good fit with the people of this parish."

The new rector, the Reverend Dr. Drew MacDonald, and his wife Carolyn Dobias on the steps to the old narthex

Anglicanism covers a wide spectrum of liturgical expression. The Anglican high-church expression with its candles, incense, and colourful vestments, is "more Catholic than the Romans," as Drew once said. In historic Ontario, Bishop John Strachan — Family Compact member and power-broker — represented that high-church Anglican expression. By contrast St. John's found its roots in a low-church expression, with its simpler ways and strong biblical focus. In some ways it is closer to a churchmanship reflected in Methodism or even Presbyterianism.

Drew describes himself as tending "toward that low-church expression." He has a deep love of Anglican tradition but, he says, "My job is to serve and grow the faith. Our culture has become so 'un-churched,' that the low-church expression just seems to make more sense to me in attracting new people." He lists his spiritual mentors as British low-church evangelicals John Stott and J.I. Packer, as well as his parish priest in Vancouver, Harry Robinson, who as stated earlier preached at his ordination. "Harry was magic," says Drew. Anglicans in the Diocese of Toronto might be familiar with Harry as the rector of Trinity East (also known as Little Trinity) on King Street East, which Drew describes as a "low-church evangelical Anglican flagship church." But, Drew had first met Harry in Vancouver. While Drew was still working in politics he attended St. John's Shaughnessy, not knowing until he researched it that he had been baptised there. When Drew began attending again as a young adult, it was one of the largest church congregations in Canada, and Harry Robinson was the rector.

When Drew arrived at St. John's York Mills, he took the hands-on approach of a low-church leader, sitting down face-to-face with people to explore the culture of St. John's. "There was a group of people who were traditionalists and who wanted to keep using *The Book of Common Prayer*, but I felt that my job, as I was ordained to do it, was not the preservation of the English language, but the propagation of the faith. Now, I appreciate that *The Book of Common Prayer* reads like Shakespeare, and it is rich, but you need to be educated to understand it." St. John's also had a rich music program that ran in two distinct and separate streams:

traditional (organ, choir, and hymns) and modern (band and contemporary worship songs). Again Drew took a direct approach.

"I said to the people of St. John's, 'Quite frankly, I don't really care whether you're listening to Bach or the Beatles. I'll tell you what I do care about: it's that you get along and respect one another.'

"It took a good two and a half years," Drew says now. "I believed that we needed to become one united congregation, as opposed to three congregations. The traditional service, numerically, was dropping. My prayerful place was that I really felt that God was saying: 'You need to come together.' The traditional and the modern need to be united as Jesus made clear in John 17."

Looking back on those early days from the perspective of the year 2015, Drew remembers the first big change that took place in the services. "We started a 10:00 a.m. service where we combined the two traditions, and it worked exceptionally well, and, finally, the congregation started to grow. But it was really hard. It's easier to pick a genre and work it, but I think that's one of the things we're uniquely trying to show people: that we at St. John's know how to get along. Quite frankly, I'm finding the place exceptionally friendly right now. I really enjoy coming to work. I enjoy the people, and we're having more fun. There's joy here … I've got good support in the church. I feel at peace."

Staunch traditionalists in the congregation — or those with a busy Sunday ahead of them — were still well served by the 8:00 a.m. chapel service. It was a quiet traditional Anglican Eucharistic service that generally attracted twenty-five or fewer people. The high-church choral tradition and liturgy remained an integral part of the 10:00 a.m. service at special times of the year. But on a regular Sunday, band music and contemporary worship songs alternated with organ, choir, and traditional hymns. It was a hybrid that really began to work and that the congregation as a whole began to appreciate.

The main service usually attracted a little fewer than two hundred worshippers, out of a parish list of some four hundred families. Outsiders may be surprised to learn that even the most devout parishioners are only in attendance two or three out of four Sundays per month. The average parishioner attends every other Sunday or every third Sunday, unlike the glory days of the church that continued right into the 1970s or even 1980s. But all of that changed significantly, especially in the 1990s.

It was in 1992 that the provincial New Democratic government of Ontario passed legislation to allow Sunday shopping. At that point, everything began to change, in some cases quite dramatically. As Drew says, "The culture just doesn't see church attendance as essential as it once did. Also, people in our congregation travel a lot, they have summer cottages, they go away in the winter, or they have children active in sport and school activities that often take place on a Sunday morning. Those kinds of activities never existed on Sunday mornings during the days of O'Neil or Garnsworthy. Times have really changed — whether we like it or not. Such are the challenges of being a community of faith in a largely secular modern world. I'm sure that my predecessor Hollis Hiscock was really starting to feel that shift during his tenure. I think he had the worst of it. Those were difficult days for everyone in mainline churches."

However, there is plenty of mid-week activity at St. John's as well. Under Drew's leadership more Bible study groups were formed (renamed Compass Groups), some at the church and others in homes. With the help of some extra funding by a parishioner, an Alpha program was offered in 2010 that led to a resurgence of people talking and learning about their faith. The Alpha program — a sort of Christianity 101 — was developed at Trinity Brompton Church in London, England. A powerful and interactive program, it is known to inspire people worldwide to renew their faith.

In his early university days, Drew encountered far too many Christians who couldn't answer even the most basic questions about their own religion. He has therefore always made sure that the congregations he preaches to understand their theology, saying: "I pride myself on the fact that St. John's is one of the most theologically educated congregations around. It is certainly the most educated parish I have ever served."

Drew also found a congregation at St. John's that was willing to try new things. Early in his incumbency, with the encouragement of wardens and the parish council, he began a new offering at five o'clock on Sunday afternoons called the Gathering. The Gathering was an intimate service of worship featuring Allison Lynn and her husband Gerald, the duo Infinitely More, as worship leaders. The Rev. Drew MacDonald would present the evening's spiritual theme followed by

The duo Infinitely More, Allison Lynn and her husband Gerald Flemming, were worship leaders at the Gathering.

a question-and-answer period. The experimental Gathering lasted for several years. But despite its enthusiastic following, it failed to attract more than thirty regular attendees and was eventually brought to a close by the wardens. Its resources were redirected to the children's ministry.

St. John's York Mills is an unusual parish in that it has a low-church Protestant ethos in one of the most affluent neighbourhoods in the country. The reason can be found in the church's origins. Joseph Shepard and his wife Catherine had come to North York in the early 1800s, and they donated the land for the first wooden St. John's church in 1816. He traded along First Nations fur-trade routes before settling down to farm a half-mile or so north of the current St. John's. The first congregation was a mix of Family Compact members such as the van Nostrands and Camerons and low-church farmers such as the Shepards and Willsons. The names of many of these families are remembered in the names

of the main streets of the area, although often with alternate spellings.

Architecturally, St. John's is clearly low-church; even the ceiling is low compared to other local Anglican churches, such as St. Paul's, St. Clement's, or Grace Church on-the-Hill. At St. John's, the oldest parish in the diocese, the connection to the past is palpable. Drew says that when he walks into St. John's, "I feel the farmers who built this place." Walter Thompson has attended St. John's since 1932. The parishioner in his late eighties remembers the time a cow stuck her nose in the front door during one Sunday service.

Drew says of the early farmers who fought so hard to establish a church in their rural area, "They were simple farmers, but they owned land and in that land there was wealth … and power." They were simple, hardworking people, and the church building itself reflects their attitude toward life and worship. This is one of the reasons why Drew feels as though he belongs here. "I personally come from a low-church background in my faith formation and that's part of the reason I think I am a fit at this church."

Architect John George Howard, who designed the original brick St. John's in

1843 and later donated his estate to Toronto to create today's High Park, was also responsible for similar churches in Holland Landing, Tyendenaga, and other Ontario towns. All were decidedly low-church. In *Hallowed Walls: Church Architecture in Upper Canada* published by Clarke, Irwin and Company Limited in 1975, authors Marion MacCrae and Anthony Adamson remark dryly that "… Howard's liturgical plans did not meet with the high churchman's notion of the seemly…."

As noted in *Hallowed Walls*, Archdeacon Bethune bemoaned the lack of a centre aisle for grand processions at St. John's when he wrote in 1847, "St. John's is an exceedingly handsome and beautifully situated religious edifice, constructed of white brick in the Pointed Gothic style. The interior too is respectably furnished but it would be improved, as I ventured to recommend, by adapting the seats in the centre to the general construction of the pews. At the same time I cannot here, or in any other church, feel reconciled to the absence of a centre aisle." St. John's did eventually get its centre aisle in one of the early renovations.

Despite its long history, deep ties to area founders, and its location in an affluent neighbourhood, St. John's faced certain financial realities. Drew MacDonald inherited a church with a deficit budget when he came to St. John's. It was another issue that required immediate attention, though certainly not an uncommon one for a church in the early twenty-first century. In finding ways to stabilize St. John's financial situation, Drew was perhaps inspired by one of his mentors, Harry Robinson. It so happens that Harry Robinson and the Robinson clan were raised in Hogg's Hollow and attended St. John's York Mills. (The story of the Robinson family is told later in this chapter.) Drew recalls in a lowered voice the moment he learned of the connection, years later. "Harry is a member of this parish and for me to be the rector of St. John's just … made me smile. I didn't know until I got here. Harry was my mentor, but I didn't ask him where he came

Facing: The simplicity of architect John Howard's design for St. John's is part of its beauty.

from. I just talked to him about God, and then I found out later that he was a little boy here and grew up and cut his teeth with McCollum and all the early rectors of this church. I'm a history buff … so the connection was very compelling."

In the late 1970s, St. John's Shaughnessy was a church with many wealthy people but a dwindling congregation. Harry Robinson helped the congregation to grow once again, and Drew credits Harry's background in York Mills and the fact that he was comfortable in affluent parishes. (Harry liked to joke that he came from "St. John's York Millions.") "Harry had come from money," Drew explains, "and he wasn't impressed by money, so he fit in Vancouver. See, that's the thing about 'fit': you've got to fit your parish."

In this area as in others, with his fundraising experience, Drew "fit" St. John's. St. John's has an annual budget of close to $1,000,000, and special fundraising campaigns also crop up from time to time.

A Visitation and Response Program such as that created by Jim O'Neil was undertaken once during the first eight years of Drew's incumbency, and it was a resounding success. In 2011 the Diocese of Toronto ran a campaign called "Our Faith-Our Hope." The funds would serve assessed needs throughout the diocese, with a total campaign goal of $50,000,000. The portion of this sum requested from St. John's was pegged at $750,000. Under the leadership of churchwardens Faye Roberts and Steve Bickley, who oversaw the mechanics, the church raised $1.1 million for "Our Faith-Our Hope."

St. John's was able to raise $1.6 million not long afterward for the renovations that were completed in 2014. This story is told in

The Reverend Canon Dr. Drew MacDonald, with his wife Carolyn and son Jamie, after his installation as a canon in 2012 at the Cathedral Church of St. James in downtown Toronto

Chapter Eleven, but the bottom line was that this new construction was completed on time and on budget, without incurring any new debt.

Meanwhile, Drew was also at work as a member of the Diocesan Council and the Diocesan Investment Committee. In 2012 Drew was appointed a canon at a ceremony at St. James Cathedral. Historically the title of "canon" is an honorific given in recognition of a priest's work as an educator or labourer on behalf of the entire diocese.

Thankfully, not all of the church's financial activities need to be expressed in large figures. Attention to detail is another key to success.

"I spend time on new-member ministry," says Drew. "When people come into our church, I spend a lot of time working with the welcome ministry. That's a whole piece that's been developed in this church. We host orientation breakfasts, bringing people to the church on a Saturday morning. I've had numerous open houses in my own home ... for all the new parishioners, spending time with them."

This focus is one of the greatest differences between Drew's world and that of his St. John's predecessors. With the help of Anne Crosthwait, associate priest at St. John's York Mills since 2011, the welcome and hospitality teams who provide the social side of each Sunday morning's services have grown to include dozens of people. They arrive early to greet people coming in the door and provide them with name tags, they prepare coffee and goodies for the after-service and in-between services, and they make newcomers feel welcome and accepted.

With a large congregation, many of whom have been attending St. John's for decades, there are always members who are suffering or in hospital. "I only have so many hours in the day but we (clergy) still make our hospital calls and do our best to visit the sick, and especially the dying. It is a work that is never finished," Drew says. That is why he makes sure to introduce new members

Associate Priest Anne Crosthwait and Rector Drew MacDonald, at a Sunday service

to long-time members, and encourages parishioners to visit the elderly and those in hospital. As Drew puts it, "The people of God visit the people of God, often with better effect than myself."

Drew sums up the first eight years of his ministry at St. John's by saying: "We finally had a growing congregation and a growing church school and that was a real encouragement."

In 2014, St. John's York Mills underwent a major renovation to the foyer, the old narthex, and the sanctuary. It was several years in the planning and the wardens of the time were anxious that it be finished before the 200th anniversary in 2016. In order to understand the background to raising money for the renovation, it is necessary to understand some aspects of the church's history.

One of the more intriguing stories in St. John's fiscal history, as previously mentioned in Chapter Two, regards the so-called "eight-foot strip" of land that once ran from the verger's lodge straight down the hill to Yonge Street.

Serious commercial development came to Hogg's Hollow in the 1970s, spurred by the northward extension of the subway. St. John's was rightfully concerned that it might one day be dwarfed by massive office buildings and condominiums lining both sides of Yonge Street. In way of protection, the church decided to hold on to whatever Yonge Street frontage it possessed for as long as possible. This way the church would have "a place at the table" when development issues were being discussed. Most parishioners are familiar with the footpath that runs down to Yonge Street from the west lawn by the Lodge to the Kaye

A view of the current footpath from Yonge Street up to the church

Lychgate. This was built in memory of William R. Kaye, a long-time parishioner and past churchwarden who was active on several Diocesan committees and the first lay person appointed an honorary canon of St. James. Many were unaware that another path had existed, and by the 1970s, it was almost completely over-grown with trees and bushes.

Although it's an intriguing story about why the church was still in posses-sion of this small strip of land slightly over eight feet wide, it would remain an interesting concern of the churchwardens for decades. The strip was originally given to the church by William Marsh in 1839 to help St. John's parishioners access the newly straightened Yonge Street. William Marsh was also the man who had sold the church his farmhouse and surrounding land in 1841 for use as the parish's first rectory. The newly formed Yonge Street ran straight north and south through Hogg's Hollow, rather than following the route of Old Yonge Street, which had been its original route when the church was built

In 1978 the church was offered $40,000 for the strip, which by then was bordering the property of a new office building at 4141 Yonge Street. The offer was turned down.

In 1985 St. John's signed a ten-year business agreement with the Canadian Federation of Independent Business (CFIB), the company that owned 4141 Yonge Street. The agreement bound CFIB to maintain the strip in exchange for first right of refusal should the church ever decide to sell. The deal was renewed for another five years in 1995, covering a period up until June 30, 2000.

But by 1995 the developers in the hollow were getting restless. Claiming that St. John's had no intention of ever using what was in essence a useless piece of land, one of the developers started rumblings in the 1990s that indicated they were thinking of initiating expropriation proceedings to force the church to sell them the land. It seems that the developers needed to attach the land to their adjacent holdings directly to the north of the eight foot strip in order to increase their footprint. They even went so far as to use then-mayor of North York,

Mel Lastman, to forcefully encourage the church to sell. But the amounts being offered by the developers were too low and the church was reluctant to sell in any event. Led by Churchwarden Dunbar Russel, St. John's rebuffed the developers and declined to sell.

The developers continued their legal salvos, however, and in 2012 they won a surprising Toronto Regional Conservation Authority decision approving a building that would significantly encroach into the steep ravine below the church. The church joined with neighbourhood associations to oppose the development. A community meeting was convened by then-City Councillor Jaye Robinson in the church's basement. It was a very rowdy meeting with hundreds of parishioners and neighbours attending. Churchwarden at that time John Bruce was a lawyer with the law firm Hicks Morley LLP. He and the Reverend Drew McDonald attended before the North York Community Council and, along with strong neighbourhood opposition, were successful in convincing the Council to oppose the development.

Then the developers appealed to the Ontario Municipal Board (OMB). John Bruce and Warden Steve Bickley attended the OMB hearings in 2013 on behalf of the church. In 2013 the OMB ruled against the developers, effectively killing their proposed large building development. In this context, after a series of meetings with parishioners and approval at Vestry, St. John's determined that the timing was right to sell the eight foot strip: its value to the church regarding restricting development along Yonge Street was now quite limited; the strip was completely overgrown and not being used by the church at all; and the land value was now large and the sale proceeds would be instrumental to the much-needed

A big topic of discussion at Vestry in 2012 was the sale of the eight-foot strip.

Left: *Churchwarden Blake Woodside addresses parishioners at Vestry in 2012.*

Right: *Churchwarden John Bruce makes a point during Vestry in 2012.*

Below: *The exterior of the church changed very little during the renovation of 2014.*

capital expenditures and renovations by the church. It should be understood that all church property is actually owned by the diocese, with the church serving as a steward. Accordingly, diocesan approvals were obtained for the sale. John Bruce and fellow churchwarden Dr. Blake Woodside sat down with the developers to negotiate the sale on behalf of St. John's and the diocese. The developers' initial offer was $200,000, far less than the church had in mind. After a protracted negotiation, the eight-foot strip was eventually sold for $600,000 in late 2013. The money from this sale was then used to help finance the major renovation of 2014, and provided much of the financial certainty that was crucial to beginning the long-planned renovation.

The beautiful result of the renovation, in updating the church's social spaces and sanctuary, has been much praised by everyone who has visited since its completion in October 2014.

The renovation of 2014 was a year of very intense work for both Drew and his wife Carolyn in her capacity as an interior designer. Carolyn was very involved in the original plans, working with the architect on many of the design items. She was also a member of the design team that worked on the overall look of the finished spaces. Both Drew and Carolyn were present at all weekly site meetings, along with the church administrator Catherine Bryant; the head of the property committee Bob Girard; the church verger Bill Dennis; churchwardens Sylvia McConnell and Maurice Bent; as well as the architect, the contractor, and site supervisors. All of this work was on top of the normal demands of parish ministry.

Once the renovation was over, but before the service of rededication in November 2014, Bishop Yu approached Drew and suggested it was time that he took a sabbatical. Drew had spent the previous fifteen years working very hard, leading parishes into a changing world, and, given

On the first Sunday after completion of the renovation, the rector was ready to welcome his flock into the new spaces.

Above: *The Reverend Canon Dr. Drew MacDonald and Archbishop Colin Johnson greet parishioners in the foyer after the service of rededication on November 2, 2014.*

Facing: *In one of the rector's own photos, we see the Vimy Ridge Memorial from the east.*

the recent demands of the renovation, he had found little time for in-depth reflection and study.

Drew's primary interest was always in the realm of what is called "practical theology." In particular, understanding the dynamics of how churches really grow was an area of special interest. He was aware that there were Anglican churches, in the United Kingdom particularly, which were experiencing phenomenal growth after years of decline. Such churches intrigued him, and in September 2014, Drew approached the churchwardens with his plan for taking a three-month sabbatical the following year. During that time he hoped not only to study, but also to visit dynamic and growing churches in the United States and the United Kingdom. Drew planned to find out what they were doing that attracted new members and enabled them to plan new churches. Holy Trinity Brompton in London, the originator of the Alpha program, was one such church.

The churchwardens of the time were very supportive and agreed to approach the congregation at Vestry with the idea of Drew being absent from the parish for four months, including some vacation time as well. The congregation was also supportive and interested in the results of his research. They looked forward to his reflections and the results of his research upon his return.

Drew began his travels and study immediately following Easter 2015. During his sabbatical, he spent most of his time in London and Oxford, but he visited France and Germany as well, since it was the hundredth anniversary of many battles of the Western Front of the First World War and also the seventieth anniversary of

Victory in Europe. He and Carolyn were also blessed to visit the Vimy Ridge Memorial to better understand St. John's deep connection to that battle in particular, and the history involved in the Guard's Chapel of St. John's.

Associate Priest Anne Crosthwait stepped ably into the void left by the rector and led the church from early April through early August, earning the admiration and praise of the congregation. More on the Reverend Anne can be found in a section later in this chapter.

On his return Drew was ready to implement some of the ideas he had encountered in his travels. In his absence and at his request, a discernment committee led by Anne Crosthwait had been considering how to foster spiritual growth at St. John's more intentionally and how to reach out to the millennial demographic. In consultation with this committee, and with the consensus of the wardens and Parish Council, Drew spearheaded another change to St. John's Sunday morning program.

Pondering the two aspects of Anglican worship, "Word" and "Sacrament" (as seen in the banner logo of St. John's), Drew had begun to see in his travels that young people today are drawn to the church to learn about

the very basics of Christianity. For these young people and others not raised in the church, "the Word" — Scripture and teaching — is paramount, while mature believers are more ready to be fed by liturgy and sacrament. Sunday morning worship had to address these diverse aspects of spiritual growth and so, after considerable consultation and prayer, a new format was launched in November 2015.

Approaching the start of the church's third century, this new format replaces the previous two services. The early morning Eucharistic service begins an hour later at nine o'clock, and offers organ and choral music, a short homily, and communion. This traditional offering is called "The Sacred Table." A time of fellowship and connection over coffee and goodies is still available after the service, and parishioners and visitors arriving for "The Open Door" at 10:30 a.m. are able to mingle and socialize with those leaving The Sacred Table. The energy and joy to be seen in the Garnsworthy Room and the foyer during the intermission time between services are often remarked on by newcomers and long-time parishioners alike.

The second offering — "The Open Door" — focuses on the Word of God proclaimed, and is a time of teaching and prayer. It is also the family service with church school running during the adult time. It is the service to which newcomers and millennials, many unfamiliar with Anglican traditions, are especially welcomed. The mood is more relaxed, the band offers contemporary music, and the sermon is central to the hour.

The Open Door is followed ten minutes later by "The Forum," at which people join the clergy for a time of thoughtful discussion of spiritual matters. The Forum has proved to be very popular, with many people staying to ask questions and discuss ideas.

These changes are still in the early stages of implementation as the church enters its 200th year. St. John's overall concern is that, while the church continues to offer flexible services to attract new people to the "Gospel Message," it must also offer a level of comfort and tradition to those raised in the Anglican Church.

Acolyte Gabi Mitchell represents the youth of the church as she carries the cross at a morning sacramental service.

The leaders of the church are aware that Sunday morning must meet the needs of a diverse community and, at the same time, bring them together as one community worshipping God.

With the continuous worship of God taking place between these walls over two centuries and the ability of St. John's York Mills to adapt to the realities of the time, the future growth of St. John's appears assured.

When asked in 2015 why he was feeling good about the future of St. John's York Mills, Drew came up with a long list of reasons why the church will continue to thrive. "It has been the most educated parish I have ever served," he says, noting that there are parishioners with Doctorates from Ivy League schools and an abundance of accomplished business people who are able to lend their considerable expertise to the church in times of need. He hesitates to put too much stock in the perceived affluence of the parish, however. "There are a lot of ordinary people who don't have a lot of money here. There's also a wide breadth and a lot of diversity in our church," a big change from the early days and one seen across the city.

St. John's has also earned a reputation as a "destination church," attracting worshippers from far beyond the parish boundaries who are drawn to the history and the message. "People come to a church because there's a product, or because what's delivered is what they want." Current parishioners come from as far away as Mississauga, Markham, and Stouffville to worship at St. John's. Drew feels it is because of the worship's solid, Gospel-informed content, saying, "It's a preaching, teaching church. I'm a teacher and that's what I really bring to the table, and that creates a community. And people really enjoy each other here."

St. John's has also been able to thrive because it is continually reaching out to all generations. "It's a family church … it's kids and bells and there are fifteen-year-olds and ninety-two-year-olds. It's a multi-generational community

Left: *Parishioner Bill Barnett, former churchwarden of St. John's, chats with parishioner Paul Warrington after a service on a sunny Sunday morning.*

Top right: *Left to right: Pamela Smith co-chair of Lychgate, verger Bill Dennis, Barbara Shearer, and Carol Ball, enjoy talking to people at Welcome Back Sunday, often held in September.*

Right: *The Rev. Canon Dr. Drew MacDonald*

church." Drew also agrees with some of the reasons that others have mentioned as contributing to the church's survival, including parishioners' pride, involvement in the community, and a sense of fellowship.

However, Drew acknowledges that, in the end, it may not be for any of these reasons that a person is drawn to church. "Who understands what it is that touches the heart, that makes a person turn to fullness in faith?" Drew asks. "My experience with the Good News of Jesus Christ as it applies to me is that,

generally speaking, it's when we hit the ditch that we finally go: 'You know what … there's got to be another route.' Blessed are the poor in spirit for theirs is the kingdom of God. It may not get you into Harvard law, but it will get you into the kingdom of God. So humility is the prerequisite, but basically we don't live in a humble culture.… So how does a church grow? I don't really know. It's a mystery."

ANNE CROSTHWAIT, ASSOCIATE PRIEST

The Reverend Anne Crosthwait joined the St. John's community in 2011 as a part-time placement. Five years later, she is still at the church, serving as a full-time associate priest.

Anne was ordained in 2003 and served as associate priest at St. Paul's Bloor Street until 2009. Before coming to St. John's, she spent two years establishing a creative offering called Contemplative Fire. This initiative reaches many people who would not otherwise attend church, but who, through Contemplative Fire, are involved in a nourishing, spiritual community. Anne brought this growing initiative with her to St. John's, where she found a supportive rector and wardens who welcomed this community into their spaces and allowed Anne the time to work with it. Contemplative Fire has four hundred people on its national database, and fifty or so people who regularly attend the worship, small groups, retreats, and teaching times in Toronto. It is currently being seeded in both the Dioceses of Ontario (Kingston) and Niagara (Burlington).

The Rev. Anne Crosthwait

Contemplative Fire celebrated the Easter morning sunrise in the St. John's churchyard.

Anne was warmly welcomed into the St. John's community and was impressed by the spirit of the church and its willingness to "try something different." She immediately developed a creative and healthy working relationship with Rector Drew MacDonald, of whom she says, "Drew has provided me with a ministry life that is never boring and always a source of spiritual growth. I would have it no other way! I am grateful for the opportunity to serve with him in tending this patch of God's garden." Both Anne and her husband Hugh were immediately plunged into the very active life of the community.

Over the years Anne took charge of developing many ministries at St. John's. Her first focus was the

further development of Compass Groups — a scripture-based, small-group ministry. Between 2011 and 2016, there were from three to five different groups with upwards of sixty people involved. Anne led one for two years at the home of Mary and Cliffe Nelles, as well as nourishing the Compass Group facilitators. The next step was the introduction of St. John's adult Christian education, beginning with the study of *The Apprenticeship Series* by James Bryan Smith. From 2014 to 2016, there were approximately ten groups with about seventy people

Above: *Mary and Cliffe Nelles have hosted a Compass Group at their home for many years.*

Right: *The Rev. Anne Crosthwait and choir member Anne Curtis enjoy a Lychgate Christmas party.*

studying and discussing *The Good and Beautiful God,* and then *The Good and Beautiful Life.* Both Anne and Drew led these study groups, as well as the Rev. Tim Taylor (Assistant Curate) and Parish Council member Paul Heersink.

In Anne's words, "Each session with each group I've led has been an experience of spiritual exploration and discovery. I have personally gained from this series as well as being privileged to walk alongside many parishioners in their spiritual journey." Hugh Crosthwait has also joined in Compass Groups and *The Good and Beautiful* groups.

At the same time, Anne was working to develop the children's ministry and was able to see the growth in Sunday church school as the children and parent volunteers learned the Bible stories and took part in dances, videos and pageants. Under the leadership of Chantal Sathi, church school blossomed, and upwards of fifty children were enrolled as of 2016. Chantal left this ministry in early 2016 to join the Ravi Zacharias International Ministries, and the church is currently conducting a search for a new church school leader.

Chantal Sathi, director of the Children's and Youth Ministries, in discussion with the Rev. Anne Crosthwait

Anne also tended to the emerging youth ministry, which began as a study group and then became a Sunday youth group. It is now a quiet but integral part of the Sunday scene at St. John's.

When Anne was asked to bring her particular organizational skills and spiritual gifts to forming a Sunday morning Welcome Ministry, she met with the leaders of the greeters, badge table helpers, and sidespersons. Out of these meetings developed a Welcome Ministry Team that works seamlessly to give a warm greeting to parishioners on a Sunday morning. The Welcome Ministry has now developed its own life and is part of the brand that St. John's offers. Hugh Crosthwait is a member of the Welcome Ministry and is often at the door on a Sunday morning to greet people as they arrive.

Hugh has also been involved in a leadership role in the Men's Supper Club, a group led by the Rev. Drew. This club brings together a growing group of men who eat and study together once a month. The Men's Supper Club is a wonderful support to the St. John's community at large, as it takes on the hosting of other events, such as guest speakers and the pancake supper on Shrove Tuesday.

In her own words, Anne appreciates "… the laughter and ease around our staff table as we meet weekly to care for the community and prepare Sunday

Left: The 2016 Welcome Team. Top row: Vicki Parrish, Hugh Crosthwait, Venetia Cowie, Cliffe Nelles, Pat Smith, John Yarker. Bottom row: Bev McLeod, Shiam Sathi, Gail Moore, Mary Nelles, Sylvia McConnell, Connie Hamson, Wendy Aspinall

Right: The Rev. Anne Crosthwait (second from the right) with Ann Dixie, Tanya Likhachov, and Gillian Mitchell at a women's retreat at L'Arche in 2016

worship. It is a delight to serve with a group who try to respect and support each other. I watch us grow individually but also as a team. We are always ready to try something and yet, not hesitant to speak up about what doesn't work."

With good reason, Anne says of St. John's as we enter 2016, "I think we are on the cusp of some interesting times. I sense some of our parishioners are waking up from a traditional faith to one that is lively and having an impact on their daily lives. The depth of our small group discussions, the extent of our outreach ministry, and the vibrancy of our Sunday mornings, are indications to me that the Spirit is at work in our midst. God is good — all the time."

THE   REVEREND HARRY ROBINSON

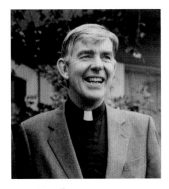

The   Reverend Harry Robinson

Although the Right Reverend Harry Sholto Douglas Robinson's time in the clergy at St. John's York Mills was brief — and long ago — his influence can still be felt today in the ministry of Drew McDonald, one of Harry's staunchest admirers and most rapt pupils.

Harry was born in York Mills on March 30, 1927, the son of respected Toronto lawyer John Robinson and his wife Elizabeth MariAn (sic) Boultbee. Elizabeth was a devout Anglican. John was a Presbyterian who never took communion. Harry's paternal grandfather was "Black Jack" Robinson, for thirty-nine years the editor of the *Toronto Telegram* newspaper. The nickname "Black Jack" did not reflect any violent or nefarious character traits, only the colour of the man's full head of hair. John R. Robinson as he was properly known, was, in fact, an unfailingly cheerful man who fought joyously from his editorial pulpit to defend the interests of the common man and rail against any private interest he suspected of selfishly exploiting the country's natural resources for personal gain.

John R. Robinson was born in the town of Guelph in 1862. At the age of three, he lost his father and was apprenticed at the age of thirteen as a printer to the *Guelph Mercury*. He worked his way up to that newspaper's editorial room before moving to Toronto to join the *Globe* newspaper. He was soon attracted to John Ross Robertson's fledgling *Telegram* and was hired there as a reporter in 1883. Within five years he was the editor — a post he held until his death in September 1928. In addition to his accomplishments as a newspaperman, he championed the public ownership of hydro-electric power generation and teamed with Sir Adam Beck to create the Ontario Hydro Electric Power Commission. He was described by *Mail and Empire/Globe* columnist J.V. McAree as being colour blind to any shade between black and white, and that "… Either a thing was something to thank God for, or it was an outrage." Black Jack Robinson was remembered as a rebel, a Protestant, and an iconoclast. His success meant that his children and grandchildren would have a better start in life than he himself had endured.

Harry Robinson the grandson of Black Jack, grew up in the family's spacious log home, which is still standing on Plymbridge Road in Hogg's Hollow. Harry was baptised, confirmed, married, and ordained to the diaconate at St. John's York Mills. Following his ordination, he briefly served on the clergy team of St. John's before being posted to Kingston, Ontario, to serve his curacy.

Harry's high school days were spent at University of Toronto Schools (UTS), where money alone didn't guarantee admission. Good marks were essential. It was there that he first showed signs of involving himself more deeply in religion when he became involved with a camping ministry in the early days of the Inter-Varsity Christian Fellowship (IVCF). Following high school graduation, in fact, Harry took some time off to work with the IVCF. He enrolled at the University of Toronto at the age of twenty-two, graduating with a B.A. in English and history, while also serving as a swim coach and a member of the varsity wrestling team. Standing 6' 5", he was a most welcome addition to the team. He lived at Wycliffe College — the evangelical Anglican college at the U of T — while he was an undergraduate and continued his involvement with the IVCF. He graduated in 1952 and spent a year studying in England at the Oak Hill Theological College, an Anglican seminary north of London. While there, he became lifelong friends with a number of young, evangelical Anglican ministers, including John R.W. Stott, then the young rector of All Souls Anglican Church in London; and Dr. James I. Packer, budding Anglican theologian. In 1953 Harry returned to Toronto, where he completed his second year of theological studies at Wycliffe. He graduated from Wycliffe in 1955 and married Frances Isobel Adams, a nurse who later trained for and practised family counselling.

Harry was ordained to the diaconate at St. John's York Mills on Sunday, January 16, 1955, by the Right Reverend Kenneth Evans, the Bishop of Ontario. He was ordained a priest in Kingston, where he was appointed rector of The

The Rev. Harry Robinson and his wife Frances

Church of the Redeemer. While in Kingston he was mentored by Canon (later Bishop) Desmond Hunt, the respected rector of St. James Kingston, a church known for its student ministry. Harry would carry this belief in the importance of ministering to students when he returned to Toronto in 1963 — the year he was appointed rector of Trinity East, or Little Trinity. Not only was Little Trinity a low-church, it was also located in what was then one of Toronto's poorer neighbourhoods on King Street, east of Parliament Street. Harry Robinson was just the rector needed for that church, and in short order the congregation had grown and a solid ministry for students was developed, particularly for students from the U of T. Harry also worked beyond the parish, as a speaker at conferences, missions, and retreats, while continuing his work with the IVCF. His next posting would take him clear across the country.

In 1978 Harry was offered the parish of St. John's Shaughnessy in one of Vancouver's wealthiest suburbs. He accepted the new position and must surely have been taken aback by just how different his new posting was from Little Trinity. St. John's Shaughnessy at that time was alternately described as high-church and wealthy or complacent and moribund. The parish list was declining and the church was in serious financial trouble. Harry was aided greatly in his efforts to turn the ship around when his old friend James Packer moved to Vancouver to accept a post as professor of theology at Regent College, founded in 1968. It was the first graduate school of theology in North America to make education of the laity its central focus. Thankfully for Harry — and the parish — James also agreed to serve as Harry's honourary assistant. It was also a blessing-in-disguise for the parish that Harry had never been impressed by wealth. Having come from a well-off family himself, he could understand and speak the truth to important citizens who may well have been able to intimidate a preacher from a more humble background. By the time Harry retired in 1992, the parish had been transformed

Harry Robinson (centre) with Dr. James Packer (left) and noted author and theologian John Stott

and was attracting what was considered the largest Sunday congregation of any Anglican church in Canada.

Following his "retirement," Harry continued to be a powerful and visible force. He continued to minister and in 1992, he received an honourary doctorate from Wycliffe College. From 1996 to 2004, he served as the first chaplain of the new Anglican Studies Program at Regent College. Although largely ignored by the church bureaucracy of the time, Harry is now regarded as one of the most influential Canadian Anglicans of the latter half of the twentieth century and the "foremost Anglican Evangelical parish priest of his generation."

Harry Robinson left this world on April 4, 2011. He had been out for a walk with a friend near his home on British Columbia's Mayne Island and, after sitting down in his car following the walk, was taken by a fatal heart attack. Eulogies and condolences universally gave thanks for Harry's stature as the most brilliant preacher of his generation.

Four days after Harry died, Donald M. Lewis, professor of church history at Regent College, wrote the following words: "Harry's success in parish ministry must undoubtedly be attributed to his genius as a preacher. While committed as a conservative evangelical, to the consecutive exposition of Scripture as the best way to build people up in the Christian faith, his highly original approach to the task reflected an innate creativity and an ability to use insightful narrative to disarm his listeners. Widely read and deeply culturally aware, his preaching combined piercing irony with deep spiritual insight and a genuine humility."

The following Annie Dillard quote from one of Harry's sermons gives some idea of what Donald Lewis was talking about. "Does anyone have the foggiest idea what sort of power we so blithely invoke? Or, as I suspect, does no one believe a word of it? It is madness to wear ladies straw hats and velvet hats to church; we should be wearing crash helmets. Ushers should issue life preservers and signal flares; they should lash us to our pews."

One day after Harry's fatal heart attack, Bishop Anthony Burton, the former Bishop of Saskatchewan, posted the following memorial on the Internet.

"The Rev. Dr. Harry S. D. Robinson, the foremost Anglican Evangelical parish priest of his generation, died of a sudden heart attack yesterday near his home on Mayne Island, British Columbia. He was 84. A gentle giant physically and morally, he combined a probing intuitive intelligence with an enormous love of people and focus on the Gospel task. He was a brilliant, original and unpredictable preacher and a perceptive critic of the interplay between the Gospel and contemporary culture. In the late 1970s he was appointed rector of St. John's, Vancouver, then a moribund, complacent, small congregation, and at considerable personal cost set it on the path to becoming Canada's largest Anglican community and one of its liveliest and most creative. As a churchman, he built bridges and encouraged friendships across the country. In his heyday he exercised an almost unrivalled degree of personal authority. A person of great warmth, charm and humility, he inspired and mentored countless vocations to the ordained ministry."

Donald Lewis of Regent College added that Harry "loved presenting Christianity to its wealthy, cultivated despisers."

Many of Harry's sermons may still be found in the archives at Little Trinity, thanks to the dedication, hard work, and generosity of his former parishioners Arthur Bennett. Arthur recorded and videotaped many of Harry's sermons, missions, Bible studies, and conferences over the years. Art spent much of his spare time copying these recordings, transferring them to CDs, and mailing them to people all over the world. Art Bennett died on April 20, 2010, roughly one year before Harry. A month before he died, he was pleased to hear that Little Trinity had accepted his generous donation of all these materials for their archives.

Harry's younger brother Tom also became a priest. The Reverend Canon Thomas Robinson, D.D., was born in 1928, one year after his brother Harry. He graduated from Wycliffe College in 1957, the same year he married Mary Smyth.

The newlyweds then journeyed to England, where Tom was the first overseas student hired by John Stott of All Souls Anglican Church, Langham Place. In 1962 the couple returned to Toronto for further parish ministry with three children and another on the way. (A fifth would follow not long after.) Tom's service would take him to all corners of Canada. He ministered from British Columbia to New Brunswick, from Yukon to Quebec, and from Labrador to the Gaspé Peninsula. He also served on the board of World Vision and was instrumental in the creation of both the Barnabas Ministries and the Essentials movement, later known as Anglican Essentials Canada. He was awarded an honourary Doctor of Divinity degree by Wycliffe College in 1996, and returned to Toronto two years later to serve as Interim Associate at St. Paul's on Bloor Street.

Tom Robinson died of cancer in St. John, New Brunswick, on December 1, 2001. He was remembered by Paula Thomas in the "In Memoriam" section of the December 2001 Wycliffe College newsletter *Insight* as follows: "Tom, the gentle giant, influenced the lives of innumerable people, and he will be lovingly remembered for his quiet, faithful presence, and a passionate, unwavering commitment to the works of God's kingdom."

Other members of the Robinson family have continued their involvement with SJYM, including Harry and Tom's brother Stony, whose 1980 photograph with Margery Pezzack and Penny Potter appears in the *Renewal 2014 Commemorative Book* that detailed that year's round of renovations at the church. Both Penny and Stony had been church school and youth group members while Margery was director of Christian Education. Descendant Jaye Robinson currently serves as a Toronto city councillor. She represents Ward 25, Don Valley West, the ward that contains SJYM.

Other members of the Robinson family buried in the churchyard at SJYM include Harry's grandmother Boultbee and several uncles and aunts.

THE DEACONS OF ST. JOHN'S

What are deacons? In the Anglican Communion, the order of deacons is a full and equal order of ministry along with that of bishops and priests. There are two kinds of deacons — those who are transitory, that is en route to ordination to the priesthood, and deacons who permanently remain deacons, previously referred to as vocational deacons.

The Diocese of Toronto describes deacons as "icons of servanthood … agents of the bishop … leaders … and prophets (alerting the church to the needs of the world and pushing it to act).… To be ordained is to choose a particular way of life, and to take public vows to accept an imposed discipline and the doctrines of the Church, and to be accountable and responsible to God and the Church for life."*

Deacons are non-stipendiary: not salaried, but they give freely of their time, talents, and treasure. They are responsible for their vestments and other tools that might be necessary for their work. SJYM has periodically provided deacons with a small honorarium that helps cover some of the expenses.

Since deacons are ordained for life and "raised up" from the St. John's parish, they serve indefinitely at the discretion of the bishop.

Bruce Williams

DR. BRUCE WILLIAMS

St. John's York Mills is a busy parish, with busy families who have less and less time to volunteer at their church. The clergy have seen their roles diversify as they spend more and more time serving a wider community of people, not just those who come to church on Sunday. The role of a deacon amidst this constant activity becomes a pivotal one to the church community.

---

*　　http://www.toronto.anglican.ca/about-the-diocese/careers-and-vocations/ordination-process/diaconate-ministry/

Two deacons have served the church faithfully and well in the twenty-first century, and each not only has an interesting story to tell, but took up very different roles within the church community.

Bruce Williams, who was deeply mourned by the entire congregation when he passed away just after Christmas in 2012, took on his role as deacon in 2000 after being installed to the diaconate at St. John's York Mills in the same year. He had undergone a process of discernment, education, screening for suitability, and preparation for his role. At the installation he made public vows for life before God, and in the presence of the gathered Church, to serve God and Church all his days.

Bruce had already been very active at SJYM and performed many of the duties of a deacon while he finished his divinity degree part-time at Trinity College. His varied career before he arrived at this point in his life was an indication of his great desire to serve.

His wife Jan Gardiner Williams takes up his and their story as she speaks about first meeting him at Queen's University in 1979, where he was doing his family residency in medicine and Jan was doing a masters in counselling. They met at a conference on "healing from the Christian perspective" at a Kingston hospi-

Top: *Bruce as a young man*

Bottom: *Deacon Bruce Williams after his installation as a deacon*

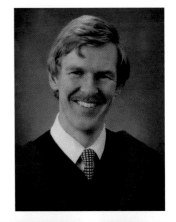

tal. Jan discovered that Bruce was actually from British Columbia, where he was born in Duncan in 1950. Jan says now that she immediately loved his red plaid shirt and blue corduroys. They were married six months later and took up work in Whitehorse, Yukon, where Bruce became a family physician and Jan a guidance counsellor.

Bruce and Jan attended the Anglican church in Whitehorse and had their first baby there, but Bruce was restless and made the decision to study psychiatry. In 1984 they moved to Toronto so he could study at the University of

Toronto. They arrived for the first time at St. John's York Mills that Christmas and stayed on, having four more children in the following years.

During the time that Bruce was a staff psychiatrist at Youthdale and also working with the Ministry of Corrections, he took up part-time studies at Trinity College to obtain a Master of Divinity. As well as assisting at services at St. John's, Bruce took on other leadership roles within the parish: organizer of the Barnabas outreach breakfast program for the disadvantaged; a mediation group leader; and initiator of a monthly ministry at the local Amica seniors residence. Bruce also took on a larger role outside the parish as prison minister with Dismas, particularly at the Don Jail. He also visited the patients at St. John's Rehabilitation Hospital. Bruce's ministry at his church and within a wider community, while holding a difficult job in child psychiatry, was a true example of Christian service.

But Bruce took time for fun as well, taking part in some of the many theatrical productions at the church and playing double bass for Boni Strang's gospel choir.

During the long years of Bruce's illness, Jan often accompanied him to work and to church to help with the walker, wheelchair, and ramp, and she became an integral part of his life as he kept up with his many volunteer activities, visiting the imprisoned and the homeless.

During the 2014 renovation, Jan Gardiner Williams donated a sum of money to help with the repurposing of the old altar and lectern into three useful pieces, one of which is the baptismal counter that stands beside the baptismal font in the reconfigured sanctuary. The plaque on the front of the font tells us that this beautiful historical piece of church furniture is dedicated to the memory of Deacon Bruce Williams from his family.

Deacon Bruce took on many roles at St. John's York Mills, including helping with the barbecue at the summer Que and Pew.

THE REVEREND DR. CATHERINE KEATING

Ministry at St. John's is a team effort, and as the parish celebrates its 200th anniversary, the Rev. Dr. Catherine Keating has become an important member of the team. As with Deacon Bruce Williams, she is also a permanent deacon of the church and serves at the discretion of the bishop since her ordination in October 2006.

Raised and baptised Eastern Orthodox, and formerly active in the Greek Orthodox Church, Catherine had "slipped away" from the church, as she says, before being welcomed by then-Rector Hollis Hiscock during a community Bible study meeting at St. John's in 1999. She was looking to rediscover her faith.

"I was seeking a new church home," Catherine recalls. "In catechism I learned that the Anglican and Orthodox faiths were in communion, so with my mom, Marlene Christopher, and later my husband, John, I started attending St. John's.… I was surprised how much my mom loved the service and both of the priests, the Rev. Hollis Hiscock and his associate the Rev. Patrick White, later Bishop White, who got to know us personally. Mom's funeral in 2002 was at SJYM with an Orthodox priest present."

Later, when Hollis laid hands on Catherine during a healing service, she says she "strongly experienced the Holy Spirit." She was then surprised to find herself feeling a call to the diaconate.

Catherine came to church leadership from the field of education, in which she worked as an educator for more than forty years, half of which she spent with the North York Board of Education as a teacher from junior kindergarten through to high school, and subsequently with the York Region District School Board, where she was an elementary school administrator. Catherine holds a diploma in Early Childhood Education from Ryerson and a B.A. and M.Ed. in curriculum from OISE. She completed her Doctorate of Education in Curriculum in 1996 with a focus on teacher development, and she is presently completing a Master of Divinity with University of Toronto, Wycliffe College.

Deacon Catherine Keating prepares for the rededication service in November 2014.

*The Rev. Catherine Keating in
the sanctuary of St. John's*

In 1997 Catherine was seconded to the Ministry of Education's Field Services Branch where she held several portfolios, ranging from elementary curriculum, school council, faculty of education university liaison, coordinator of inspections of private schools in the Toronto area, Literacy Numeracy Secretariat, and liaison for several district school boards in the Toronto area.

After Catherine was ordained a deacon by Bishop Patrick Yu at St. John's in 2006, she dedicated herself to the service of the church. She serves God through a number of ministries: assisting in services, providing pastoral care, leading Bible studies, providing Eucharist for people in care facilities, visiting hospital patients, supporting the Outreach ministries, providing prayer support for St. John's Barnabas ministry, conducting funerals, and, perhaps most significantly, co-ordinating children's ministry.

With the Rev. Tay Moss, incumbent of the Church of the Messiah, Catherine says, "We founded the Centre for Excellence in Christian Education (CECE) to resource children's ministers." In 2010 the CECE presented its first Sladen Award, named in honour of St. John's parishioner Kathleen Sladen, to recognize exceptional volunteer Sunday school teachers. In 2011 CECE hosted its first annual Leading Children's Ministry Conference, an event that is open to all denominations.

On Christmas Eve 2015, the St. John's children's ministry presented a video project called, "The Christmas Story as Told by the Children of SJYM." The ambitious project was not without its challenges and many people were thanked by Catherine in the spring 2016 issue of *The Link* for their contributions to making the production a success. The next video project from this dedicated group is to be titled "The Resurrection as 'Witnessed' by the Children of SJYM," and is scheduled for Easter 2017.

The Barnabas ministry is another part of life at St. John's that Catherine finds especially important. On the last Wednesday of every month, the St. John's Barnabas ministry provides Holy Communion for the less fortunate in our

*Deacon Catherine with parish
council member Peter Miller*

community. A nourishing hot breakfast is provided as well as subway tokens and food vouchers. There are usually fifty or so attendees at these services, and at Christmastime, they are provided with special gift packages. "It is my privilege to serve in the Barnabas ministry as part of the prayer team," Catherine says. "It never fails to amaze me what our Barnabas guests have to endure." And yet, she says, "As we pray together, their thoughts turn to the SJYM family, in thanks for our caring and ministry to them. They come with woeful stories but never complain.… Recently, one of our guests was asking for prayers for the refugees who will be coming to Canada and for the poor within our city — the jobless, the sick, the weak, the homeless.…"

Catherine knows what it feels like to be homeless. "I remember when my mom and I lost our home. It was a scary time. I was nine years old. My godmother opened her heart and home to us, and we stayed in the safety and

loving care she provided for eight years. She certainly more than fulfilled her baptismal vows to me. I have never forgotten her for this and for her faith; she was an inspiration."

Catherine married John Keating in 1982. They have no children but are blessed with many nieces, nephews, and cousins in Canada, the United States, and John's home Australia. They both love to travel and, as much as possible, they try to keep in contact with extended family

Above: The Barnabas helpers: Front row (left to right): Diane Thornton, Yvonne McGregor, Jane White, Beverley Salmon, Beverley McLeod, Ify Okwuosa, Margaret Cunningham, Sylvia Raynham, Norma Anderson, Josephine McDougall; Back row (left to right): Guggi Way, Joanne Lang, Russ Carrington, Keith Way, Doug Lee, Olivia Lee, Aleksandra Harrington, Liz Keddie, Catherine Keating

Right: The Reverend Catherine Keating assists Bishop Yu at the Rev. Tim Taylor's ordination in May 2016.

and friends through occasional visits. John and Catherine have their resurrection site in the churchyard with this inscription:

> "… if we love one another, God lives in us and His love is made complete in us."
>
> 1 John 4:12 NIV

CHAPTER FIVE

The Verger, Bill Dennis

Verger Bill Dennis prepares the altar for a service.

As St. John's York Mills celebrates its 200th anniversary in 2016, Bill Dennis is celebrating an anniversary of his own — his thirtieth year as verger at this, the oldest parish in the city. Much has changed during his time at the church. While his years of service may not yet rival those of his most famous predecessor John Page Squire, who served for more than sixty-eight years, it must be noted that Bill has managed to keep the place humming during some of the most trying times in the church's history. He has taken on more duties and responsibilities as the parish battles declining attendance and budget deficits, and yet he has somehow managed to keep his sense of humour. When asked to give a list of his duties, he laughs and says, "It's massive. I have a job description, and it tells you all kinds of things and then at the very bottom it says, 'other duties as assigned,' so there's a great deal of flexibility in that." One of his core duties is to tend to the maintenance of the church and church property, a task to which he is well suited.

In the 1970s and 1980s, Bill was working in residential property management in Niagara Falls and St. Catharines at a time when interest rates were skyrocketing and large regular rent increases were the order of the day. One of his more onerous tasks involved dealing with senior citizens and retirees who were unable to pay their rent, a job for which he was singularly unsuited. "I'm not Simon Legree," he recalls. "I don't do that kind of thing terribly well."

Bill decided to find a new job, and his thoughts turned to working at a church. "Well, I was a cradle Anglican actually," he says. "My entire life I've been active in the church." The problem was that there weren't many churches around that could offer someone like Bill a full-time job *and* a living wage. It was while on vacation in North Bay in 1984 that Bill picked up a *Toronto Star,* and while perusing the want ads, saw an ad for a building superintendent at Yorkminster Park Baptist Church on Yonge Street, north of St. Clair. He applied for the job, not really expecting to get it, but get it he did. The church even paid to move him from St. Catharines to Toronto.

"I enjoyed the work there," he says. "It was a much larger plant than this one [SJYM], more staff, but I really missed the Anglican tradition. My job on Sundays there was … to sit in the narthex and guard the coats. It was a decent fit, but it wasn't my favourite and then I just happened to see the ad for 'a North Toronto Anglican church' and I thought, well, I'll try it." The church, although the ad didn't specify, was St. John's York Mills, advertising for a new verger. Bill submitted his resumé and in short order, the job was his.

Unlike the last few rectors at St. John's, Bill had the luxury of learning the ropes from his predecessor Ernie Peters. Ernie had been at St. John's for about five years, after retiring from a school board in southwestern Ontario, and though Bill didn't officially begin his job at St. John's until the end of September 1986, he was able to spend a month or so of spare time visiting with Ernie and learning the basics of his new job. It's doubtful that Ernie would recognize the job today, for in addition to inheriting the normal custodial duties that come with the verger's position, Bill soon found himself taking on an increasingly heavy workload as St. John's struggled to adapt to a changing world.

One of the first new duties Bill had to embrace involved the operation of the churchyard.

"When I started here, it was just the building maintenance," he remembers, "but the churchyard secretary back then was somebody from outside … and we ended up with a situation here one summer when he was ill and in hospital, and the records weren't even kept on-site at that point in time. They were kept in his apartment, and we wanted to have a burial, and we were frozen. We were locked. We didn't know what to do, so within a matter of months the rector at that time, Jim O'Neil, decided that it would really be best to have a staff person taking care of that sort of thing from now on, and so they tacked it onto my job." Bill then had to hit the books to learn the Cemeteries Act in order to be certified for his new duties.

St. John's is blessed to have its very own churchyard, a feature that sets the church apart from most other parishes in the Diocese of Toronto, where land has long been at a premium. The terms *churchyard*, *graveyard*, and *cemetery* are often thought to be interchangeable, but there is one important distinction, and that is the fact that a churchyard is located on the same property as its church, while cemeteries and graveyards stand alone. This distinction is most keenly felt during a funeral service, where the procession need not venture onto public roads on its way to the burial site. Rather, the entire service at St. John's takes place within sight of the beloved historic church and within earshot of its familiar bells. No traffic

Left: As part of his responsibilities, Bill Dennis cares for the churchyard. It is a beautiful and tranquil spot in all seasons.

Right: The churchyard is a historic part of St. John's, as many of the area's early pioneers are buried here.

jams to offend the time of mourning. No prying eyes to glimpse a solemn and private moment.

The policy at St. John's has long been to offer spaces in the churchyard only to parishioners and their families, and even then, only at the time of need. The rector is the only individual who can grant interment to a non-parishioner. The spaces here cannot be purchased in advance. Small wonder, then, that a challenge to this tradition was met with immediate resistance in 2003.

In the May 2003 issue of *The Link*, an article by the chairman of the churchyard committee stated that, "In view of changing demographics and general church population, the Committee is considering opening up the use of the Churchyard to other selected parishes." Opposition was swift and strong. The proposal was quickly abandoned, allowing the churchyard at St. John's to remain a blessed oasis in a mega-city that grows ever less comforting.

The verger Bill Dennis discusses the upcoming 200th anniversary celebrations with Linda Grasley, chair of the anniversary committee and longtime chair of the churchyard committee.

Much of Bill's time is spent handling the logistics for the numerous functions that are held at the church. This can run the gamut from setting up meeting rooms with tables and chairs to arranging audio-visual equipment for special presentations, or overseeing the equipment and operations necessary for meal preparation and clean-up. In addition Bill is responsible for all liturgical supplies: wine, candles, silverware, and vessels. His church background allowed him to become involved with the Chancel Guild, helping with Sunday morning communion set-ups, hangings, and seasonal changes of liturgical colours and vestments. The Chancel Guild "basically folded a few years back," Bill remembers, "so *everything*, all the liturgical (items) for every service, all the hangings, everything comes under me now…." He takes special pride in maintaining the church's impressive silver collection.

"We have a lot of really good silver here," Bill says. "We're very fortunate. They were commissioned pieces. Doug Boyd was a well-known silversmith in the city and Greg Merrall, who teaches up at Seneca (College) still, they've custom-crafted pieces. Andrew Fussell was another one. They've custom-crafted pieces for us and they were all done as memorials on a commission basis. Somebody came in and they said, 'we want this,' and so they would go to the silversmith and have them custom made, so we've got a nice selection of fairly contemporary silver pieces, all in sterling. The processional cross was another piece that was custom made … so all those items we have to keep an eye on and make sure they're shiny."

Verger Bill Dennis and sexton Mark Anderson are hard at work on a Sunday morning.

The "we" he refers to here includes sexton Mark Anderson and sacristy attendant and parishioner Judith Adam, adding that the verger's job as it stands today is "much too big for one person. We've got another full-time person [Mark] on with me as well." When Bill eventually retires, the church hopes that Mark Anderson will take on Bill's massive job.

The extensive renovation, completed in 2014 at a cost of $1.6 million, is a project that Bill is particularly proud of. He praises the new, flexible seating as "a real innovation" and fought against any cutbacks that would have created problems down the road. "What we're trying to do at this point in time," he says, "is create flexibility … and we tried to foresee electronically. I mean, we've got data cables and everything else running

Above: *After the completion of renovations in the sanctuary, the 1889 baptismal font had to be reassembled in a new location.*

Left: *Bill Dennis inspects the digging for the foundation of the patio during the 2014 renovation.*

everywhere that can be tied into. I said, 'We don't want things that are nailed down and fixed; we want total flexibility through this thing,' so that way, twenty years down the road, we don't have to go through this again. When things change a little bit, we just have to move some furniture." He values the flexibility that was built into earlier renovations as well and looks forward to future improvements.

"They're talking about a phase-three renovation at some point," he says, adding that, "They've done a nice job here. They've done a nice job on the worship space, but the Sunday school wing is getting a little tired, and it's 1950s wiring and all that sort of thing in it. We did update it and made all the washrooms barrier free, but it really needs to be more flexible, that space. Right now it's all tiny little classrooms, so it doesn't have a huge amount of flexibility."

Bill goes on to praise the architect and St. John's personnel of the time for their foresight. "They built the auditorium first then they put the top two floors on it afterward. The beauty of that is that the only [load] bearing walls are the north and south walls. Everything in between is supported on 40-foot I-beams so you can gut each floor out completely to the four outside walls and completely rework the inside of it … really well thought out and designed when they did it." Bill also looks forward to the restoration of the old barrel organ, which he still plays on special occasions. The organ, a high point in the history of the parish when it was shipped from London, England, and installed in September 1847, cost less than £82, fully installed. Although this may seem like a small sum today, it should be noted that it took the parish until March 1848 to collect the full amount from the congregation. The barrel organ was first restored in the early 1960s at a cost of $850 — money raised by the Women's Parish Guild. Restoration costs in 2016 are estimated at $20,000 and Bill is confident that a donor will step forward with the full amount. The status of the barrel organ is just one of many changes in the life of the parish of St. John's.

When asked to comment on how St. John's role in the community has changed since he first came here, Bill is unequivocal. "It's very different," he says.

"It's a different world…. When I first got here, this was very much a community church. Everybody in the neighbourhood came here, they all knew about it. If you didn't come to church here on a Sunday morning, you maybe came to the Wednesday morning mothers drop-in, you would come to extra events that the church would put on, and you're certainly not seeing that [today]…. The church doesn't affect the community as it once did. When I first came here someone said to me, 'What are the three most exclusive clubs in North Toronto?' and I said 'Pardon?' and she said, 'Well, the Granite Club, the Rosedale Golf and Country Club, and St. John's York Mills.'"

Bill says that although the church was once very much community-anchored, "Our people are coming from pretty far-and-wide now, but our church is not affecting the community as it once did, but then the church in general doesn't, period; it's not just this place. On the flip side, for whatever reason, the parish, compared to many others in the diocese, certainly in the city, is very healthy. The numbers are increasing. We meet budget. You're operating on close to $1 million a year and that's a healthy operating budget for a church."

The image that St. John's projects into the community is not the only thing to have changed dramatically during Bill's tenure. The church's image of itself is also quite different. "The biggest thing that has changed here is the openness to embrace change," Bill believes. "When I first got here, very certainly things were status quo and traditional and all that sort of thing, and it was fine then, but it doesn't attract people nowadays. I think that one of the reasons why we are still healthy is that — under Drew — things have totally changed." While change used to be met with some grumbling and resistance, Bill says that "It's just like water off a duck's back now in most cases. [Parishioners] just accept it as a matter of 'life changes,' so I think that is most definitely the biggest change that I've seen since I've been here." When pressed to define the most notable *constant* in the last few decades, Bill is harder to pin down, almost giving one the feeling that change *is* the new constant. He even believes that the concept of fellowship at the church has changed.

The barrel organ dates from 1847 and still works, although its condition is not optimal.

Top: *Churchwarden John Bruce chats with Robin Bickley at one of the church's many social events.*

Bottom: *Venetia Cowie, former churchwarden and chair of the 2016 Doors Open Toronto, discusses the upcoming event with Bill Dennis.*

"When I first arrived here there were fourteen active women's groups. We're down to one now. The congregation was too large to embrace the thought of fellowship on a Sunday morning. We had three distinct congregations. You had your 8:00. You had your 9:30 and 11:00. Coffee hours? You couldn't, because you created a traffic jam in the parking lot. The 9:30 service had to end at 10:30 sharp, so that they could get out and the 11:00 people could start coming in. So," he pauses, "I think in some ways, the group fellowship idea, the *fragmented* fellowship of individual factions has gone by-the-by and a total-congregation sense of fellowship is developing because you do … have basically one main service now…."

After thirty years at St. John's, Bill has certainly seen an incredible array of parishioners come and go, some more memorable than others. When asked about Nora Wedd he replies, "She was just amazing. Olga Burgess would have been another one … Helen Kayes…. There was a group of older women when I got here that I referred to as 'the dowager duchesses' and they were lovely, genteel women, just so gracious and kind. If I thought for a few minutes, I could probably come up with a list of twenty or so of them. There were no airs. They were sweet but they were classy. They were really classy people and they had a definite opinion on what should and shouldn't be done … so I have a huge appreciation for that. I learned to appreciate those folks a very great deal."

When asked why he feels that St. John's York Mills has been able to thrive while other parishes have faltered, Bill offers up a most refreshing answer. "Honestly and truly, one of the reasons why this parish does so well is because the wardens had the foresight, back in the forties, to pay $2,500 for that parking lot…. At the time, members of the congregation wanted to lock them up. They were insane. Why would you spend that kind of money? There would never be a need for it." This sentiment was expressed at a time when many parishioners still walked to church. These days, however, the parking lot benefits not only the parish but the diocese, other dioceses, and the non-churchgoing public as well. Bill lists some of the functions that the church could not host without its parking lot: "Diocesan functions, synods, and all kinds of stuff happens here because of that parking lot. I don't care what anybody says. That's a huge drawing card. There are a lot of churches downtown — lovely, wonderful, welcoming places — but people don't want to go to them, because they don't have any place to park. If they can't park and they have to walk ten blocks, they're not going to come. No, those people back in the forties, they were really smart."

Currently, about thirty parking spaces in the lot are rented to the public at a cost of $100 per month each, meaning that the parking lot repays its original purchase price every three weeks. The proximity of the church to both Highway 401 and the Yonge Street subway has made the lot so popular with commuters that there are always more people wishing to rent spaces than there are spaces.

Bill may have a particular affection for this St. John's facility, since his current home, known as the Lodge, was built near the southwest corner of the parking lot, on the edge of the valley in 1958. That was the year in which the church property had been valued at $350,000 — a tremendous sum for the day — and concerns had arisen over the fact that there was no one living on-site to keep an eye on things. A special vestry meeting was held in April 1958 where it was decided to build a permanent residence on the property. Parishioner and noted architect Bruce Napier Simpson Jr. was hired to design the new home, which was completed in October 1958

The 1958 Lodge, recently having undergone some interior renovations, stands on the grounds of the church and is home to the verger.

at a cost of $20,000. It was initially used as the verger's residence, and although it was subsequently home to assistant curates, it is now the verger's residence once again. In 2015 the Lodge underwent extensive renovations, including new washrooms and a new kitchen, which undoubtedly cost more than the original construction.

Like current rector, Canon Drew MacDonald, Bill has an abiding interest in history in general and the history of St. John's York Mills in particular. He is keenly aware of the pioneer families who created the church in the first place, and he is a wellspring of information when questioned about the subject. He talks of Bill Marsh, whose ancestors sold the first rectory to the church in 1841; of Jesse Ketchum and his brother Seneca, both buried in the churchyard; and of the van Nostrands, Jefferys and others. "Bill Marsh was the last one (of the Marsh family to have any contact with St. John's). He and his second wife lived in Orillia. They used to have family reunions here. We actually have a book in the archives … that

Bill did up when he was alive, and it's the Marsh family and all of their relatives as they came to Canada."

He mentions that, in the spring of 2015, Toronto was thinking of naming a street in North York after the van Nostrand family. The city came to St. John's for assistance, and Bill was able to provide contact information for Innes van Nostrand Jr. — at that time the principal of Appleby College in Oakville — and direct them to Peter van Nostrand, still living on long-held family farmland near Vandorf, Ontario. Members of the Mercer family, who came to York Mills in 1794, are still alive. Seneca Ketchum, who married a Mercer, is actually buried in the Mercer plot in the churchyard. The names Shepard, Willson, and Harrison are some of the other familiar pioneer names that dot the headstones, mute testament to families who were farming in York Mills while Beethoven was still performing in Europe.

Current Rector Drew MacDonald has often mentioned how important it is for a rector to "fit" the parish. If the same thing applies to vergers, then Bill Dennis must be considered a very good fit indeed.

Verger Bill Dennis is considered to be the historian and institutional memory of St. John's.

CHAPTER SIX

Music at St. John's

I t's quite possible that nothing better illustrates the changes at St. John's York Mills over the last fifty years than the changes that have taken place in the music department. In 1966 the "swinging sixties" were just starting to swing, and they certainly hadn't swung anywhere near the Anglican church. Solemn robed choirs and organ music were very much the order of the day. Fast forward fifty years and you find a very different scene indeed. Guitars, drums, handbells, saxophone, trumpet, and percussion are now leading a completely reinvented service. Through it all, St. John's has been blessed with passionate, talented, educated, and dedicated musical directors who have reflected the tone of their times while invoking the power of shared musical experience to bring the congregation closer to God. Maurice White — musical director in 1966 when St. John's celebrated its 150th anniversary and the Beatles played their final shows at Maple Leaf Gardens — led the congregation in song for more than thirty-seven years.

MAURICE WHITE

Maurice debuted as the musical director at St. John's in January 1964, and retired in June 2001. He served with Lewis Garnsworthy, James O'Neil, and Hollis Hiscock. His time at the church spanned a genuine revolution in the way people live their lives and relate to one another, as well as the way they relate to music and the church. Maurice's involvement with church music began at a very early age. It seems that his rector overheard him playing piano at a young people's event one day and asked Maurice to try his hand at the church organ. He took to it immediately, and although he had no family background in music, Maurice decided to make it his life. His musical education is impressive. He holds the following diplomas:

> Associate of Trinity College of Music, London, England
> Associate of the Royal Canadian College of Organists
> Associate of the Royal College of Organists, London, England

He taught musical theory at The Royal Conservatory of Music, in all branches of music, both secular and sacred, from 1969 to 1999. He lists Healey Willan as his main influence. Healey Willan was an internationally respected composer and organist. He was born in England in 1880 and died in Toronto in 1968. He composed more than eight hundred musical works in his lifetime, including hymns, symphonies, operas, and concertos.

Maurice has a long list of personal favourites, including organist David Briggs, violinist James Ennis, baroque orchestra Tafelmusik, and the Elora Festival Singers. He lists Johann Sebastian Bach as his favourite composer. It should come as no surprise then to realize that Maurice is a staunch traditionalist when it comes to the music of the church. When asked what his musical aspirations were he replied, "Preserving the rich Anglican choral tradition and its important role in the church." When asked about the most rewarding part of his career he replied, "Assisting others to appreciate the richness of the musical heritage that exists in the Anglican church and how the heritage can still be a powerful force in worship." Maurice feels that the handbell program has been successful in keeping young people involved with church, and credits the choir as well, saying, "When there was significant involvement of children in the choir program, it is interesting how many of these children went on to keep their connection with the church."

Maurice's own connection to St. John's ended with his retirement in June 2001. The very next year, he was named assistant organist at St. Simon-the-Apostle Anglican Church on Bloor Street East, where he continues to this day, also serving as interim director of music when duty calls. As St. John's York Mills celebrates its 200th Anniversary, it is worth noting that for well over *one-quarter of that entire time*, Maurice White has been bringing congregations closer to God through the sacrament of music.

Robin Davis, music director at St. John's from 2001–2011

ROBIN DAVIS

Following Maurice's departure, Robin Davis signed on as the new musical director at St. John's, a position he would hold for the next ten years. Like Maurice, Robin says that church music has been a part of his life since childhood. "I actually recall singing at one of my first choir rehearsals at St. Martin's Anglican Church in Pickering," Robin says of one particularly vivid childhood experience, "and the reaction of one of the ladies in the choir: that I had no problems reading the music, but was having trouble reading the words. For me, engaging in traditional sacred music is being in my worshipping place. I also realized as a young person that in order to keep my love of it healthy, I should pursue a livelihood/career outside of music." Robin has stayed true to this early decision, studying mechanical technology and mechanical design in college and graduating to a successful career in heavy-machinery sales.

Robin graduated with a Bachelor of Music in Organ Performance from the Faculty of Music at the University of Toronto, where he studied under John Tuttle. He also studied in Wupertal, Germany, under Professor Hartmut Klug. When asked in 2016 about any plans for further musical education, he mused, "It would be fun to be immersed in the United Kingdom cathedral life with the daily liturgies and level of excellence experienced in that setting." He feels that the biggest challenge facing Anglican musical directors these days is separating the wheat from the chaff when it comes to selecting what to play from the overwhelming number of new musical compositions that are currently available. He says the reward is "the knowledge that you have helped others connect with God in a profound way."

Robin Davis in 2016, rehearsing the choir at St. Simon-the-Apostle, where he is the music director.

Robin fondly recalls his time at SJYM, calling it "ten wonderful years!" He made the most of his time there, recording a number of the church's musical performances, including the memorable CD *Ring in Christmas*, recorded by St. John's handbell ringers in autumn 2001. He also directed the St. John's choir at a performance of Handel's *Messiah* with the Canadian Sinfonietta at the CBC's Glenn Gould Studio in Toronto.

Robin plays pipe organ, piano, and harpsichord. During his time at St. John's, the musical performances on a typical Sunday morning consisted of choir and organ, with Robin conducting the choir from his organ console on pieces that required organ accompaniment. He recalls a number of special performances with particular fondness. "Between 2000 and 2009, the St. John's Chorale, our moniker for the eleven o'clock choir, presented annual Passiontide concerts. Many of these included collaborations with orchestral musicians. Some of the most memorable were Bach's *St. John Passion* with Marc DuBois, the Mozart and Duruflé Requiems, and two African masses. Also memorable was a production of the children's musical *Once Upon a Starry Night*." Other internationally renowned musicians such as David Roth and Laura Albino also performed at St. John's during Robin's tenure. It wasn't all serious, though.

Parishioner Gwen Denney dressed as a witch for the Spooktacular fundraiser

"The cabaret fundraisers with the leads from both the Chorale and the Gospel choir were lots of fun," Robin says. "I seem to recall lots of laughs at a combined music department Spooktacular costume fundraiser. Annual July choir weekends at the van't Hof's cottage were always a great time." When asked what advice he would offer a younger musician wishing to follow in his footsteps, Robin replies, "Strive to engage your choir and congregation with the best quality and calibre of music possible. Challenge your choir to learn and 'raise the bar,' but mostly remember it's about worship."

Over the years Robin has been a conductor, guest organist, organ consultant, and harpsichordist, as well as serving as chairperson of the Royal Canadian College of Organists, Durham Region Centre. He left St. John's in 2011, following a farewell luncheon on Sunday, March 6. He then joined Maurice White at St Simon-the-Apostle Anglican Church where he remains as musical director.

Patrick Dewell became St. John's next musical director in September 2011, after serving as musical director at Grace Anglican Church in Markham for the previous five years.

BONI STRANG

Working concurrently with both Robin Davis and Maurice White was Boni Strang. She became an integral, passionate member of the music team at St. John's York Mills in the early 1990s and was a beloved music director for almost two decades.

The parish wanted a more contemporary service at the 9:15 a.m. worship, especially focusing on more upbeat music. Boni had recently joined the parish and brought extensive experience and talent, and appeared to be the right person at the appropriate moment. Boni was known for her joyful spirit and her passion for sharing the Gospel message in song.

The Gospel choir brought together a group of young professionals and volunteers who came for a warm-up before the 9:15 a.m. service, held their choir practice after the worship, and generally concluded about midday. They sang a full repertoire of Gospel songs, contemporary praise, and classic Anglican hymns with the goal of encouraging enthusiastic congregational singing.

The Gospel choir's involvement beyond worship also included acting and singing in *The Real Christmas Story*, providing entertainment at many parish functions, and combining with the other musical

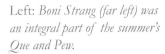

Above: *Boni Strang (left) director of gospel music at the family service, and Carolyn Martin the handbell director, often worked together on musical events at the church.*

Left: *Boni Strang (far left) was an integral part of the summer's Que and Pew.*

groups for special worship services—Christmas and Easter carol services – and MusicFest. Boni was part of the team that organized Gospel Vespers, a late afternoon worship service based on gospel stories, drama, and appropriate music.

Que and Pew, a weekly summer program centred on a barbeque meal and a short worship of prayer, music, and dramatization of a Bible character, was also part of Boni's responsibility at St. John's.

In addition to planning and leading music for worship, Boni was an artist who did a lot of work beautifying the church school wing with paintings and murals. Her Bible-themed murals can still be seen in the Sheppard Room today. She also played handbells, was a member of Lychgate, and actively participated throughout the parish. Boni retired in 2008 and died a few years later of ALS. She is greatly mourned by all her church family.

Gospel music director
Monique Ingalls

MONIQUE INGALLS

Monique Ingalls was the Gospel music director at St. John's from July 2009 to June 2011 — a short time, but she left her influence on the music program and was greatly missed when she left the church to further her studies in Cambridge, England.

Monique and her husband Jason moved to Toronto from Nashville, Tennessee, for Jason to attend Wycliffe College as part of his training for the priesthood. Monique had recently completed a Ph.D. in musicology at the University of Pennsylvania, where she focused on the development of contemporary worship music in American churches. Initially, Monique was hired to build a contemporary worship team for the five o'clock service with Allison Lynn and Gerald Flemming as assistant worship leaders. Less than two months into her position, she was also tasked with overseeing the music in the morning contemporary service.

Two of her main goals were encouraging more participation in congregational singing, and building a community of musicians. To encourage congregational singing, the worship team under Monique's leadership introduced the congregation to a repertoire of approximately forty new songs. These songs were chosen for their "singability," their robust expression of Christian truth, and their fit within Anglican spirituality. The new song repertoire consisted not only of contemporary praise and worship songs, but also modernized hymns, Taizé choruses, and contemporary service music written by Allison, Gerald, Monique, and other Anglican musicians.

Secondly, Monique sought to encourage the formation of a Christian community of musicians. She began each rehearsal with a brief time of devotion and prayer and penned a mission and vision statement, relating the worship team's calling to other ministries of the church. She organized social gatherings, including a monthly potluck after the 5:00 p.m. service, an annual music ministry cookout, and a church music workshop. Under Monique's leadership, the worship team at St. John's expanded from three paid staff members to include twenty volunteer musicians on a rotating schedule. Monique left St. John's in 2011 to take up a post-doctoral fellowship at the University of Cambridge in England, and is now a professor of church music at Baylor University in Texas. Though her time in Toronto was brief, when contacted recently for a contribution to this book, she fondly remembered her friends at St. John's and is looking for any excuse to visit.

INFINITELY MORE

Allison Lynn and Gerald Flemming, the music duo Infinitely More, studied and led worship in Nashville for three years. While there, they earned extraordinary opportunities, such as writing with Grammy-winning songwriters and performing in concert with Gaither Homecoming artists. Upon returning home to Canada, the Rev. Drew MacDonald offered them the positions of assistant worship leaders under Monique Ingalls. They would become the full-time worship leaders two years later, after Monique left.

Over the course of their four years there, they contributed primarily to the Gathering service. Because this was a Sunday evening or late-afternoon service, when most church musicians had the night off, an extraordinary band consisting of some of the best church musicians in Toronto was slowly but surely assembled. The seeds of discipleship were at the heart of this service. This showed itself particularly on holidays such as Easter and Thanksgiving, when the band members were told to go and spend those evenings with their families. But they would show up anyway, always ready to serve.

Every year, St. John's would send Infinitely More to Break Forth, a world-class Christian music conference in Edmonton. There they studied with many more talented Christian worship leaders and songwriters. When they returned to St. John's,

The reverends Drew (far left) and Anne (right front) join Infinitely More's Allison Lynn and Gerald Flemming and the Worship Band at an Easter Gathering service. The other people in the photos are (left to right) musicians Jonny Smith, Steve Parr, Jess Nee; the tech team, Derwyn Costinak, and James McNeish; music director Patrick Dewell

they would hold workshops with the music teams and share their new-found knowledge, expanding the possibilities of worship at St. John's.

Special events such as Easter, Christmas, and MusicFest were always unique places for Infinitely More to contribute. The Christmas carol service, which also featured Infinitely More's original songs and arrangements, was recorded and now makes up the live portion of their Christmas album, *Tonight, Everywhere Is Bethlehem*.

After leaving St. John's, Infinitely More became a full-time, nationally touring music ministry. At the time of writing, only three years into this new chapter of their career, the duo has been nominated for ten national music awards, including five Covenant Awards and an East Coast Music Award for Gospel Recording of the Year.

Gerald and Allison hold the time spent at St. John's York Mills dearly. They are forever grateful for the depth that was contributed to their ministry by the wonderful ministers, musicians, and congregants of St. John's. A song Gerald wrote that was inspired by St. John's 200th Anniversary is called "The House Where Prophets Speak."

Stones carved by the Builder
And placed at the base of a wall
Generations have prayed here
They've listened and learned and loved above all
The promise for us is the same
Perfect glory through His grace.

This is the house where prophets speak,
This is the air where angels fly
This is the cross where He gave His all for you and me
And here is where we seek …
The House Where Prophets Speak

Infinitely More tours the country as part of their music ministry.

PATRICK DEWELL

Music Director Patrick Dewell

Current musical director Patrick Dewell, very much a man of the twenty-first century, seems to be the ideal person to steer the church's musical ship into new waters. For while he may be a product of the digital age, his heart is firmly rooted in the traditions of the church. "Music-making is the birthright — scratch that, it's the responsibility! — of every Christian," Patrick wrote in the winter 2014–15 issue of *The Link*. "The Bible calls us again and again to offer our praise to God through music." He then lists a series of passages in the Bible that illustrate his point and, in so doing, offers proof positive that his musical knowledge is only part of the knowledge he draws on to spread the word of God. He cites Psalm 96, verse 1, which says, "Sing to the Lord, all the earth," to support his belief that *all* are welcome in the music programs at SJYM. "There's no distinction between "beginner" and "advanced" musicians, between "amateurs" and "professionals," he points out. "It simply says 'all the earth.'"

Patrick's "a-ha" moment of musical epiphany came at a relatively early age. It seems that he was in grade eleven at Clarke High School, located on Highway 35/115 between Newcastle and Orono, when he sat back on his stool after a group performance. He was playing the stand-up bass and although his part had been particularly challenging, he also found it most rewarding. As he sat there, a sense of accomplishment washed over him and he said to himself, "Yeah, I can see myself making music every day for the rest of my life."

Patrick comes from a musical background so it should come as no surprise that he chose a life in music. His father is a retired music consultant for the Kawartha Pine Ridge District School Board, and his mother is a piano teacher who made sure that Patrick and his three older siblings obtained their Grade Eight Piano and Grade Two Theory through the Royal Conservatory of Music. Both of Patrick's parents are also church musicians. After high school, Patrick enrolled at the University of Toronto where he graduated with a bachelor's degree in music and a Master of Sacred Music. His musical education remains ongoing as he continues to take regular organ lessons. He says he would love to take further courses in composing, conducting, and methods of vocal teaching.

Patrick is less active now in the world of secular music than he used to be, an evolution he feels happened naturally, saying that, "While I believe that all music

Patrick and the choir at a morning service before the renovation in 2014; Back row: Justin Grenier, Dave Finneran, Blake Woodside, Rob Ellis; Front row: Elizabeth White, Laura Peetoom, Anne Curtis, Pat Stephenson, Patrick Dewell

is inherently sacred, the music of the church has always captivated me and so now most of my time is spent playing or singing for worship services." However, he can occasionally be found outside the church walls directing a secular choir or playing jazz piano at a private function. Patrick can play many instruments, including piano, organ, flute, recorder, clarinet, marimbas, timpani, violin, and string-bass, and says, "I would *love* to play the harp, harpsichord, accordion, and banjo!" Sunday services find him playing piano and organ as well as conducting and singing, sometimes all at the same service. When asked what he considers the biggest challenge he faces as musical director at SJYM, his reply echoes the feelings of the last two rectors, Hollis Hiscock and Drew McDonald.

"My biggest challenge? Not only striking a balance between traditional and contemporary liturgical music, but also breaking down the barrier between the two. Diversity is the key to the musical success that we've achieved here at SJYM.… I would argue that our blended worship style is unique and what makes us stand out from our contemporaries. I am absolutely convinced that SJYM is the only Anglican parish church in Toronto that has such a diverse, yet fully integrated music program." When asked about the greatest *reward* in directing the music program at SJYM, Patrick offers a more visceral response.

"I am convinced that if there is at least one piece of music in the service that you can really *belt out,* then you will be more inclined to try singing a piece of music that you are not familiar with," he says. "The result is that it breeds more than just 'tolerance' or 'polite endurance' of different styles of music. It cultivates a spirit of openness and acceptance which in turn opens our hearts to love *unconditionally*, to accept and celebrate each other for who God created us to be." Small wonder then, that every service includes at least one piece that everyone can really "belt out."

Patrick's personal musical favourites are eclectic to say the least. "My favourite classical composer is Johann Sebastian Bach," he says, "his organ works in particular. I'm also quite fond of chant (all styles and from all parts of the world), Tudor church music, big band and smooth jazz, reggae, funk, and, last but not least, video game soundtracks. It's one of my aspirations in life to compose a musical score for a video game." A product of the digital age indeed! When asked who has most influenced his actual musical direction however, the list quickly narrows to just one man, Patrick's organ teacher John Tuttle.* "Like any good teacher," Patrick says, "John met me where I was on my musical journey and helped me unlock the vast musical potential inside me. After studying with him, I decided that I wanted to be not just a professional organist but a professional *church* organist. John inspires me daily and every time I sit down at the organ bench to practise, play, or perform, I always tell myself, 'Make John proud.'"

Patrick is equally willing to share the glory when it comes to the music program at St. John's. When asked if he feels that the handbells and chimes groups have helped keep young people involved with the church, Patrick gives credit where credit is due, saying that "Carolyn Martin has really spearheaded this initiative

---

*   John Tuttle graduated from the Curtis Institute of Music in Philadelphia. Following gradua-
      tion, he joined the U.S. Army and served as organist and choirmaster of the Post Chapel at the
      United States Military Academy in West Point, New York. In 1971 he returned to Philadelphia
      to serve as organist and choirmaster at that city's First Presbyterian Church. In 1975 he moved
      to Toronto where he ran the musical program at St. Paul's Anglican Church. In 1985 he
      moved to St. Thomas's Anglican Church on Huron Street, where he remains to this day. In
      1979 he was appointed organist to the University of Toronto and adjunct associate professor
      at the university's Faculty of Music. From 1981 to 2005 he conducted the university's Hart
      House Chorus. In 1981 he also became the founding conductor of the Exultate Chamber
      Singers, a nationally known twenty-voice ensemble that he led for thirty years. From 1985
      to 2000 he was the musical director of the Canadian Children's Opera Chorus, a group that
      toured both Canada and the United States. In 2006 he was appointed organist and director of
      music at the University of Toronto's Trinity College. He has a Fellowship Diploma from the
      American Guild of Organists, and honourary Fellowship diplomas from the Royal College of
      Organists (United Kingdom), and the Royal Canadian College of Organists, where he served
      as president from 1986 to 1988. In addition to his duties at St. Thomas' Anglican Church, he
      continues to play concerts and teach master classes in organ playing and choral conducting in
      both Canada and the United States.

Patrick Dewell played the organ at Doors Open Toronto 2016 for the many guests who toured the church.

with the handbells and chimes program that we have here at SJYM. Through this unique music ministry, children and young people have the opportunity of learning the basics of music as well as giving back to our parish and the wider community through the gift of sharing and performing music." He also points to bandleader Rob Ellis and the established band and choir members who welcome and mentor newcomers. "Many of our band and choir members are already professional musicians," he says. "Some take vocal and piano lessons (while others teach both!). Some are professional studio musicians and producers and some sing in community choirs and other choral groups." He acknowledges and values the contribution that these more-experienced musicians make to ensuring that the music programs at SJYM remain as inclusive as possible and says, "I strongly believe that the church should be a safe place for anyone to experience for themselves the joy that music can bring into their life."

In fact, Patrick believes that the integration of all the various parts of the musical program at SJYM is the greatest change in the past fifty years. "The biggest change at St. John's, from *my* perspective," he says, "is how seamlessly we have been able to combine all of our musicians into a single, unified musical team. The band, the choir, the handbells, the organ — we're all in this together! Our music leaders, me, Rob Ellis, our bandleader, and Carolyn Martin our handbells and chimes director, really enjoy collaborating with each other. We are constantly exploring new ways in which we can combine and showcase the wealth of different musical resources we have here at SJYM."

The seamless integration that Patrick refers to involves the combination of the following on any given Sunday: one organ, one piano, a six-to-twelve voice SATB (s̲oprano, a̲lto, t̲enor and b̲ass) choir, two or three solo vocalists, two or three guitarists, one bass guitarist, one percussionist, one tenor saxophone, one accordion, one trumpet, as well as chimes and handbells from four different handbell choirs. And don't forget the voices of the congregation!

The more modern side of the musical department is reflected not only in the updated instrumentation and musical selections but in the very way in which these sounds are conveyed to the congregation. The latest round of renovations to the church added two large video screens at the front of the chancel that face the congregation and display the lyrics to the musical selections — hymn books on the big screen!

Music director Patrick Dewell plays the piano and sings with the Worship Band.

The Casavant organ was wrapped in plastic to protect it during the renovation.

The voices of the choir are now captured by microphones and amplified through a sophisticated sound system, and much of the sheet music in use by the various musical departments is downloaded from the internet.

At the back of the church sits a state-of-the-art digital mixing board where the sounds coming from the stage are balanced for an optimum listening experience. It is this new technology that also allows for both audio and video recording of the proceedings. Not even the venerable old Casavant Brothers pipe organ has escaped the technological revolution.

It was enhanced with new digital capabilities in the 1990s and today, more than 50 percent of the sounds it produces are digitally created. Today it is properly known as a Walker-Casavant Hybrid Organ. Still, not even digital resources are infallible as long as human input is required. Many in the congregation may remember the day when the lyric "Lord of all *clam*" appeared on the big screens instead of "Lord of all *calm*."

ROB ELLIS

Bandleader Rob Ellis has been at St. John's York Mills since 2013, drawn here in large part by the church's reputation as innovative. He realizes that it is sometimes a challenge for a church to introduce new ideas — musical or otherwise — into the church culture, but he feels that St. John's is more than up to the challenge. Rob says, "there's an open-mindedness and level of forward-thinking that one might not always expect in an Anglican setting."

Like Patrick, Rob has a sound grasp of traditional church music and is currently working toward his Master of Sacred Music at Canada Christian College in Don Mills. He has always been drawn to music, and although he can't point to one specific moment where he chose to make music his life. He says, "Music has always grabbed me and inspired me more than anything else."

Rob first learned to love music through his father — a Presbyterian minister, vocalist, and respected musician who liked to play piano and sing hymns at home for his own enjoyment. Rob has an undergraduate degree in music from the University of Guelph and taught vocal lessons

Rob Ellis is at home playing on the steps of the chancel.

for many years at a private music school. Despite his formal education, he also credits a type of osmosis for much of his musical knowledge. "In many ways you simply soak it in from all around you as you go." He adds, "There's always a need for Biblical grounding, theological intelligence and genuine spiritual inspiration in our music. However, no song is complete in and of itself and was never meant to be. The Psalmist said, 'Sing a new song to the Lord,' so that's what we'll continue to do…. There's much value in the musical traditions of the past, just as there is with new styles and ideas, but we must do it without ever pretending that the musical world has stopped turning and we can settle ourselves a little too comfortably in one place." Rob is a firm believer in the idea that a blended worship, which embraces new music and attitudes, is a great way for the church to relate to the world beyond the parish and to "those we want to reach with God's grace and truth."

Rob has been a fan of contemporary Christian musicians such as Petra and Stryper since an early age and cites a significant influence from Michael W. Smith,

Rob Ellis and Dave Finneran, a choir lead, work together at a Sunday morning rehearsal.

an American Christian singer, songwriter, and musician who has sold more than eighteen million albums. He is also impressed by certain secular musicians, such as the band U2, when they make music that he finds revolutionary or pioneering. Rob plays guitar, piano, and "to a lesser extent" drums, bass, saxophone, recorder, and percussion. Sunday services usually find him singing and playing guitar. He is also a songwriter with a large backlog of songs that he is looking forward to recording and sharing with others.

When asked if he feels that the music program is a good way to keep young people involved with the church after confirmation, Rob offers a thoughtful response: "Of course, not all young people are musical, and we can't assume that music will be a catch-all solution," he says. "But for those who *are* musical, church music programs are vitally important because they can often be the one thing that keeps them (the young church-goers) connected to the church. Church has the potential to be a very accepting and affirming venue in which to develop and share their talents. And even for those who aren't musically inclined, it can be a draw that still works well when combined with other ways of being involved and using their gifts. That said, I believe musical interest among young people is increasing. In short, music in church can do far more than provide a soundtrack for people to sing along to. In some cases it can be a real lifeline."

There are always challenges and rewards involved in running a church music program. Rob's reward comes from being part of the team involved in leading the worship. "So often a service finishes, and I feel really good about the music I just played as well as the people I'm playing it with." He feels that the music

Left: *The Worship Band rehearses before a service, with lead singer Monika Burany, band leader Rob Ellis, Dr. Carol Redstone on guitar, and Charlene Sathi in the background on violin.*

Below: *Brian Hull on percussion and Ambrose Swanston on bass round out the regular Worship Band, which is also joined by other players from time to time.*

program "stands out as one that is welcoming and inclusive, as well as being musically accomplished" — two things that don't always go together. One of his challenges involves dealing with the digital revolution and the new big screens added to the church during the latest round of renovations. "It's created more demands and, I confess, it can be hard to keep up to," he admits. "For example, there was a time when all people had to do was pick up a hymn book and sing. Now someone has to prepare slides on a weekly basis, not only for the music, but for readings and other visuals." Still, even here there are rewards, for as Rob says, "With the overhead slides, the big screens now have people looking up, as opposed to having their noses buried in the hymnals. I think it has a very unifying effect when we're all looking up and in the same general direction instead of staring into individual books."

If any young people are interested in pursuing a life in church music, they can only benefit from following Rob's advice. "Don't take yourself too seriously. Learn to take your *craft* seriously so you're able to give it your best, but be wary of your own ambitions…. Set them aside as an act of humility and reverence and remember that it's about the worship experience for everyone present, and not for you or your goals. Your value is not tied to how well you perform or the legacy you create for yourself. Instead, your focus should be on helping people to experience God's presence. Prepare for the moment but always be *in* it as well, as your own act of worship."

HANDBELLS, CHIMERS, AND RINGERS

The third section of the current music department includes four handbell choirs and one chimes group, led for the past twenty-six years by parishioner Carolyn Martin. Though born of tragedy, the handbells have taken the message of SJYM to more people in more places than any other parish initiative. The first handbells, a three-octave set of Schulmerich English Handbells, were donated by the estate and family of parishioner Shirley Ingram, who, as mentioned in an earlier chapter, had been killed in a traffic accident while visiting Bishop John Robinson at his home in England. The bishop, an internationally known New Testament scholar and author, had been invited to preach at SJYM in September 1976, and while in York Mills, he stayed with Shirley Ingram at her home in Hogg's Hollow. Before returning to England, he invited Shirley to visit him there at his home as a way of repaying her hospitality. Shirley was innocently walking along the sidewalk in the seaside town of Hastings when an out-of-control car mounted the curb and killed her instantly. Her family used money from her estate to establish the Churchyard Sustaining Fund, which maintains gravesites in the churchyard, and to purchase that first set of handbells. This was a fitting gift, as Shirley was an American who grew up with the tradition of handbell ringing in her home church. The first handbell choir was made up of women from the parish and directed by Dorothy Galilee. Sadly, it only lasted for a few months. The next attempt would be much more successful.

JOANNE FLINT

In 1980 Joanne Flint — parishioner, one-time city councillor, and wife of the Reverend David Flint who was an associate priest at SJYM — became director of handbells, a position she would hold for the next decade. She began by approaching all of the teenagers at St. John's to see who might be interested in forming a new choir. Eleven brave souls agreed to give it a try: Tracy Stephenson, Heidi Kjollesdal, Alexandra Ross, Heather Fraser, Sarah Flint, Heidi Hunt, Steven Way, Doug Palm, Michael Grasley, Craig Gordon, and Marshall Ross.

Joanne Flint was director of handbells for ten years and was the person who firmly established the tradition of handbell ringing and chimers at St. John's York Mills.

Joanne Flint says, "The subsequent launching of the handbell program at St. John's York Mills throughout the 1980s was due to two concurrent and interwoven factors: eleven young teenagers who, by dint of their focused weekly practice and commitment to each other, made handbell ringing fun and popular; and St. John's membership in the American Guild of English Handbell Ringers (AGEHR). The AGEHR network exposed the ringers to the best American directors, a wide range of music, and opportunities to participate in exhilarating festivals and mass ringing events. As a result, the young people strived for — and achieved — a remarkable and acknowledged high degree of excellence. Two additional octaves of handbells were purchased, the choir expanded to fourteen ringers, and a culture of good ringing was established at St. John's." The new group decided to call themselves the Festival Choir because their initial goal was to attend a handbell festival in Calgary at the end of their first season — a goal they achieved.

"They made it," Joanne says, "thanks to fundraising and wonderful financial support from the wardens. In Calgary they rose to the occasion of a solo performance at the opening ceremonies, and then finally experienced the thrill of ringing with others. The trip was expanded to include a trip to visit Kananaskis Country, the Glenbow Museum, a Hutterite colony near Lethbridge, and ringing for St. Andrew's Anglican Church where they were billeted with parish members during the off-festival time of the trip." It should be noted here that the handbell festivals are not competitions. They are actually three-day collaborative events, at which attending choirs work together on music they have previously

The Festival Handbell Choir were in Vancouver in 1986. Front row (left to right): Kim Winter, Heidi Hunt, Heidi Kjollesdal, Tracy Stephenson, Alexandra Ross, Patti Barber, Heather Fraser; Back row (left to right): Michael Bakker, Craig Gordon, Doug Palm, Sarah Flint, Michael Grasley, Marshall Ross, Steven Way, Peter Wismath

VANCOUVER
BRITISH COLUMBIA

VANCOUVER
city of the century

Photography by Siwik Productions
P.O. Box 5148 Vancouver, B.C. V6B 4B2

1986

rehearsed on their own before performing together at a festival-ending concert. The three-day event also includes lectures, workshops, and smaller concerts. Although the hours are long and the work is hard, most of the choirs in North America are associated with Christian churches and the overall spirit at a festival is one of caring and sharing.

During the years immediately following the Calgary festival in the mid-1980s, the St. John's Festival Choir performed at two Ontario festivals, numerous festivals in the United States, Expo '86 in Vancouver, and an international festival in Exeter, England. While in the United Kingdom they also performed in a number of English cathedrals and gave a solo noontime concert at the Church of St Martin-in-the-Fields in London. No ringers quit the choir during the 1980s. In fact, more young parishioners were becoming interested in joining all the time, attracted by the camaraderie and the adventure of travel. All of the teen choirs at the time were comprised of an equal mix of males and females, providing a strong sense of balance, moral support, and a very creative dynamic. Joanne stresses how important each individual ringer is to the choir: "Each ringer is responsible for five or six bells. There are no back-ups. Thus, each ringer is absolutely essential to the success of the choir. Attendance at practices and performances is compulsory."

In 1983 four Ontario handbell directors from Toronto, Mississauga, London, and Niagara Falls met in the Garnsworthy Room and formed the Ontario Guild of English Handbell Ringers (OGEHR) to promote handbell ringing in Ontario. Today the OGEHR has more than one hundred members and is a major influence in the North American handbell community. Meanwhile, the St. John's program itself was expanding.

A choir comprised of adults of mixed ages and genders was formed. Dubbed the Ingram Choir, it focused on performing timeless musical pieces for seniors' groups and festival workshops and was always invited back to perform again. A teenage choir called the Brass Choir was also formed. This choir specialized in sight

The first Brass Choir: Front row (left to right): Jamie Shone, Shawna McAuliffe; Middle row (left to right): Pamela Martin, Matthew Jukes, Lianne Furlong, Warren Cherry, Jennifer Lee; Back row (left to right): Kevin Way, Sheila Jones, Peter Wismath, Daniel Nelles, Peter Moore, Fiona Oliver, David Otter

reading: seeing a piece of sheet music for the first time and being able to play it on sight. They became so adept at this that they were invited to be the demonstration choir at a meeting of the American Music Distributors annual conference, held at the King Edward Hotel. Brass Choir members would often go on to join the Festival Choir, replacing members who had gone away to university. Finally, the O'Neil Choir was formed to attract the youngest boys and girls. Joanne Flint took the program a long way in less than a decade. It comes as no surprise then that she is able to look back on many highlights.

"The biggest thrill for me, as director," Joanne says, "was to witness teenagers, who may not have known each other well at the beginning, or were not very familiar with music, develop into musicians worthy of representing their country. And along with that, to see them find within themselves — individually and collectively — a depth of character that enabled them to make the best of situations in which they found themselves and to accept the responsibility of leadership. Every ringer was aware, at home or away, that they were ambassadors for St. John's."

She cites a number of instances in which members of her choirs made bad situations better, such as the time a power failure at an Ontario festival in Peterborough left everyone in a dark, silent auditorium until one of the St. John's ringers started a sing-along that became the highlight of the festival; or the deadly-slow river rafting trip in blazing Wyoming heat that was saved by the antics of the Brass Choir. Some moments were more special than others. Joanne remembers the time when "Heidi Kjollesdal rose to the pulpit in

Liverpool Cathedral — the largest cathedral in England — and, in her clear soprano voice, sang *No Man Is An Island*, accompanied by the Festival Choir. The music soared and echoed throughout the cathedral and into the hearts of everyone who heard it."

One of the most memorable moments of all happened at home, in the familiar embrace of St. John's sanctuary. "One Sunday morning in the mid-1980s," Joanne recalls, "Avril Helbig magnificently sang every note of *The Holy City*. Cheryl Buckingham played the challenging piano score perfectly and, in harmony with Avril, Sarah Flint rang solo twenty-three handbells without missing a beat. Three exceptional teenagers combined their talents in one very difficult piece of music and produced an unforgettable moment of magic and praise. No one wanted to break the silence that followed." In 1990 current director Carolyn Martin took over this remarkable program from interim handbell choir leaders, which included Heidi Hunt and Peter Wismath.

CAROLYN MARTIN

From the time she was a grade eight student at McKee Avenue Public School, North York, and was allowed to help look after the younger children when teachers were out of the classroom, Carolyn Martin wanted to be a teacher. She later graduated from Toronto Teacher's College, and her desire and love of teaching never changed. She taught at Owen Boulevard P.S. in North York, and then in Halifax and Montreal, as she and her husband made career moves. She enjoyed being a stay-at-home mom with Daniel, Pamela, and Andrew.

When Andrew was in nursery school, she began a new career holding music workshops with a partner in schools and libraries in North York and Thornhill. Carolyn also performed for many years in a community theatre group and concert choir.

Carolyn Martin

Carolyn Martin's grandson Sean (third from the left in the second row) was a member of the Rockin' Ringers in 2014.

Carolyn and her husband Peter and their family joined St. John's in 1984. Baptism, confirmation, marriage, and a funeral all deepened their family's roots at St. John's. Now her grandson Sean is a server and a Rockin' Ringer!

Over the years, she has been involved with music in the Sunday school and worked with drama director Sally Armour Wotton on Holy Day programs for children. As a retired schoolteacher with a passion for music and a love of young people, she is delighted that directing handbell and handchime choirs allows her to combine the two through a unique musical medium.

After Carolyn and Peter and their three children joined the parish in 1984, their children soon became servers or handbell ringers. Their daughter Pamela joined the junior choir and handbell choir in 1986, and four years later Joanne

Flint asked Carolyn to take over the Ingram Ringers. Today there are four choirs: the Chimers for those in grades three through six, the Rockin' Ringers for grades six through nine, the Brass Ringers for teens and adults with some musical background, and the Ingram Ringers for adults. The choirs are in action from the week after Labour Day until June. The St. John's handbell choirs are members of the Ontario Guild of English Handbell Ringers and have travelled widely in Canada and the United States, where they are frequent participants in festivals sponsored by the Handbell Musicians of America. To date, St. John's handbell choirs have performed in Michigan, Indiana, Maine, Texas, Vermont, Wyoming, New York, and the United Kingdom. They have also performed at other churches in Canada and the United States. Here in Toronto, they have appeared on City TV, Global TV, CBC-TV, CTV, and TV Ontario. They have also performed with the Toronto Youth Wind Orchestra and at the Distillery District Christmas Market, as well as at local hotels, corporate events, and the annual Fenelon Falls Santa Day. In autumn 2000 six of the most experienced ringers recorded a television commercial for Swiss Chalet restaurants that appeared on TV for the six weeks leading up to Christmas, with "St. John's York Mills" appearing in small print at the bottom of the screen while the commercial played. The commercial ran for three Christmas seasons.

In 2001 the handbell program took another step forward. "In the fall," Carolyn recalls, "with the commitment of thirty-nine ringers and their families and the help of Robin Davis, our new organist, we went forward with the plan to record a Christmas CD. Three exhausting but fun seven-hour recording sessions in our church were constantly interrupted by the rumble of the subway! It was constant stop and start for our ringers as we completed the pieces bit-by-bit between subway trains! Editing with our recording engineer, Ed Marshall from CBC, obtaining copyright, taking pictures, writing a brochure, and finally ordering a thousand CDs, filled the spring of 2002. We celebrated our completion and distribution at our MusicFest performances in May." The CD *Ring in Christmas* was an instant success. By December 1,200 copies had been sold and an order for a further thousand copies was placed. To date *Ring in Christmas* has sold more than three thousand copies and has proven to be a most-effective fundraiser.

In 2003 Carolyn directed eight handbell choirs in a cold and blustery Nathan Phillips Square to celebrate the lighting of Toronto's official Christmas tree. In 2004 Carolyn recalls the ringers marking a more solemn occasion. "In the spring of 2004, we had a chaplain from the Toronto Firefighters Association who had been to New York City at 9/11 come and speak to us to prepare us for a special trip we had planned to honour the 9/11 fallen. Our teenagers travelled to New York City and played at St. Paul's Chapel at Ground Zero, offering our music for those lost or affected by the tragedy. We visited Steinway Hall, saw how pianos were made, and visited the basement area where great artists getting ready to play in Carnegie Hall can come to practise. We then drove to Morris Plains, New Jersey, to ring with another choir and be billeted by them. It is a wonderful experience to meet other teens and adults with similar interests and join with them in producing beautiful music."

For the remainder of the decade, the handbell choirs maintained their busy schedules — schedules that could not have been maintained without the dedication of tireless volunteers from the parish. "Over the years," Carolyn says, "Charlotte and Tim Orser and Brenda Parkes have been wonderful planners and drivers for our ringers. Jan Williams, the Richards, Diana Kennedy, and Boni Strang, also joined us on some of our road trips." Susan Shone, parent of an O'Neil ringer (from an earlier choir) made red stoles for the ringers that are still in use today, twenty-two years after she made them.

In August 2004 Toronto hosted more than six hundred experienced English Handbell Ringers from around the world for the biennial 11th International Handbell Symposium. With ringers in town from Korea, Japan, China, Australia, the United States, and the United Kingdom, interpreters were required to make sure that rehearsals ran smoothly. In May 2006 St. John's ringers travelled to

Montreal to perform for and be hosted by the congregation of St. Lambert United Church. In May 2007 the ringers returned to New York City where they performed for a midnight Eucharist and slept over on the gymnasium floor of St. John the Divine, before returning to New Jersey where they performed for and were billeted by one of the churches in Basking Ridge.

Following MusicFest in May 2008, the ringers travelled to Quebec City where they rang at St. Anne de Beaupré and Notre Dame de Québec Cathedral. MusicFest 2010 holds special meaning for Carolyn and her husband Peter. "MusicFest 2010's 'Jukebox Memories' was a great success," Carolyn remembers. "I will be forever grateful for the way all the ringers and others pulled together to handle rehearsals and all the set-up required when our son Daniel suddenly passed away just four weeks before. How wonderful to be part of an extended family of people who care. That December we had our first Sing and Ring in Christmas."

In the spring of 2011, the Ontario Guild Handbell Festival was held at McMaster University in Hamilton, where ringers stayed in the residences while the festival was happening. Some of the ringers enjoyed the experience so much that they later chose McMaster for their post-secondary education. In 2012 the church was presented with a somewhat unusual opportunity to appear in yet another television show. Carolyn says, "St. John's was contacted by Sinking Ship Entertainment (yes, I questioned the name, too!) in October 2012. I was asked if I would like to teach the young host of the show, Scarlett, how to ring bells for an episode of the program *This is…*. My answer of course was *yes*, but with one provision: that our eight chimers could be part of the experience. The production team talked about it and came back with a *yes*! The filming date was set for December 10, 2012. Cameras, lights, sound equipment, and more all moved into our sanctuary. There were many takes and retakes as they attempted to get six-year-old Scarlett to do and say what they wanted for the filming. I had great fun and the chimers really enjoyed being part of such a unique experience. As I write this article (2016), the episode is still being played on TVO…."

That December, Sing and Ring raised $1,000 for World Vision and $700 for bicycle ambulances through Anglican Gifts for Missions. The first chimer sleepover was held in the church in February 2013 and has since become an annual tradition. MusicFest during the 2014 renovation was subtitled "Hard Hats, Hammers, and Hallelujah."

Carolyn Martin summarized her feelings on the handbells and handchimes program with the following thoughts in early 2016:

"It has been wonderful, over the years, to work with a variety of talented St. John's music directors: Maurice White, Boni Strang, Robin Davis, Monique Ingalls, and, most recently, Patrick Dewell. Our band is led by Rob Ellis. Collaboration with band and choir for our big performances is a wonderful opportunity to bring us all together.

"My greatest pleasure over the years has been working with children, watching and being a part of their 'growing up' years, writing letters of recommendation for jobs, rejoicing in engagements, marriages, and births, and growing 'mature' with a group of very special people.

"A program begun with a donation of three octaves of handbells by the Ingram family has enriched the lives of hundreds of ringers who have passed

Left: The handbells and chimers rehearse for the service of rededication in November 2014.

Right: The entire music department at St. John's performs together every May under the leadership of Carolyn Martin. Pictured here: MusicFest 2015, the first one held after the renovation was completed.

through it — a program that has challenged and enriched my life for twenty-six years. It has been a blessing to me and a source of pride for our church.

"To God be the glory in all that we do and thank you for the memories!"

There are currently thirty-nine ringers in the four choirs. The current inventory of handbells includes the original three-octave Ingram set of Shulmerich English Handbells, a complementary five-octave set of Shulmerich English Handbells, and four and five-and-a-half octave sets of Malmark handchimes. Somewhere, one likes to imagine that Shirley Ingram must be very proud of the way that Carolyn Martin and Joanne Flint have taken her bequest and turned it into an indispensable part of St. John's heritage.

IN CONCLUSION

It should come as no surprise that none of this music-making would be possible without a regular rehearsal schedule, a tricky bit of coordination that Rob Ellis mentions as another "challenge." The band rehearses on Sunday mornings from 8:15 a.m. to 9:45 a.m. The choir rehearses Thursday evenings from 7:30 p.m. to 9:00 p.m. and on Sunday mornings from 8:30 a.m. to 9:00 a.m., while the paid choir leads hold an extra half-hour rehearsal on Thursdays from 7:00 p.m. to 7:30 p.m. The band and choir hold a joint rehearsal on Sunday mornings from 10:00 a.m. to 10:30 a.m. Handbells and chimes groups hold weekly rehearsals on Sunday afternoons and Monday evenings. In addition to these regular rehearsals, additional rehearsal time is required to prepare for special concerts such as MusicFest or Sing & Ring, and special services for Christmas, Holy Week, and Easter. The paid choir leads mentioned above have become an integral part of the music program at SJYM.

Patrick Dewell explains, "Our three choir leads, Emma Burns (our soprano lead), Laura Peetoom (our alto lead), and Dave Finneran (our tenor lead) are paid choral professionals who have an interest in both church music and music ministry. They provide strong vocal leadership at our Thursday night rehearsals, our joint Sunday morning rehearsals, and, most importantly, during our 9:00 a.m. liturgies. Not only do they serve as informal mentors to members of our existing choir, they are also just really nice, compassionate people! We are so fortunate to have these three singers in our midst every week and I'm so grateful to the congregation for their financial support. It demonstrates to me that the faith community of SJYM really cares about music!"

Patrick relaxes by practicing Bikram Yoga, a discipline where classes run for ninety minutes and always consist of the same series of twenty-six positions and two breathing exercises. He likens the experience to the Anglican order of service, which contains a sequence of recurring liturgical items. He also feels comfortable with yoga, as the practise requires that you "be in the moment," a state of mind that Patrick likens to a musical performance. "Creating music, whether playing for a religious service or a recital, is an activity that exists only in the present," he says. "As both a church musician and organ recitalist, many hours of my life go into planning and preparing all kinds of liturgical and concert music. Yet, plan and prepare as I may, the act of making music always occurs in the present, in the now!" The Bible makes note of this, especially in Psalms, Patrick says. "If you take a look at the Psalms, you'll notice that not only are many of the verses written in the imperative but also in the present tense: 'Come, let us sing for joy to the Lord; let us shout aloud to the Rock of our salvation.' (Psalm 95: 1); 'Sing to him, sing praise to him; tell him of all his wonderful acts' (Psalm 105: 2)."

When asked his opinion on the biggest constant in the musical program, Patrick is quick to reply, "The Anglican liturgy and its unique ability to both pique the curiosity of the seeker and deepen the faith of the believer." It is this respect for tradition that determines many of the musical selections that are currently performed on a regular basis. "Because we are a sacramental church," Patrick says, "we do Communion every Sunday, and with the Anglican Communion liturgy also comes the opportunity of singing specific parts of the service. At SJYM we often sing a Gospel acclamation ("Alleluia"), a Sanctus ("Holy, Holy, Holy Lord"), and the Lord's Prayer ("Our Father in Heaven"). Sometimes we sing a Kyrie ("Lord Have Mercy") and an Agnus Dei ("Lamb of God") during Advent or Lent."

The hand-cranked barrel organ, installed in September 1847, is still used on special occasions, such as the recent Doors Open Toronto. Rob Ellis finds another type of constant in the music program. "For me, it's been the accepting and encouraging spirit that continues to prevail among our musicians, staff, and congregants, despite any challenges or hardship. I would go so far as to say that St. John's stands out from any other church I've been a part of for the way people truly love and care for each other."

Who knows what the next fifty years will hold for the music department at SJYM? All Patrick can say for sure is that "I would like to see both our band and choir ministries grow in size. The more the merrier!"

CHAPTER SEVEN

The Women of St. John's

The last fifty years have seen an almost seismic shift in the structure of the women's groups at St. John's York Mills. In 1966 there were fourteen such groups in operation with a total of 277 members. Today there is only one, the Lychgate Group, named after the historical lychgate at the entrance to the churchyard.

It is hard to determine exactly how many groups were active at any given time, as records often disappeared when the groups disbanded, though it is known that there were at least twenty-four different groups over the years. Although there were many different "sub-groups," there were only three main groups: the Women's Parish Guild, the Sanctuary Guild, and the Women's Auxiliary.

The Women's Parish Guild was formed in 1927 with the stated purpose "to assist the Rector and Wardens in every way possible." The sub-groups that formed under the wings of the parish guild were autonomous in every way, except when it came to spending the money they raised. Regular meetings were held from September to May, with groups taking turns handling the catering. An annual meeting was held every January, at which time new officers were elected to the council. Many of the sub-groups took their names from streets or

Top left: *In 1946 the annual bazaar was opened by Mrs. Ray Lawson, the wife of the Lieutenant Governor of Ontario, and bazaar convenor Margaret Brophy.*

Top right: *In the early 1960s the Birtle family organized a bottle drive to aid the scout troop that met at St. John's.*

Left: *The Women's Guild organized a picnic on Centre Island in 1928.*

neighbourhoods in the area. Not all members were parishioners, and the groups were very fluid, forming, merging, or disbanding as situations demanded. The scope and variety of their fundraising efforts, however, were breathtaking.

They held bake sales, book sales, plant sales, jam, jelly, and pickle sales, auctions, and bazaars. They hosted fashion shows, square dances, a children's fun fair, film nights, theatrical performances, garden parties and teas, bridge luncheons, bridge marathons, yoga classes, pot-luck lunches, cooking classes, cottage getaways, seminars on income tax and estate planning, murder mystery dinners, and scenic bus tours to out-of-town locations. They canvassed friends and neighbours for good used clothing they could sell for money, which they then donated to charity. They made blankets, quilts, and knitted goods for northern churches. They held Valentine's Day parties for residents of Cummer House Retirement Residence. They baked cookies and packed cookie tins that they delivered to the elderly and shut-ins at Christmas. They made dressings for hospital patients. They sponsored underprivileged families and supported them with bedding, clothing, and furniture, as well as providing them with special Easter, Christmas, and Thanksgiving dinners. They produced and sold cookbooks. They made cloth diapers for underprivileged children. They volunteered at Sunnybrook Hospital. They collected grocery store tapes and green stamps, and redeemed them for cash to buy food for St. Peter's Church programs and the Downtown Churchworkers Association. At Christmastime they packed gift boxes for the children in Bloorview Children's Hospital, wrapped and distributed parcels to charitable organizations, made Christmas decorations for hospital patients, and collected canned goods for distribution to needy families. Their efforts on behalf of St. John's itself were no less spectacular.

In 1948 the Reverend Arthur McCollum praised them for providing more than $28,000 to enlarge the church and purchase the new pipe organ. In 1949 they supplied new shutters to decorate the exterior of the rectory. They provided pews and other furniture to the church. In 1966 they donated $5,000 to assist in the publication of Audrey Graham's book, *150 Years at St. John's, York Mills*, on the occasion of the church's 150th anniversary — a book the guild members were also responsible for selling. That same year they also provided a new electric typewriter for the church office, as well as new furniture, hymn book repairs, and drapes that they had sewn themselves. In 1967 the Women's Parish Guild, the Sanctuary Guild, and the Woman's Auxiliary, amalgamated under the new title of Anglican Church Women (ACW). The good work continued.

In 1968 the annual bazaar raised money to refurbish the main kitchen at a cost of $5,290, and to buy a new stove and fridge for the Garnsworthy Room. In 1969 the ACW provided forty new gowns for the junior choir, each gown cut, sewn, and individually fitted by ACW members themselves. The women also took on the responsibility of decorating the church for all special occasions and catering clergy luncheons for up to 150 members at one sitting.

As the decades passed, however, the combination of a declining parish list and an increasing number of women joining the workforce would bring inevitable change to the ACW. In 1968 three of the groups under the ACW banner disbanded. In the 1970s two more joined them, followed by four groups that disbanded in the

Above: *The Lychgate Group organized a fundraising cabaret in 2002. Worship music director Boni Strang (far left in the back row) was an essential part of the team.*

Left: *Jay Burford, costumed as the Town Crier, stands by a plaque in the sanctuary commemorating the work of the Anglican Church Women's guild in refurbishing the pipe organ and furnishing the chapel.*

1980s, and two that disbanded in 1991. It was clear that the nature of the women's groups was changing. The groups that lasted into the twenty-first century, only to fold before the end of the first decade, were the Metro Group, the York Group, and the Twenty-One Group. In 1970 a group of young mothers from the community started a Wednesday morning drop-in group. By the end of the 1970s, this had grown into the Lychgate Group. In the beginning it featured badminton, guest speakers, a nursery, and, of course, coffee! Larger fundraising events were planned that could raise larger amounts of money from a single event, as it was clear that people no longer had the time to devote to the smaller, more numerous fundraisers of the past. These new events often included well-known guest speakers such as Doris Anderson, author and then-editor of *Chatelaine* magazine, who was the guest speaker at the 1974 spring luncheon. Ontario Lieutenant Governor Pauline McGibbon was the spring luncheon guest speaker in 1976. In 1978 the Lychgate Group was formally instituted as a women's group of St. John's York Mills, and it was the first to begin meeting in the evenings to accommodate the number of women who were working.

On the occasion of the 160th anniversary of the church in 1976, the women's groups of the day celebrated with a "Ramble in a Country Churchyard," where period-costumed ACW members stationed themselves in the churchyard, entertaining attendees with the stories of the church's pioneer families. There was also a strawberry social on the lawn of the Old Rectory, which offered tea, wine, and beer.

In the 1980s, members of the ACW, the Lychgate Group, the York Group, and the Metro Group, were responsible for refurbishing the Garnsworthy Room — used as a common social room — as well as the main washrooms.

Change continued throughout the 1980s, however, and while a new parenting program drew interest in 1987, the traditional Welcome Back Tea in the fall was cancelled the following year for lack of interest. The ACW continued to be represented at the Toronto Diocesan Anglican Church Women's annual and general

meetings. Members were also active in the World Day of Prayer every March and even hosted this event, which is held in a different denominational church each year. In 1990 ACW meetings were moved from afternoons to evenings to accommodate younger businesswomen in the area. Meetings opened with a cocktail reception followed by a sit-down supper, business meeting, and guest speaker.

At the suggestion of the Rev. Jim O'Neil, Lychgate ran a rummage sale for many years that was part outreach function for the disadvantaged — including sponsoring city children for the Moorelands summer camp — and part fundraising support for St. John's. The Christmas bazaar was a major fundraising event for all of the women's groups for many years, selling used books, mincemeat, jams and jellies, pinecone centrepieces, and door wreaths. There was also a toy stall for children and handmade Christmas decorations. Lychgate sponsored the Olde Lantern Café, where attendees at the bazaar could purchase a bowl of hamburger soup followed by Christmas goodies to sustain them during their shopping.

Other events in which various groups participated were the cabaret evenings put on by the music departments and Lychgate, and two Mardi Gras evenings and silent auctions that raised more than $10,000 each. Lychgate also hosted a number of ladies fashion shows.

Left: *The annual Christmas bazaar was a popular event for many years and all the women's groups and the men's group, under the leadership of Anne Bawden, helped to make it a success. Here, the ACW represented by Yvonne Aziz, sold jam in 1993.*

Right: *Sometimes the men are invited to join the Lychgate parties. Here we see (left to right) Bruce Snell, Vern Barney, Bill Dewberry, and Peter Oliver at the final June party.*

Above: *The Reverend Hollis Hiscock and parishioner Brian Hull as the town crier open the bazaar in 1992.*

Above right: *As one of the bazaar activities, the Lychgate Group ran the Olde Lantern Café in 1992 and for many years afterward.*

As the church enters its third century, the Lychgate Group has been gathering the women of the parish together for over forty years into a community of support — support for each other and support for the church at large. Many of the women in the group, the young mothers of the 1970s, are still attending the monthly meetings, and several members who now live out of town still join the group for the Christmas party and the June barbecue. In 2016 Lychgate is still meeting once a month to listen to speakers, discuss books, plan events, and, of course, socialize.

The women of Lychgate, joined now by the men of the Men's Supper Club, can still be counted on to host special events, such as the speaker series for the 200th anniversary, and the reception after the service of celebration planned for the fall of 2016. The role of Anglican women has changed over the years to respond to the changing times, but the goal of learning together, praying together, supporting each other, and serving their church community remains the same.

Top left: *A fashion show hosted by the Lychgate Group with (left to right) models Venetia Cowie, her daughter Jennifer, Yvonne McGregor, Liz Keddie, and Connie Hunt Hamson*

Left: *A 2007 fundraising book sale is staffed by Karen Barnett.*

Top right: *Some of the members of the Lychgate Group in 2016: Back row (left to right): Judy Arsenault, Shiam Sathi, Ellen-Jean Dewberry, Anne Curtis, Sylvia McConnell, Mardi Saunders, Jane White, Sharon Barney, Yvonne McGregor, Venetia Cowie, Sylvia Raynham, Pamela Smith (chair), and Karen Barnett; Front row (left to right): Carol Barney, Gillian Gillespie, Gail Moore, Liz Keddie, Linda Grasley, and Connie Hunt Hamson*

CHAPTER EIGHT

Walter Seymour Allward

It is doubtful that there is a monument anywhere in the world that can stir the Canadian soul more deeply than the Vimy Ridge Memorial in northern France. Canadian troops opened the Battle of Arras at Vimy Ridge on Easter Monday, April 9, 1917. The attack on the German-held ridge began in driving sleet at 5:30 a.m. It was the first time that all four divisions of the Canadian Corps had joined together in the same battle. The battle raged for three more days, with the Canadian Corps capturing the final German position on the ridge in blowing snow on April 12.

The battle is often pointed to as the moment when Canadian nationhood was born, and while the story should probably be required reading for all Canadians, it is far too complex to be properly conveyed here. The memorial at Vimy Ridge, designed and constructed by Walter Seymour Allward over a period of twelve years, is one of the most awe-inspiring monuments in the world. Parishioners of St. John's York Mills have a particular interest in the memorial and its designer, as Walter and his family were also parishioners at St. John's. Since Walter was largely self-taught, his background and early years gave no hint as to the exalted place he would one day occupy in the history of his country.

The Reverend Drew MacDonald shared a story from his recent visit to the memorial at Vimy Ridge during his sabbatical in 2015. There he took a tour and was visiting the underground tunnels at the closest point to the enemy lines, when he shared some of his personal history with the tour guide. Drew's grandfather immigrated to Canada from Wales in 1909 at the age of sixteen. When the war broke out in 1914, he was twenty-one and immediately signed up. Because he was from the "old country," he was assigned to the Princess Patricia's regiment. As he told his story, the tour guide stared at him and then said, "The Princess Pats were right here, ninety-eight years ago, right here on this spot. They were the elite troops and they were the first ones out." Drew cannot describe how he felt at that moment, but he says, "I did feel a part of history and thankful that he survived, but also mindful of those not standing with me whose fathers had not survived. Such are the mysteries of life and death."

The Vimy Ridge Memorial, approached from the north

Walter Allward was born in Toronto on November 18, 1876, to parents who had recently moved to the city from Newfoundland. His carpenter father taught Walter woodworking at an early age, but the youngster's interests already lay elsewhere. For even as a young boy he was interested in architecture and design. The problem was that the city had no art school at the time that addressed his particular interests, so he began to teach himself, augmenting what he could learn from books with Saturday morning classes at the Art Gallery of Toronto (now the Art Gallery of Ontario).

In 1894 while still a teenager, Walter landed his first job when he was hired by the Taylor family. The Taylors' Don Valley Pressed Brick Works, founded twelve years earlier on the site of today's Evergreen Brickworks, was manufacturing more than 114,000 bricks a day. The company shipped its wares all across Canada as well as to cities in the northern United States. By 1916, the renamed Don Valley Brickworks was the largest brickworks in the world. It continued manufacturing bricks at the same site until 1984 under the name of the Toronto Brick Company. In addition to bricks, the company also manufactured a wide array of other products, primarily terra-cotta pipes, tiles, urns, chimneys, and architectural embellishments. This is where Walter's eye for design proved invaluable. The year he arrived, the company won a gold medal for their display at the Toronto Industrial Fair.

Walter then took another step along his career path when he found employment as a draughtsman in the office of architect Henry Simpson. He would return to the office after supper to practise drawing by copying images from the books in the company's library. He also took lessons in painting and sculpture in Toronto before travelling to Paris and London to broaden his horizons. In 1898 he married Margaret Patricia Kennedy. The couple honeymooned in Paris so Walter could continue his studies.

Shortly after returning from his honeymoon, Walter won a competition to design a figure-of-peace sculpture for installation in Queen's Park as a memorial to the battles of the Northwest (Riel) Rebellion of 1885. He would later design a number of other Queen's Park sculptures, including of Lieutenant Governor John Graves Simcoe (1901), Sir Oliver Mowat (1905) who was Ontario premier when the Parliament Buildings opened in 1893, William Lyon Mackenzie (1937), and Queen Victoria on her throne. Walter never had to work at another job to support his art. He was able to make a living as a sculptor all his life.

In 1907 Walter completed one of his most poignant memorials. This monument, titled *The Old Soldier*, stands in Victoria Memorial Park on the northeast corner of Portland and Niagara Streets in downtown Toronto. The memorial was sponsored by British army and navy veterans to commemorate soldiers who died in the War of 1812. It depicts an unknown older soldier holding his helmet in his hand and looking skyward with a yearning gaze. It's impossible to stand in front of this sculpture and not feel sympathy for this fictitious figure, so great was Walter Allward's talent.

In October 1921 the Allwards were living at 76 Walker Avenue, between Yonge Street and the campus of De La Salle College on Avenue Road. At that time Walter was chosen by the Canadian Battlefields Memorials Commission to create the Vimy Ridge Memorial. Walter's design was chosen from more than one hundred entries by Canada's finest sculptors and architects. The commission could not have made a better selection. From the very beginning, Walter's commitment was deep and moving.

The Old Soldier, *Allward's work from 1907, stands in a park at the corner of Portland and Wellington streets in downtown Toronto.*

After his design was chosen, he revealed that his inspiration had come to him in a dream while the war was still raging. "When things were at their blackest in France, I dreamed that I was in a great battlefield. I saw our men going by in thousands and being mowed down by the sickles of death…. Suffering beyond endurance at the sight, I turned my eyes and found myself looking down on an avenue of poplars. Suddenly, through the avenue I saw thousands marching to the aid of our armies. They were the dead. They rose in masses, filed silently by, and entered the fight to aid the living. So vivid was this impression that when I awoke it stayed with me for months. Without the dead we were helpless. So I have tried to show this in this monument to Canada's fallen, what we owed them and will forever owe them."[*] More than 66,000 Canadian soldiers perished in the First World War. The bodies of more than one-quarter of those men were never recovered. Approximately 3,600 died capturing Vimy Ridge between April 9 and April 12, 1917. The names of

---

[*]   "Vimy Clippings," box 2, 5055, Allward Fonds, Queen's University Archives (QUA).

A close-up of the names on the memorial to the 11,285 missing men

11,285 men are engraved on the Vimy Ridge Memorial — soldiers who died in France and whose bodies were never recovered. More than one hundred bodies have been recovered since the panels were engraved.

The monument, begun in 1924, had a budget of $1.5 million. It took more than twelve years to complete. Such was Walter's dedication to the project that he moved his family to London, England, to be closer to his work. By 1931 he was actually living at the site. It is interesting to note that Vimy Ridge is less than one hundred kilometres from the English Channel, and the sound of the guns that launched the Easter Monday battle in 1917 could be heard as far away as London.

It took two years just to find the right type of stone for the monument: white limestone that was found in a formerly abandoned quarry in Yugoslavia; and white stone to represent the snow and ice of a Canadian winter. A special road was constructed to convey the six thousand tons of stone from the main road between Lens and Arras to the construction site on Vimy Ridge. This task alone took two-and-a-half years, slowed tremendously by the land mines and underground tunnels that still pockmarked the battlefield. The monument is surrounded by 107 hectares of former battlefield, land given in perpetuity to Canada by a grateful France. Old trenches, tunnels, and bomb craters are still there, preserved as part of the memorial. The rest of the land has been lovingly reforested to repair the absolute devastation of warfare.

Critics of art and architecture feel that Vimy Ridge is where Walter Allward really came into his own as a sculptor. Laura Brandon was the curator of war art at the Canadian War Museum in 2005 when she told the *Toronto Star* that she could see the influence of Rodin and Michelangelo in this work, and that Walter was at that time working in a style that was "more emotive, rigorous, and vibrant than his earlier work…."[*] The monument far transcends the single battle it was meant to represent. It makes no reference to victory, but rather to the goal of

---

[*]   Debra Black, "Old Soldier recalls past glory" *Toronto Star*, April 1, 2005.

good, the cycle of life and death, and the hope of resurrection. The religious imagery is strong, with two massive pylons, one for Canada and one for France, and a space between them that offers a gate to eternity. In addition to more usual influences, such as classical Greek and Renaissance architecture, Walter admitted to being influenced by the style of medieval French cathedrals. At certain times of the day, the light shines through the two pylons in such a way that the monument appears almost as an open-air place of worship.

The religious imagery of both the battle and the monument was embraced immediately and has changed very little in the ensuing years. The sacrifice of the pious soldiers; the fact that the battle began on Easter Monday; the ridge that took the soldiers closer to God; the wooden crosses that marked the graves; the feeling that the dead soldiers were resurrected in the birth of a new sense of nationhood; the overwhelming need for comfort in a time of great loss; the volumes of prose and poetry that made this battle the most memorialized of the entire war — all of these things can be seen and felt in the Vimy Ridge Memorial. In addition to the two pylons and the massive fortress-like base that joins and protects them, the memorial contains twenty separate statues, each designed to

Left: *The two pillars give a suggestion of the great cathedrals of France.*

Right: *A sculpture of a male mourner reclining on the steps of the approach*

Canada Bereft *looks down at an empty sarcophagus.*

Facing: *A statue representing the idea that Canada defends the helpless*

represent a human virtue or demonstrate a Canadian sacrifice; each sculpted on-site in its own separate studio. Working from half-scale plaster models that Walter had painstakingly constructed in London and transported to France, some of the finest sculptors in the world helped him realize his dream.

One approaches the monument from the rear. The first two figures you see are a female mourner reclining on one side of the stairs, and a male mourner reclining on the other. Looking up you see angels on top of the two pylons, guarding the gate to eternity. As you near the front of the monument, there are two figures between the pylons, representing sacrifice and the passing of the torch. Once through the gate, you turn around to see a set of figures at the base of each pylon. One set represents truth and faith with justice above them. The figures on the other pylon represent knowledge and charity. Above them is peace. Turning back to look out over the Douai Plain, you see the largest statue on the memorial: the four-metre high statue known as "Canada Bereft" or "Canada Mourning Her Dead," facing the plain but looking despairingly downward.

Walking down the great stairs to the front of the memorial and turning around, you are forced to raise your eyes heavenward to see over the fortress wall to the angels on top of the pylons. There at the base of the monument are several more statues. On your left are three figures: one breaking a sword to depict the defeat of militarism, and two gazing skyward in poses of defiance. On the right base are four more figures, one standing tall to protect the other three. This statue is alternately known as "The Sympathy of Canadians for the Helpless" or "Canada Defending the Helpless." Only one statue remains — an empty sarcophagus sitting in the centre of the fortress wall — directly on the battlefield. Looking up again, you suddenly realize that this is what the figure of "Canada Bereft" is looking down at. Painstakingly engraved on the walls of the memorial are the 11,285 names of Canadian soldiers killed in France during the First World War and whose bodies were never recovered.

Walter Allward's own emotional connection to the memorial was horribly magnified when his son, who was working on the project alongside his father, was killed in a car crash not far from the site. The memorial suddenly took on new meaning for a heartbroken Walter Allward.

On July 26, 1936, as planes from the Royal Air Force flew across the sky, the Vimy Ridge Memorial was officially unveiled by King Edward VIII. It would miraculously survive the Second World War.

The Allwards returned to Toronto following the unveiling and built a new house that Walter designed at 33 Old Yonge Street, in the parish of St. John's York Mills. The house, which contained a spacious studio for Walter, still stands in its original location. In 1938 Walter received a parliamentary vote of thanks from the Government of Canada for his incredible achievement. In addition to the sculptures that have already

A portrait of Walter Allward

Walter Allward is buried in the St. John's churchyard.

been mentioned, Walter's works can be found across Toronto and Canada, including the South African War Memorial on University Avenue in Toronto, and the memorial to Alexander Graham Bell in Brantford, Ontario. Some of his smaller works are in the National Gallery in Ottawa, and some of the models he made for the Vimy Ridge Memorial can be found in the Canadian War Museum. The Reverend Drew MacDonald recommends visiting and viewing the plaster models in order to appreciate the fine detail work, which is so hard to appreciate in the final renderings because of their immense size.

The Reverend Drew shared some further compelling memories of his visit to Vimy. "Visiting the monument feels almost sacred; Allward's work is so moving. He presents the themes of justice and character and mercy, as Mother Canada weeps over the destruction caused by war. The monument does not in any way glorify war, but it is a testament to the sacrifice: some 3,600 boys died in three days. That would be 1,200 a day or almost fifty an hour, or one Canadian a minute. Staggered as I was, leaving the grounds, I felt as though I were leaving Holy Ground, a sacred place. Months later at our Remembrance Day service, I was in conversation with Jeremy Diamond, the director of the Vimy Ridge Foundation. He said he felt the same way, and he came up with the analogy of taking leave of royalty. When in the presence of the king or queen, one never turns one's back. You leave walking backward, out of respect for the office. This is the image that stays with me as I remember the sacredness of the Allward monument. It is holy and sacred ground, a place every Canadian needs to visit."

The Allwards were parishioners at St. John's. Son Hugh Allward (1897–1971) was also a well-respected architect and a partner in the firm of Allward and Guinlock. Some of his better-known works are Sunnybrook Hospital (1943–48), the Veterans Memorial Building in Ottawa (1948), and the Tudor-style Locke House — a wedding gift from George S. Henry to his daughter and son-in-law. It was built in 1933 and still stands on the southeast corner of Leslie Street and

Highway 401. Hugh Allward also designed a house for himself, which is still standing in the parish of St. John's, at 27 Beechwood Road, just around the corner from his father's house on Old Yonge Street. Walter Seymour Allward died on April 24, 1955, and is buried in the churchyard at St. John's York Mills.

In December 2004 a team of international artisans began the massive task of restoring the Vimy Ridge Memorial. When the team found out where Walter Allward was buried, they contacted St. John's to see if the church would be interested in having a piece of the original monument that was being replaced during the restoration. The church was indeed interested and, following a special memorial service led by the Reverend Hollis Hiscock, St. John's was presented with a piece of the original monument, a "very large piece," as Hollis recalls. The piece can be seen today in the museum cabinet in the chapel, a tangible link to a defining moment in Canada's history and a poignant reminder of one parishioner's extraordinary accomplishments.

The procession to Walter Allward's tombstone is led by parishioner Jay Burford and the Rector Drew MacDonald.

In 2007 there was an initiative, begun by Branch 165 of the Royal Canadian Legion, to honour Walter Allward on the nineteenth anniversary of the capture of Vimy Ridge. As a result of their efforts, a bronze plaque was dedicated by the Reverend Drew MacDonald on November 27, 2007. The ceremony was attended by members of the Allward family, St. John's parishioners, and members of the Legion. The plaque now stands beside his grave in the St. John's churchyard.

Members of the Allward family with the new plaque, accompanied by a member of the Legion

CHAPTER NINE

C.W. Jefferys House

The house known as the C.W. Jefferys House at 4111 Yonge Street, while not actually on St. John's property, is impossible to ignore when considering the history of the parish. For one thing, it's still there at the bottom of the footpath, having moved only once in the last 183 years. For another thing, it was home to St. John's parishioners until just a few short years ago. The church's history and the history of the house have intersected a number of times throughout the years. The story of this house is integral to the history of York Mills in general and Hogg's Hollow in particular.

The physical make-up of the hollow had a profound impact on the way the area was settled. Upper Canada's first Lieutenant Governor, John Graves Simcoe, decided that a road was needed from the town of York on Lake Ontario to Holland Landing, which was on the Holland River near Lake Simcoe. The proposed road was needed both as a strategic military route and as a means of opening the area up to settlement. Work began in 1793, with a band of Queen's Rangers led by Deputy Provincial Surveyor Augustus Jones. But when they reached Hogg's Hollow the following year, it became clear that they could not continue north in a straight line as they had intended, owing to the steep hills and the swampland at

the bottom of the valley. Their solution was to follow the contour of the east wall of the valley down to the river—today's Donwoods Drive—then across the river and back up the east wall of the valley along today's Old Yonge Street. From there the road followed the valley's edge in a northwesterly direction until it could head straight north once again, as imagined on the original survey. The earliest houses and schools were built along this route, as well as St. John's York Mills, while mills were built on the West Don River. It took five years to clear the 20-foot-wide path through the wilderness as far north as Steeles Avenue. Yonge Street would eventually stretch all the way to Rainy River, near the Manitoba border, and be heralded as "the longest street in the world." By the 1830s, stage coach traffic, which served settlements as far north as Holland Landing, had become so heavy that the hollow came to be viewed as a real impediment to settlement and commerce. A plan was hatched to reroute Yonge Street to run straight north through the hollow.

In 1833 Rowland Burr was hired to oversee construction of the new road. The scope of the project was such that Rowland decided to build a house in the area to allow him to be more closely involved. In 1833 he built the house that is now known as the C.W. Jefferys house. As constructed in 1833, it was a single-storey Georgian cottage.

Rowland's crew graded the hills, drained a swamp that stood near the mills, and filled in part of a bog so they could lay a stable roadbed through the hollow. By 1835 the newly straightened Yonge Street was ready to be "macadamized" — an expensive and time-consuming process that involved covering the roadway in a compressed surface of small stones that men with hammers broke from large rocks that had been placed along the roadway.

Rowland Burr also owned farmland on the north side of Finch Avenue East, between Bayview Avenue and Leslie Street, as well as a farm in Vaughan Township. In 1854 William Marsh bought Rowland's house in Hogg's Hollow as a wedding gift for his daughter Anna Maria and her new husband John van Nostrand. (William Marsh had sold St. John's the original rectory in 1841.) In 1864 the van Nostrands sold the house to Andrew McGlashan III. The McGlashans also had a long history with St. John's York Mills.

Andrew's grandfather Andrew I first moved to Hogg's Hollow in 1815 after farming near today's Harrison Road in York Mills from 1804. Shortly after arriving in the hollow, he built the house that came to be known as the Goodwin House, after local carriage maker William Goodwin who purchased the house in 1844. On March 11, 1862, John Page Squire became the sexton of St. John's York Mills and shortly afterward moved into the Goodwin House — directly across Yonge Street. The house remained the property of the Goodwin family until finally purchased by John Squire in 1908. John died there on January 25, 1931, at the age of eighty-seven. He had served St. John's until late in 1930.

After John's death the Goodwin House was sold to Arthur Tunnell — the publisher of *Who's Who in Canada*. Arthur and his family would remain there until he died in 1980. By 1981 the house was boarded up and facing demolition to facilitate the widening of Yonge Street. It was saved, mere hours prior to demolition, by Mike Singleton — an employee of the Federation of Ontario Naturalists — and moved to their premises behind the historic Locke House, on the southeast corner of Leslie Street and Highway 401.

Back across Yonge Street, in 1864 Andrew McGlashan III offered his newly purchased house to the York Mills Presbyterian Church for use as a manse. The church, built in 1859 on land donated by Andrew McGlashan II near today's Eastview Crescent, was demolished in 1885 and its churchyard abandoned. In 1955 construction crews widening Yonge Street unearthed a number of human bones, and work was halted until the remains could be re-interred in York Cemetery. Arthur McCollum, then-rector of St. John's York Mills, gathered up pieces of the broken headstones and stored them safely at St. John's as a way of showing unity with another pioneer church. In 1876 descendant John McGlashan vacated *his* home near today's Lorreto Abbey, so it could be rented to St. John's new rector Henry Bath Osler because the condition of St. John's Rectory on Old Yonge Street at the time was so poor. In 1872 Andrew McGlashan III sold the C.W. Jefferys House to James Armour. It was James who added the second storey and the gable front.

Charles W. Jefferys was a well-known author, teacher, painter, and illustrator. (Some of his illustrations appear in Audrey Graham's book, *150 Years at St. John's, York Mills*.) He first came upon the house on Yonge Street in 1910, falling in love with it immediately. He rented the house as a summer place for his family, but it soon became their permanent residence when he bought it in 1922. During those years, the house frequently hosted some of the most important names in Canadian art and literature, including members of the Group of Seven. In 1912 the Jefferys's daughter Elizabeth (Betsy) Jefferys was born in the house. In 1941 she married Dr. Alexander Fee, who then bought the house. The Fees would raise their three daughters there. C.W. lived with them until his death on October 8, 1951.

The house that was built in 1833 by Rowland Burr, who oversaw the straightening of Yonge Street, is moved back to accommodate the widening of the street. St. John's Church can be seen on the hill behind it.

In 1955 the house was expropriated for the widening of Yonge Street, but the Fees weren't so easily dismissed. They took the matter to arbitration and won, on the condition that they move the house back sixty feet on its lot to accommodate the new construction.

The Fees raised their family in the house while Betsy immersed herself in local history, serving as a founding member of the North York Historical Society, and being instrumental in the creation of Black Creek Pioneer Village. She was a long-time parishioner of St. John's, where she worked with Audrey Graham to establish the church's archives.

Betsy Fee died in the house on October 15, 2010 — one hundred years after her family first moved in. She was ninety-eight years old and still the honourary president of the North York Historical Society. Betsy was interred in the churchyard at St. John's beside her parents, husband, and daughter Judy. The house remained in the family's hands for a time, before being sold to a buyer who then decided he wanted to develop the land. Thankfully, his efforts were thwarted by the fact that the house had been historically designated by Toronto City Council on October 6, 1997, under Part IV of the Ontario Heritage Act. This is the section of the act that protects buildings deemed to possess cultural heritage value. The house was subsequently resold and remains a private residence. No alterations or demolitions that would affect the heritage value of the house can be undertaken unless they are specifically debated and approved by Toronto City Council.

CHAPTER TEN

The Generosity of Connie Comer

When long-time parishioner Constance Louise "Connie" Comer died on January 6, 1980, she left her home at 11 Don Ridge Road to St. John's York Mills. This incredibly generous gift was also accompanied by a bequest of $250,000 in various investments. Some of the money was put to use for much-needed repairs to the footpath, while the house — eventually known as "Comer House" — would serve the parish in a number of interesting ways to the present day and beyond.

The first new occupant of the house following Connie's passing was a family of refugees from South Vietnam — "boat people" as they were known in the parlance of the times. Their resettlement had been arranged by parishioner Donovan Lowry, who contributed to St. John's image beyond the parish by working to arrange for a number of such families to find new homes in Canada. His efforts were heartily encouraged by the rector Jim O'Neil and the churchwardens of the day. Once this family had established themselves and moved on, Comer House would be home to a number of prominent members of the Anglican clergy from across the country when they came to spend time in Toronto.

First was the Reverend Dr. Tom Traynor, followed by the Right Reverend Mark Genge. Mark was the retired Bishop of Newfoundland who came to Toronto in September 1990 to accompany his wife Maxine while she completed her Ph.D. in education at the University of Toronto's OISE. Mark was an old friend of St. John's new rector Hollis Hiscock, and was appointed as a pastoral assistant at St. John's during his stay in Toronto. Comer House would later be home to the Reverend Frank Lee, the Reverend Dr. Patrick White, and the Right Reverend Victoria Matthews. All would recall their time at Comer House with fondness while continuing their journeys through the Anglican Church. Patrick White went on to become the Bishop of Bermuda. Victoria Matthews, who was a former Bishop in the Diocese of Toronto, would later continue her work as the Bishop of New Zealand. Allison Lynn, one of Hollis and Helen Hiscock's two daughters, moved into Comer House in 2010 with her husband Gerald Flemming three years after her father retired from St. John's. Allison and Gerald were the musical duo called Infinitely More. They led the worship at the evening Gathering service for several years in addition to leading the Worship Band for select Sunday morning services and other holiday services throughout the year.

Left: *Infinitely More held occasional fireside concerts during the time they lived in the Comer House.*

Right: *The Comer House in 2016 after its sale by the church and renovation by the new owners*

Connie Comer's house was sold by the church on May 15, 2013, for $1,250,000 and, wonder of wonders, it wasn't demolished to make way for a monster house! It seems that the couple who bought the house had been looking for a small house in the neighbourhood all along and, after some renovations, the house still stands — backing onto the churchyard for all to see, a continuing testament to Connie Comer's generosity. Although the diocese was entitled to 50 percent of the sale proceeds, they only took 20 percent, or $250,000. The remaining $1 million paid for more than half of the beautiful church renovations that were completed in 2014. One likes to think that somewhere, Connie Comer is smiling.

CHAPTER ELEVEN

The Renovations of 2014

The congregation of St. John's is blessed to be greeting its third century in a newly renovated and enlarged edifice. The latest round of renovations began in February 2014 and were completed by October that year. The brick church, originally constructed in 1843, was rededicated by Archbishop Colin Johnson on November 2, 2014. Many parish volunteers worked long, glory-free hours to effect the transformation. All agreed it was well worth the effort.

The church had not seen any significant changes since 1968, when the last round of renovations was completed to mark the 150th anniversary of the parish in 1966. Initially though, the congregation of the time was divided as to how to celebrate such an auspicious occasion. Some supported the idea of improvements to the building, while others favoured the idea of raising funds for Outreach programs. In the end an impassioned speech by parishioner Marshall Davis convinced the congregation that a growing parish list could only be served by immediate improvements to the church building itself. A building and finance committee, co-chaired by churchwardens Alan Tully and Edmund Bovey, was created to oversee the project. Parishioner Derek Buck, a senior partner at the venerable Toronto architectural firm of Page and Steele, was hired to draw up the plans.

The newly renovated church was rededicated on Thursday, November 21, 1968, by the Right Reverend George B. Snell, then-Bishop of Toronto. The new addition was christened the Arthur C. McCollum Wing, to honour the previous rector of St. John's. New facilities included increased office space, an enlarged narthex, and main-floor washrooms and cloakroom. There were also new areas on the lower level for a warden's vestry and choir practice room. The centrepiece of the renovation, however, was a large new meeting and reception area on the east side of the church, overlooking the churchyard. This area, which included an attached kitchenette, would eventually be known as the Garnsworthy Room, after then-rector Lewis S. Garnsworthy, who was consecrated Suffragan Bishop of the Diocese of Toronto on November 30, 1968 — nine days after the rededication. The diocese kindly allowed their new bishop to remain at St. John's until the end of the year.

Fast forward nearly half-a-century and it was clear that renovations were again long overdue.

Once again it was time to form committees, recruit volunteers, draw up plans, and raise money. Only this time there would be no rapidly expanding parish list

Left: *The original brick church of 1844 as it was before any additions took place. Carriage sheds can be seen at the left rear of the church.*

Right: *The construction of the McCollum wing began with the laying of the cornerstone and the relocation of the 1843 cornerstone by the Right Reverend Leslie E. Strading, Bishop of Johannesburg, and the Reverend Canon Garnsworthy.*

Above: *The chancel before the renovation of 2014*

Above right: *Architect David Parker attending the rededication service after all the work was done.*

Right: *The sanctuary before the renovation, showing the enclosed chapel that was opened up during the renovation and the balcony that was removed.*

to cushion the financial blow. But this time St. John's had a guardian angel — and it was a good thing, too, for these renovations would prove to be the most ambitious yet. Virtually every square inch of the main floor was about to be altered, and not just in the physical sense. For St. John's would soon find itself completely rewired to "plug in" to the new digital world of the twenty-first century.

The renovation focused on common areas accessible to all parishioners, including the chancel, chapel, transept, sanctuary, narthex, foyer, entranceway, kitchen, Garnsworthy Room, cloakroom, washrooms, and offices. In addition a brand new patio was planned, overlooking the valley to the west and accessible from the entrance hall. Once the decision to renovate had been reached, churchwardens John Bruce and Blake Woodside were put in charge of gathering the funds for the project. David Parker of Parker Architects in St. Catharines was hired to draw up the blueprints and an initial team was formed to work with David. This initial team included churchwarden Steve Bickley, head of the property committee Bob Girard, the Rev. Drew McDonald, and interior designer Carolyn Dobias. As a result of the departure of Steve Bickley, who had to return to the United States just before construction actually began, churchwarden Sylvia McConnell was brought in to be the wardens' liaison and to coordinate the design team. The renovation was ultimately overseen by two separate but co-operating teams.

A parish team was assembled to oversee the church's interests and the day-to-day construction. Part of the team's mandate was to make sure that transparency prevailed by holding regular parish Q-and-A sessions — often with slides — and by providing regular written and verbal updates. The parish team included the Rector Drew McDonald, verger Bill Dennis, churchwardens Sylvia McConnell and Maurice Bent, design committee member Carolyn Dobias, property committee head Bob Girard, and church administrator Catherine Bryant. Though not all parishioners agreed with every decision, they at least had a chance to make their opinions known. Members of the parish team sat in on the weekly site meetings with the architect, contractor, and site supervisor to oversee the work as it progressed.

Left: *Church administrator Catherine Bryant kept everyone organized during the construction.*

Right: *Churchwarden Maurice Bent speaks at a vestry meeting.*

Facing top: *Choosing the design and the fabric colour for the pew chairs took hours of work by the property and design committees.*

A design committee was formed that included staff liaison Carolyn Martin, interior designers Sharon Barney and Carolyn Dobias, parishioner Yvonne McGregor, and warden liaison and coordinator Sylvia McConnell. The design committee worked on every aspect of the design for the renovation. For example, they chose the colour and material for the new pew chairs, and selected furniture for the new foyer and Garnsworthy Room, and appliances for the kitchen.

They decided what colour to stain the floor in the redesigned chancel, and were also responsible for choosing paint colours and ordering altar rail cushions. They had input into the design of the sound cabinet at the back of the sanctuary. They worked tirelessly, shopped often, and attended a seemingly endless parade of meetings. Verger Bill Dennis and sexton Mark Anderson were also on-site every day, lending valuable muscle and expertise. Their eye for detail and their knowledge of the church building were invaluable to all aspects of the renovation.

Before the first hammer swung in February 2014, the project was divided into two separate sections to allow the congregation the use of the sanctuary for as long as possible. Renovations to the offices and the Garnsworthy Room were tackled first, while offices were temporarily moved to the second floor in the south wing. The second phase of the project involved the renovations to the foyer, narthex, chancel, and sanctuary, while construction of the patio would wait until the arrival of warmer weather. When construction started on the sanctuary in the spring months, the basement auditorium became the new home for Sunday services.

This space, which had previously hosted teen dances in the 1960s, as well as

Bottom left: *The work began in February. The green construction waste bin and the porta-potty were to greet parishioners for many months when they entered the church.*

Bottom right: *The rubble in the foyer as construction began*

many special church functions, classes, and meetings in subsequent years, was transformed every Sunday by the presence of a congregation that gathered to worship the Lord. Though the room was plain, it was intimate, and many who gathered there in worship remember it fondly as one of the high points of the year. Although there was no organ, choir loft, stained glass, or pulpit, the community spirit felt there each Sunday morning made it clear to all that God is much more than bricks and mortar.

Basement auditorium services were packed with parishioners enjoying the informality of the space.

The church was in complete disarray for much of 2014. Old walls were coming down while new walls were going up. Giant sheets of clear plastic were hung in a vain attempt to keep drywall dust from permeating every corner of the building. Saws, hammers, and nail guns kept up a constant racket, while power was turned on and off to allow for the complete rewiring of the building. The rewiring included all sorts of cables for data transmission, as well as the usual plugs and light switches. Bill Dennis made sure that the wiring was installed with an eye to technical changes. "What we're trying to do at this point in time is create flexibility," he said. "We don't want things that are nailed down ... we want total flexibility ... so that way, twenty years down the road, we don't have to go through this again." Staff continued to work in cramped, temporary office space on the second floor while the transformation progressed.

The renovations cost $1.6 million, money supplied primarily through the generosity of parishioner Connie Comer. Additional funding came from the sale of the eight-foot strip of land that once ran from the parking lot down to Yonge Street. Money also came from the diocese, as promised to those who donated to the diocesan-wide "Our Faith-Our Hope" campaign. Forty percent of the funds raised by St. John's parishioners in that campaign were returned to the parish.

As the church headed into phase two of the renovation, it became clear to the design team that the original budget had underestimated the cost of furnishings and appliances for the offices, Garnsworthy Room, kitchen, sanctuary, and family room. Just before the old sanctuary was cleared out, music director Patrick Dewell approached the committee with the idea that this would be the perfect time to

Above left: *The sanctuary cleared for action*

Above right: *The chapel is opened up and the balcony removed, revealing an unexpected steel beam*

Left: *One of the major changes to the nave was the extension of the chancel to accommodate the expanded music program at St. John's. Bill Dennis and the Rev. Anne examine the work.*

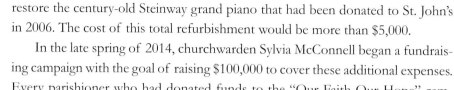

Sylvia and Peter Raynham show off the new Commemorative Book in the newly finished foyer. One of the pieces of furniture, designed using the panels of the old lectern, is behind them and over it hang photos of the church by Paul Heersink.

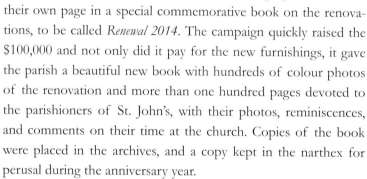

restore the century-old Steinway grand piano that had been donated to St. John's in 2006. The cost of this total refurbishment would be more than $5,000.

In the late spring of 2014, churchwarden Sylvia McConnell began a fundraising campaign with the goal of raising $100,000 to cover these additional expenses. Every parishioner who had donated funds to the "Our Faith-Our Hope" campaign, from which funds were returned to St. John's for the renovation, as well as anyone who donated at least $100 to the new fundraising campaign, was offered their own page in a special commemorative book on the renovations, to be called *Renewal 2014*. The campaign quickly raised the $100,000 and not only did it pay for the new furnishings, it gave the parish a beautiful new book with hundreds of colour photos of the renovation and more than one hundred pages devoted to the parishioners of St. John's, with their photos, reminiscences, and comments on their time at the church. Copies of the book were placed in the archives, and a copy kept in the narthex for perusal during the anniversary year.

One of the major projects funded by this special campaign was to repurpose the old altar and lectern into three beautiful new pieces: a baptismal counter for the sanctuary, a reception desk in the foyer to display the church's literature, and a beautiful welcome table to accommodate the badge boxes on a Sunday morning and the drinks and food at special events and services. The pieces were designed and built by woodworker Dean Hansen of Cambridge, Ontario. The completion of the work was greeted with "ahhs" of delight as people contemplated the fine detail of each piece and their ultimate adaptability to the many uses of the foyer and sanctuary. Jan Gardiner Williams donated a large portion of the funds for these repurposed pieces in memory of her husband Deacon Bruce Williams. These three pieces are stunning reminders of the heritage of the church.

Instead of purchasing expensive artwork, the design team asked parishioner Paul Heersink to take photos of out-of-the-way or quaint areas of the church that might not be so familiar to the congregation, such as the bell pull, the old door handles, and the sundial. A selection of these were framed and hung in the foyer, in the Garnsworthy Room, and down the hallway, along with some of the church's heritage art pieces. The result, combined with the repurposed furniture, was a modern yet traditional look to the new social areas. Decisions about the placement of more heritage pieces are still ongoing, but the team hopes to have all the work of redecoration completed by the anniversary celebration in September 2016.

The new front doors lead into the foyer and entranceway described above. To the right is a refreshed cloakroom. Just beyond that are the doors to the inviting new patio, which expand the church's event space to the great outdoors. To the left of the entrance is a brand new Garnsworthy Room, a new and larger kitchen, new washrooms, a photocopy room, and new offices for both rector and church staff.

At the end of the foyer stands the new sanctuary, which was opened up and transformed by a fresh coat of white paint, and a chancel that extends into the

Left: *One of the repurposed pieces — the welcome table in the foyer — using the panels of the pulpit*

Right: *This view of the chancel area before the renovation shows the pulpit on the left and the lectern on the right. Both pieces were repurposed into two beautiful and practical pieces of furniture for the foyer, and a baptismal counter for the new baptismal niche.*

Left: *The new Garnsworthy Room takes full advantage of the beautiful windows overlooking the front garden.*

Right: *The niches for the relocation of the angel windows from the foyer are prepared.*

previous seating area. Extra sitting room was added by opening up the chapel into the main sanctuary and removing the balcony, where the stained glass windows above, hidden for many years, are now revealed. One of the windows high up on the chapel's north wall still retained its original pale tinted glass, in marked contrast to the vivid colours of the other stained glass windows. Parishioners Heather and Ian Stewart commissioned a stained glass window to replace the coloured glass. It was produced by Susan Obata and dedicated to the Reverend Jim O'Neil in August of 2015 at a special service.

Two large video screens were installed high on the walls of the chancel, facing the congregation, where the words to songs and hymns, plus visuals to accompany the sermon, are now displayed. A sophisticated new sound system was also installed at this time, including an array of new microphones and a state-of-the-art digital mixing console.

Two windows from the chapel were placed into the previously blank wall at the back of the sanctuary to provide light and sightlines for the old narthex. This became a family room and sitting area, where parents can retire with restless children to a mostly sound-proof room in which they can enjoy the service on a television set while watching the proceedings through the large windows.

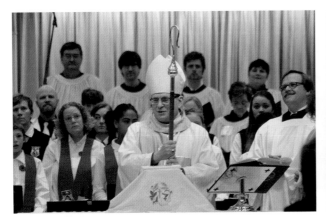

Above left: *Archbishop Colin Johnson, backed by the St. John's choir and ringers, presided at the rededication service held in November 2014.*

Above right: *The rededication service was a moving and joyous occasion.*

Left: *The first vestry meeting to be held in the newly renovated spaces was in October 2014.*

The foyer was utterly transformed with a new, lighter tile floor and by the removal of the angel windows from the west wall into the sanctuary, where they now hang — backlit and ethereal — for the enjoyment of all during the services. The west wall of the foyer is now a row of clear windows and doors overlooking the patio and the ravine.

The Garnsworthy Room could be accessed directly off the foyer, opening up the social spaces and making the whole McCollum wing a welcoming place for gatherings and social activity.

The renovations were completed by the end of October 2014. When the stunning new sanctuary was rededicated by Archbishop Colin Johnson on November 2, 2014, two cakes, baked for the occasion, were proudly lettered with the words "On Time" and "On Budget." The church had been truly transformed.

THE STORY OF ST. JOHN'S GRAND PIANO

St. John's Steinway grand is a Model "A" grand in mahogany, made by Steinway and Sons in New York City. Each of their grand pianos took a year to build. St. John's Model "A" was sold by Steinway in 1904 to the A.S. Nordheimer Company in Toronto — the company that represented Steinway in Ontario at the time. The piano's history from that time on is really the history of one family.

Noted Toronto publisher and philanthropist Sir William Gage, bought the piano sometime in 1904 or 1905. It lived at the family home on Bloor Street West, where the Holt Renfrew store stands today, until the family moved to Walmer Road. Sir William gave the piano to his daughter Irene when she married William Martin Griffith, and the piano went with her as she moved to the United States and then back to Canada, settling at 64 South Drive in Toronto in 1949.

Irene Griffith eventually gave the piano to her daughter Diana, when Diana and her husband Charles Tisdall bought the home from Irene in 1953. The piano remained in the house until 2003, when it followed Charles to 500 Avenue Road where he moved after Diana's death in 2000.

Three great-granddaughters of Sir William Gage have been parishioners at St. John's York Mills over the years: sisters Martha (Tisdall) Smith and Marilee (Tisdall) MacFarlane, and their cousin Vicki Parrish.

In May 2006 Charles Tisdall and his daughters Martha and Marilee donated the piano to St. John's for all to enjoy. On Mother's Day in May 2006, the piano was dedicated by Rev. Hollis Hiscock to the glory of God as a gift from the Tisdall family. In 2014 the piano was restored to its former glory by Robert Smit of Robert Smit Keyboard Services in Whitby as part of the new renovations.

The hundred-year-old Steinway, ready from its restoration, is moved back into the chancel by the team of sexton Mark Anderson, handbell director Carolyn Martin, and music director Patrick Dewell.

CHAPTER TWELVE

Beginning the Third Century

As the people of St. John's York Mills look forward to the third century of worshipping and learning about God in their historic and beautiful church, and serving their diverse community, they are filled with optimism about the future and enthusiasm for the task of bringing more people to the understanding of the love of God.

The move from morning worship as the main service on Sundays, to the nine-to-noon offerings of the Sacred Table, the Open Door, and the Forum, is still in the early stages. Although each one of the offerings can be attended on its own, many people are choosing to stay for the entire morning, to be nourished at nine o'clock by the rich Anglican Eucharistic tradition, and then to stay on for the teaching offered at the Open Door at ten-thirty, followed by the discussion format of the Forum. People who stay for the entire morning call themselves "nine-to-nooners."

Six months after implementation it would appear that the new Sunday morning format is a success, as the energy in the foyer at intermission attests to the enthusiasm of the people of St. John's in embracing the new nine-to-noon model. Parishioners of St. John's through the years have shown themselves to be open to change. Early estimates from the welcome team are that the greeters are welcoming more visitors through the doors every week than in the past, and the badge table team is producing more new "official" badges a month than previously.

In the first quarter of 2016, St. John's is blessed to have three full-time clergy plus a deacon.

In the spring of 2015, the diocese asked that St. John's take on a curate to join Rector Drew MacDonald and Associate Priest Anne Crosthwaite. He would be attached to St. John's for two years and ordained in May 2016. The church community was excited to welcome Curate Tim Taylor into their midst. Arriving in July 2015 during the Reverend Drew's sabbatical, the Reverend Tim was instantly involved in summer activities at the church. As Drew returned and the fall schedule began, Tim took on new responsibilities and quickly made himself a strong voice in the community.

The four clergy of St. John's in 2016: the rector Reverend Drew MacDonald, deacon Reverend Catherine Keating, associate priest Reverend Anne Crosthwait, and curate Reverend Tim Taylor

A group of hard workers from St. John's headed to Jamaica in the summer of 2015, under the leadership of Michele Mcdonald and Damien Benedict. Here the team is installing a new bathroom in the elementary school in Sandy Bay.

Tim Taylor said of his arrival at St. John's, "I feel that I have won the curate's lottery by being asked to be curate at St. John's York Mills during the anniversary celebrations! First of all, I inherited Drew's old office, so I have a great space. But, more importantly, I have landed in your midst as you step out into a third century of ministry — full of energy, brimming with a commitment to 'Know Christ and make Him known.'"

Tim quickly became responsible for the monthly service held at Amica — a local seniors' residence. He also began offering special courses for parents on parenting teens, and, later in the year, a marriage course. He took on a small group studying *The Good and Beautiful Life* and became a part of the marketing and communications team in the office that was to help promote the 200th anniversary celebrations and other events.

Late in 2015 the Syrian refugee crisis became a priority for the church. St. John's had, just the year before, taken on the role of helping a primary school in Sandy Bay, Jamaica, with reconstruction and mentoring. The outreach project to Sandy Bay, led by Michele Mcdonald and Damien Benedict, organized its first trip to Sandy Bay in the summer of 2015 to do some reconstruction work in the local school there and were to return to do more work in the summer of 2016. At its completion, the parishioners of St. John's agreed that they wanted to make an ongoing commitment to the Sandy Bay school, and the Rev. Drew and Carolyn Dobias took a group of people from St. John's to visit the school in May of 2016 to further evaluate the work that needs to be done.

When the Syrian refugee crisis happened later that fall of 2015, with Rev. Tim Taylor's help, the church set up a refugee committee to examine how St. John's might sponsor some Syrian refugees. At the time of this writing, with Tim's organization, the community has helped sponsor a Syrian family, a family fleeing war in Burundi, and another family from Colombia.

Damien Benedict, team leader of the Jamaica project, spoke in June 2016 at an Outreach Sunday about his work with Habitat for Humanity and his ongoing work in Malawi. He stated that each outreach project that he and/or the church undertakes has a "trickle upward effect," that enriches not only the people the church works with, but the people of St. John's.

Speaking about St. John's role in reaching out to others beyond the community, the Rev. Tim said, "It is obvious to me that the SJYM community is well on its way to transforming from the 'maintenance' mode of Anglicanism to the 'mission' mode. This is a transition that does not happen overnight, and the work that you have been doing in liturgical renewal, in Compass Groups, including *The Good and Beautiful God* series, as well as the outreach activities in the neighbourhood with the Barnabas breakfasts, Flemingdon Park, the Downsview Homework Club and now moving globally with refugees and the Sandy Bay project, is an inspiration."

Curate Reverend Tim Taylor

The Reverend Tim will be at St. John's until the summer of 2017, seeing St. John's through its anniversary year. "I am blessed to be able to walk alongside you during this reawakening. What a wonderful way to celebrate the commencement of a new century of service!"

In May 2016 St. John's York Mills was the site of Tim Taylor's ordination. It was a wonderful service, attended by many in the church family.

In 2016 the church school continues to grow as young families join the congregation. Church school numbers are now up to fifty children per Sunday. Rector Drew MacDonald has recently begun a new teen group, tentatively called the Youth Forum, to nurture young people. They will meet over pizza after the services on Sunday morning, or on a Monday evening during the school year. The teens will be invited to submit their questions ahead of time or just come ready to engage in open discussion.

More small groups are studying together in Compass Groups and adult Christian education groups offered by the clergy and members of the community.

The Men's Supper Club, which studies and socializes together, is a strong component of community building in the same way that the women's Lychgate Group continues to offer special activities and speakers to its members, who also work together to help host many events for the entire congregation. A new women's group has formed, called the Yarn-Yarn Sisterhood. The welcome team is another buoyant group that is at its post early on a Sunday morning, while the hospitality team makes coffee and lays out pastries and cookies for intermission and after services.

Another initiative that the leadership of St. John's has been tasked with is a role at the nearby parish St. Leonard's, which is faced with a declining congregation and the threat of their church closing. St. John's was granted diocesan funds to help mentor St. Leonard's and begin to rebuild its congregation. Located in a community with many families, St. Leonard's is perfectly positioned to begin a rebuilding process under the guidance of St. John's York Mills.

Preparations for celebrating the 200th anniversary year are well underway. Throughout the year special guest speakers will be on the roster of events, helping the congregation to understand their place in the history of the area, as well as helping the church to focus on what it is being called to be in the twenty-first century.

On Sunday, September 18, 2016, the focus of St. John's will be on a Service of Thanksgiving. The entire parish will be gathered together to celebrate the anniversary of the laying of the cornerstone for the first church building that took place on September 17, 1816. The founder Seneca Ketchum, the Rev. Dr. John Strachan, later Bishop of Toronto, and Lieutenant Governor Francis Gore were all in attendance that day. For the special day of celebration in 2016, Archbishop Colin Johnson will be celebrating, and parishioners from far and wide will be gathering. All the musical resources of the

Above: *The Men's Supper Club meets once a month in the Garnsworthy Room to share a meal and discuss spiritual matters.*

Left: *The Nelles's Compass Group has been meeting twice a month for more than half a dozen years to study Scripture.*

Facing: *The Reverend Tim Taylor smiles after his ordination at St. John's.*

Right: *Parish Council, clergy and other church leaders met at a retreat in April 2016 to discuss the church's vision for the future. Back row (left to right): Martin Block, Jennifer Hull, Ian Bowles, Paul Heersink, Peter Raynham, James Parrish, Hugh Moore, Damien Benedict; Middle row (left to right): Giovanna Sirianni, Para Sathi, Max Dionisio, Suzanne Sutherland, Tony Martino; Seated (left to right): Anne Crosthwait, Drew MacDonald, Tim Taylor, Catherine Keating*

Below: *The sign at the entrance to the church is lit in the evenings to welcome all.*

church will be making a joyful noise, with the Lychgate Group hosting a reception to follow the service.

A finale to this special year will be the publication of this book, *200 Years at St. John's York Mills*, in fall 2016.

PART TWO

HIGHLIGHTS OF HISTORY PAST

BY JEANNE HOPKINS

INTRODUCTION

I began work on an early history of St. John's Church some years ago and was encouraged by many members to continue this research with an eye to the 200th anniversary in 2016.

Much of my information for this book has come from Audrey Graham's book *150 Years at St. John's, York Mills*, written for the church's 150th anniversary in 1966. Audrey was the church archivist for many years, and her father Dr. T. Howard Graham (1886–1966) is buried in St. John's churchyard. Since Audrey Graham's book is back in print, I hope my section will give additional information and more human-interest, and to that end, I have organized my material to tell those interesting tales.

Much of my research has come from history files for which I was responsible while working in the North York Public Library's Canadiana Department for more than twenty-five years and writing articles for the *Bayview Post*. Today we can use the *Globe and Mail* (since 1844) and the *Toronto Star*'s "Pages of the Past" (since 1894) on the internet, so a lot of additional material has come from these sources.

St. John's Anglican Church York Mills is the oldest parish church in York County. Many members of St. John's and their neighbours served in the War of

1812, the Rebellion of 1837, and the two World Wars, and are buried in St. John's churchyard. Of course, I have not been able to research all of these families, so for those who are omitted, I apologize.

Over the years, St. John's has undergone many additions and renovations (the last in the past two years) and members of the clergy and their families have gone on to serve the Church of England as archbishops, archdeacons, and bishops of Toronto, York County, Ontario, and beyond.

Many streets and landmarks in the York Mills area bear the names of the early members of St. John's. I hope this book brings back memories as I have focused on the people who helped build St. John's to the great church it is today.

I also wish to thank many at St. John's who gave their encouragement and answered my many questions, including verger Bill Dennis, and the reverends Drew MacDonald and Anne Crosthwait. I also thank Sylvia McConnell who has allowed me to write the highlights of the past "my way." I hope you will enjoy it and perhaps learn a little more about this wonderful church.

CHAPTER THIRTEEN

Early History of York Mills

Many early histories of Upper Canada were written for or by the local churches. York Mills is no exception as St. John's York Mills was the first church to be established north of the Town of York, and many of its earliest settlers and their descendants are buried in St. John's churchyard: Camerons, van Nostrands, Humberstones, Mercers, Willsons, Harrisons, and Shepards. The history of St. John's is an important part of the history of the York Mills area.

Yonge Street was laid out by Lieutenant Governor John Graves Simcoe, beginning in 1793, to open the area for settlement and to create a military trail from York Mills to the Holland River. As he was making plans to transport men and supplies north to Lake Simcoe, he used the transport route of the North West Company that had travelled the West Don River to where it met Old Yonge Street, using this junction as a transfer point for their supplies. From there, they loaded their supplies onto *bateaux* (flat-bottomed boats) on wheels and hauled them thirty miles overland to the mouth of the Holland River, then on to Lake Simcoe and the Upper Great Lakes.

At York Mills, the hills were too high and the river too wide for a proper bridge to be built, so the route went down the hill to Valliere's Inn. There, troops

Hogg's Hollow and the church on the hill, St. John's, as it looked approximately 1920

and their horses could for stop for rest and refreshment. These troops of the Queen's Rangers had been hired to build Fort Penetanguishene on Georgian Bay to protect the Upper Great Lakes from any attack.

As mills developed around the Don Valley, farmers came on the main concession routes to have their wheat ground into flour. Soon they too needed a place for rest, and water for their horses and themselves. Valliere's Inn was the first to be built on what is today Old Yonge Street.

Local sawmills in the valley provided lumber for the new settlers' houses while gristmills were constructed to grind the farmers' grain into flour. The mills were set up on the west branch of the Don River. They were owned by Samuel Heron (1804), Thomas Arnold (1817), Cornelius van Nostrand II (1837), and others. In 1824 James Hogg emigrated from Scotland and bought Thomas Arnold's mill and farm. He added a distillery and soon began calling his property "York Mills." The Hogg family operated a number of other businesses in the valley, including an inn where the first York Mills Post Office was established in 1836.

The first "wave" of settlers — those loyal to the British Crown — had come after the American Revolution (1776–1783) to settle in Upper Canada because of the free land. They built homes, and set up businesses and stores. Many had belonged to the Church of England and around 1807 they began establishing a church. After the War of 1812, late Loyalists came for the free land and their descendants stayed for the many opportunities. They built more stores, housing for the mill workers, and a post office. The York Mills Baptist Church was built in 1832 on the concession road that later became York Mills Road, and the York Mills Presbyterian Church was built on Yonge Street in the valley in 1836. Even though many belonged to the other churches, all friends and neighbours pitched in to help whenever they were needed for building.

Finally, in 1835, Yonge Street was reconfigured to run straight through the valley and a proper bridge was built over the West Don River. When James Hogg died in 1839, his sons were too young to inherit his property. But by 1851, when his sons came of age, John and William Hogg developed their property along Yonge Street into a hundred and one building lots to attract more settlers. Cottages were built for the mill workers, two of which can still be visited

Left: The York Mills Baptist Church manse on York Mills Road in the mid-1800s

Right: The first bridge over York Mills Valley as seen in 1897

today, as they were combined to create the local restaurant Auberge du Pommier. The brothers called their new subdivision "Hogg's Hollow" and, although the project was not a great success at the time, the name endured. The original Yonge Street route became known as Old Yonge Street, the street where Valliere's Inn and Hostelry as well as the active St. John's Church stood. By that point in time, St. John's Church had grown to be the largest Church of England north of the Town of York.

CHAPTER FOURTEEN

Early History of the Church of England in York

In the early 1800s, the Methodist Church used saddlebag preachers or circuit riders to travel around Upper Canada and preach to those of any religion. The Yonge Street Circuit included York to Lake Simcoe, with services held in settlers' homes. These circuits could be extremely large, involving hundreds of miles and taking four to six weeks to complete. Saddlebag preachers were so-called because they travelled on horseback through dense woods with only a compass to guide them. They carried a saddlebag of clothes, some hymn books, and Bibles. At first they preached in log cabins. Then, when a few larger congregations gathered, camp meetings were formed.

One of the largest and most popular in York County was in Willowdale and was called the Cummer's campground. It was located in a valley on the East Don River on land owned by Jacob Cummer in 1819. The area was also known as Scripture Town or Angel Valley. These meetings were also attended by Native people from as far away as Lake Simcoe. Meetings could last up to four days, and they continued for years until proper churches were built in the area. Strong fences up to ten feet high guarded the grounds, which were also patrolled by "camp meeting police." A preacher's stand was set up among the tents.

Instead of using circuit riders, the Church of England held services in private homes around York County. Until a proper preacher could be assigned, these services were ministered by lay readers, missionaries, or members of the military, such as the chaplains of the forts. Members of the ministry visited the private homes once a month to perform baptisms, marriages, or funerals, and conduct "proper" services. Many members of the Church of England, who had served in the War of 1812, were given land north of York: families such as the Sibbalds, Raines, Bourchiers, and Johnsons on Lake Simcoe, and further south the Hollingsheads, Parsons, Thomases, and Millers of Thornhill.

In Upper Canada the Church of England preferred districts, or a collection of communities such as York with their own little churches. The first Church of England to be established in York County in 1803 was St. James in York (later Toronto), which today is the Cathedral Church of St. James. The second was St. John's Church York Mills in 1816.

When Upper Canada was laid out, the Constitutional Act of 1791 decreed that one-seventh of all land be set aside for the support of a Protestant clergy. These plots of land were called "clergy reserves," or "Glebe." At first, there was much bitterness as Protestant — which actually referred to all non-Catholic Christians — was generally taken to mean Anglican in the Upper Canada of the early nineteenth century. Methodists, Presbyterians, Lutherans, Quakers, and others felt excluded and marginalized.

Local farmers, whatever their stripes, were also angered by the fact that many of the road allowances on clergy reserves remained uncleared — a task the farmers would have had to complete on their own land grants before receiving their deeds from the Crown. These uncleared road allowances greatly impeded travel in the primitive pioneer wilderness and were one of the main triggers leading to the Upper Canada Rebellion in 1837. Thankfully St. John's York Mills did clear and improve its land.

On January 16, 1836, the Crown granted half of St. James's original four hundred-acre endowment to St. John's York Mills, a transfer formalized by Dr. Strachan in 1838. This land was established as the "second Parsonage or Rectory within the said Township of York, otherwise known as the Church of St. John in Yonge Street." The reserve stretched from Bayview Avenue, east to Leslie Street, one-quarter of a mile south of Sheppard Avenue East — a lot formally known as Lot 14, Concession 2-East. The Reverend Charles Mathews was named as the Incumbent, the first rector of St. John's York Mills.

The Reverend Charles Mathews, serving St. John's first as a missionary and then as its first rector, 1830–1841

When the Rev. John Strachan arrived in Upper Canada from Scotland in 1799, he set himself up as a champion of education and of the Church of England in Upper Canada and York. He had first gone to Kingston where he tutored eleven children of the upper classes in a one-room schoolhouse. In 1803 he was ordained a priest of the Church of England, fulfilling his mother's dream that one of her six children would become a minister. After he moved to Cornwall and married Ann McGill — the widow of Andrew McGill — the Rev. Strachan devoted himself to the church; teaching classics, English, and science; and debating with the children of prominent families. He believed that Upper Canada should be ruled by high-minded men and so was strongly against the Reform Party.

In July 1812 John, Ann, and their children moved to York, where John was appointed master at the grammar school, chaplain of the Fort York Garrison, and a member of the Legislative and Executive Councils of Upper Canada.

Even though he wasn't wealthy, John did well as a leading member of the Family Compact, made up of members of the Legislative and Executive Councils, and of the wealthy of the town. Most members of this elite group, who had served with Strachan in the wars, were granted prestige park lots along the lakeshore in the Town of York and larger lots north of the town.

CHAPTER FIFTEEN

St. John's York Mills Church 1816

In many early communities, histories were written for and by local churches and cemeteries. Such is the case with York Mills.

York Mills, one of the earliest villages on Yonge Street north of the Town of York, had its beginnings in 1794 when it was settled mainly by loyalists who came to Upper Canada after the American Revolution. Their closest house of worship was St. James Church, six miles south in York. After the War of 1812, many British came to Upper Canada and worshipped at St. James until they were able to support a church of their own. In the new settlement of York Mills, they set out to build their own church.

These pioneers began their Churches of England with meetings in local homes or schools conducted by lay readers or merely those who were interested in the Church of England. The reverends George Okill Stuart and Henry Scadding visited homes in York Mills monthly.

Early members of the Church of England in the York Mills area included the Camerons, Humberstones, Harrisons, Willsons, Mercers, Shepards, and van Nostrands — all of whom have family buried in St. John's churchyard.

Seneca Ketchum, who was a devout member of the Church of England, was tired of walking the six miles down to St. James. He decided to start Church of England services in his home in North Toronto. When gatherings became too large, they moved to a small schoolhouse in Hogg's Hollow on land that Seneca later bought from Thomas Mercer. The ramshackle schoolhouse where people planned to meet had a leaky roof with no chimney (smoke escaped through a hole in the roof). Furnishings included a school-form broken chair and table, and services were often conducted while rain dripped from the roof. Farmers drove their carts or sleighs along muddy roads to worship in the new church hidden in the dense woods, leaving their horses and carts in the driving sheds of nearby Valliere's Inn or Samuel Heron's Inn in Hogg's Hollow.

Left: *The tombstone of William Harrison and his wife Elizabeth, early pioneers in the area, can be seen in the churchyard at St. John's. He took part in the Upper Canada Rebellion of 1837.*

Right: *Seneca Ketchum began the first Church of England services in his home. He was the driving force behind the establishment of St. John's York Mills.*

By 1816 St. John's York Mills was established as the first outpost mission of St. James Church in York. Services were held each Sunday afternoon in the roughly built schoolhouse just east of where the Miller Tavern stands today. Services were conducted by divinity students with Seneca Ketchum himself helping and the Rev. Stuart or the Rev. Strachan visiting monthly.

In 1816 Joseph and Catherine Shepard donated 2 3/4 acres of land for a church and a churchyard. Over the summer plans were put in place for a church to be built on the hill facing Yonge Street, later to become Old Yonge Street. With the help of friends and neighbours, the land was cleared of underbrush and trees were cut, and the larger ones squared for use in the new church. The original timbers can be seen today in the old narthex of St. John's Church. Even though money was scarce, the church received donations in cash and time from friends and neighbours, much of it from Seneca Ketchum.

On September 17, 1816, a cornerstone was laid by Lieutenant Governor Francis Gore and Dr. Strachan, with many people attending, including the Hoggs, Humberstones, Harrisons and Camerons. They sat on boards set on timbers around the site. The cornerstone included a half-penny and a medal minted during the reign of George III. A rude unpolished stone was placed over it. Since it was pouring rain, causing many to take shelter under the trees, the Reverend Dr. Strachan delivered that address to only two or three people.

Then, the building of the church began, using the squared timber cut by neighbours. Over the summer and fall, raising bees were held each Saturday with friends and neighbours helping. The first thirty-by-sixty-foot church was completed and ready for services by December 30, 1816. Pews were built and the church could accommodate 256 people.

By August 4, 1817, the new St. John's Church was finally completed enough to be formally opened. The Reverends Allan Macaulay, George Archbold, and

On land donated by Joseph and Catherine Shepard, the community came together to build the first church, with timber cut by neighbours. It was formally opened in August 1817.

John Strachan served as missionaries until 1836, when the Rev. Charles Stephens Mathews was appointed rector of St. John's.

The congregation continued to grow steadily and on June 16, 1829, St. John's York Mills was officially consecrated. As there was no vestry room, the clergy had to robe themselves in a nearby shed. The next day, confirmation services were held with Lady Elizabeth Colborne, her sister, children, and tutor coming up from York in two carriages, with one son riding horseback behind them. On the way they stopped for a rest at the farmhouse of Seneca Ketchum.

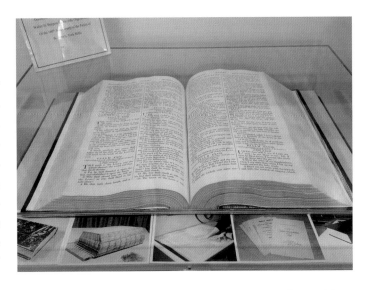

This Bible, printed in 1819, was presented to St. John's by Chief Justice Powell in about 1820. It is still in possession of the church and brought out for special occasions.

In 1836 Lieutenant Governor John Colborne asked Lord Goderich, the colonial secretary of the Imperial Government, to assign four hundred acres of land to each of the parishes in York County. St. John's York Mills received a two-hundred acre Glebe farm on Bayview Avenue in 1838, formalized by the Reverend Dr. Strachan.

After St. James Church burned in 1839, the members of St. John's wondered if their church could meet the same fate, so plans were put into place to build a stone or brick church on their land in York Mills.

CHAPTER SIXTEEN

The Second St. John's York Mills

Over the years, St. John's continued to grow and flourish, surviving a cholera epidemic in 1832 and the Rebellion of 1837. The graves of many of those who took part in that rebellion can be found in St. John's churchyard.

In 1835 Yonge Street was straightened, setting a new course through the valley, which resulted in Valliere's Inn and St. John's now lying on (Old) Yonge Street. Then when St. James Church was destroyed by fire in 1839, and fire threatened the St. John's frame chapel, then twenty-three years old, the congregation thought it was time to consider building a better church. On Easter morning 1840, some worshippers had gathered around the stove to visit and a loose floorboard had dislodged the stovepipe, causing a small fire. Luckily, the fire was easily extinguished, but members realized they needed a proper, more stable church building.

It seemed logical to hire John George Howard of High Park, the architect of St. James Church and other churches in Upper Canada, to design the new building for St. John's. The exterior was identical to that of Christ Church in Holland Landing, also built in 1843. The new commodious church, forty by sixty feet, was also a plain simple construction, but plans included opportunities for future additions.

Several meetings had already been held to discuss building a new church. On May 20, 1843, the foundation stone was laid to the west of the old church building, in a newly cleared area on the brow of the hill. Although the day was wet and rainy, a large crowd had assembled in the old church. At noon John Strachan, Lord Bishop of Toronto, conducted the service with the Rev. Alexander Sanson reading the prayers.

Afterward Bishop Strachan administered the rites of confirmation to four candidates, one of whom was the parish clergyman who had never been ordained — the Rev. Alexander Sanson. After the confirmation the bishop and the new clergymen walked across to the site of the new church in the pouring rain. Only about one-third of the congregation braved the rain to follow them.

Meanwhile, William and Dinah Marsh, who owned land south and west of the church property, granted an acre of land, roughly L-shaped, to extend the grounds westward to allow for an eight-foot pathway to be built up the steep hill from the new Yonge Street.

A building committee of twenty men of the parish, including Rev. Alexander Sanson as chairman, Cornelius van Nostrand II as treasurer, and Col. William C.

Left: *Although this photo was taken later in the 1930s, the carriage path up the hill to the new church, on land donated by Dinah and William Marsh, had changed little from its beginnings.*

Right: *The footpath and steps end today in this gateway at the bottom of the hill. It's a route used by the community to access the subway at York Mills.*

Rochefort as secretary, went to work raising funds and confirming plans for the design of their new church.

Churchwarden Henry George Papst and builder George Brown were awarded the building contract, to be assisted by volunteers from the church and community.

The building committee and architect had finally decided on a design: a Gothic style, simple plan with four lancet-style (tall and narrow) windows with pointed tops on each side. Many thought it would be cheaper to use red bricks, but when members of the congregation found an unusual vein of blue clay in the nearby Don Valley, they decided to use this clay to make the church's distinctive burnt-white bricks, even though these cost a little more. The extra cost was covered by two ladies of the parish.

In addition to his clerical duties, Rev. Sanson took an active interest in the building of his new church, inspecting it daily. After the outside of the building was completed, bees were held every Saturday to add the finishing touches to the grounds and interior. Men used their carts and horses to haul away brush, while the women cleaned and arranged the pews and furniture inside, and provided food and drink for the many helpers.

Architect John Howard also designed a Holy Table, pulpit, and reading desk, to be built by Paul Sheppard (no relation to the Shepards of Lansing), who had carved the Golden Lion statue for his brother Thomas's Golden Lion Hotel on the southwest corner of Sheppard Avenue and Yonge Street. Extra costs were paid for by Mrs. Duncan. The pulpit and prayer desk were made of walnut from trees found on the property.

Facing: The Norman-style bell tower is still impressive today.

Below: A view of the second St. John's Church as it would have looked in 1844. It dominated the landscape in the early years.

The new building also featured a Norman-style bell tower, as did John Howard's other churches in Upper Canada. The church had been built high on the western edge of the hill, so it could be seen by people in Hogg's Hollow and the Town of York.

On November 22, 1843, the Rev. Sanson went down to Toronto to visit the firm of Thomas D. Harris, an ironmonger on King Street, to order a bell for the new tower. It weighed four hundred pounds and cost about $400. A month later the Rev. Sanson visited the store again to order two stoves, ninety-six lengths of stove pipe, and six elbows, for a total cost of $30. The bell and stoves were hauled up Yonge Street by a team of oxen.

While the new church was being built over the winter and spring, services were held in the old church. By the following summer, the new St. John's York Mills, although not completed, was officially opened — on another wet, rainy day. Pews from the old church were moved to the new church and cleaned up by volunteers. Bishop Strachan visited periodically to conduct confirmation services and check on the construction of the church.

Even though the new church was still not fully completed, opening services were held on June 11, 1844 — again in the pouring rain. Bishop Strachan and the Rev. Sanson delivered addresses and sermons, followed by a collection in aid of

the building fund. Music was performed by a quickly assembled choir seated on chairs in the gallery, under the leadership of Daniel Grigg (Gregg) Hewitt, who used a tuning fork to begin the hymns.

At the vestry meeting of 1845, they decided to sell off the old church building. Fearing another winter storm could cause the roof to collapse completely, the building was sold to Edward Pease, who rebuilt it as a shed on his father Elihu's farm on the southeast corner of Yonge and Sheppard. That farm was eventually sold to Joseph Christie Bales in 1896, and in 1921 Mr. Bales dismantled the shed and stored the timbers in his barn. In 1948 when the Bales family heard that St. John's was renovating the church, they donated the timbers to be used in the new addition. These can still be seen in the narthex today.

Two years later Henry and Elizabeth Papst were given an acre of land on the clergy reserve on Bayview Avenue in appreciation for their work.

A winter view of the church as it stood on the hill

One of the first major alterations took place just a few years later in 1848, when the old pews in the gallery were slightly altered to add to the choir members' comfort, and the front of the gallery was lowered and a brass rail installed. Even today, additions and alterations are being carried out to add to the comfort of parishioners, without altering the historic facades of the original St. John's Church of 1843.

Left: *The chancel area before electrification, with gas lamps lighting the altar*

Right: *A view of the chancel after electrification*

CHAPTER SEVENTEEN

The Men and Women of St. John's

Facing top: *The cornerstone for the second church was laid in 1843. This date can be seen over the original west entrance.*

Facing bottom: *The Camerons often opened their home for church socials. Called Lindally, it stood on the corner of Old Yonge Street and The Links Road. This photo was taken in 1956.*

The men and women of St. John's were active in serving the church and community, individually and in groups. Over the years, men and women worked together to refurbish the interior and exterior of the church and make renovations and restorations when necessary.

After the land was donated by Joseph and Catherine Shepard, members and neighbours gathered to clear away the underbrush and burn the tangled bushes and shrubs. The trees were used in the new wood-framed church. The larger trees were squared on-site, while others were sent to the nearest sawmill — that of Samuel Heron. Local farmers did the hauling with their oxen or horses and donated their carpentry skills. The women provided food, while men brought in lavish supplies of whiskey.

A generation later they decided that a larger, more permanent building was needed, and a cornerstone was laid in 1843. As the new church was being built, work meetings were held inside and outside. Pews from the old church were too short for the new larger sanctuary, so new pews had to be built. The stronger parishioners moved the old pews into the gallery.

The women, including Elizabeth Sanson, wife of the rector, cleaned and polished the old pews and the sills. Because there was no regular sexton until 1842, the women of the parish such as Catherine Shepard, Mary van Nostrand, Ann Mercer, Margaret Willson, Elizabeth Harrison, and Katherine Cameron, had been busy in the old church scrubbing the pews and floors after each Sunday service, wedding, and funeral. They also hosted those who conducted the services, feeding them in the afternoons and often offering an overnight bed.

When heavier work needed to be done, the church paid people on an individual basis to perform tasks, such as cleaning the stoves and stove pipes, splitting wood from trees in the churchyard, and digging graves.

Most of the women of the parish opened their homes for fundraising events such as festivals and bazaars, serving food and drink afterward. After the corner-stone was laid, Katherine Cameron opened her home, called Lindally, for a reception. This was the first of many garden parties, festivals, picnics, strawberry festivals, and oyster suppers. As the congregation grew, these were held in the Golden Lion and Hogg's Hollow hotels or at the local York Mills public school. Musical concerts were sometimes held in Lindally and other large homes in York Mills. Later even non-members, such as Levon Babayan and Frederick Nichols, opened their estates for St. John's.

Above: *This 1915 painting of John Page Squire was recently unearthed from the vault at St. John's.*

Left: *John Squire shows off the barrel organ. The crank that he turned to make the music resound throughout the church can be seen on the right-hand side of the barrel.*

Right: *A close-up of the barrel in the barrel organ*

St. John's first sexton was Henry Collins, appointed in 1842 at a salary of £6 a year. When he died in 1852, his son served St. John's for the next two years, at which time the job passed to John Strong, who was sexton until 1861. He was followed by the longest-serving and most popular sexton John Page Squire. When he retired in 1930 at the age of eighty-eight, he was the oldest sexton in Canada and had served St. John's for nearly seventy years.

The Squire family immigrated to Canada in 1862 and, shortly thereafter, their young nineteen-year-old son John Page Squire began work as a sexton. He was expected to be on duty every Sunday to ring the bell, crank the barrel organ, and light the candles and lamps in the sanctuary. During the Rev. McCollum's tenure in the 1920s, John's duties included stoking the stoves in the front and the back of the church with firewood. If cold weather made it necessary to stoke during the service, that often caused the blowing of pipes and the clanging of doors, drowning out the rector's sermons and prayers. John would collapse afterward into a rattan chair at the back of the church, often in a fit of coughing and laughter.

John Squire was described as a "little old man with a high-bridged nose and old-fashioned whiskers." As sexton, he was supposed to wear a long, black gown and three-cornered hat, but he refused to wear the uniform. He said he was fearful that someone would try to knock the hat off his head.

In 1908, John and his wife Mary Ann Leeder (1845–1915), and their three daughters, Mabel Ann, Katherine, and Blanche, moved into the William Goodwin (Godwin) house on the east side of Yonge Street, south of York Mills Road, just down the hill from the church, so John would be close to his work. The family was very active at St. John's, and daughter Blanche played the old barrel organ and sang in the choir for many years.

Above: *Parish Council member Peter Rayhnam is costumed for Doors Open Toronto 2016 in the kind of outfit that John Squire was expected to wear on Sunday mornings.*

Left: *John Squire stands in front of the church he served for 69 years.*

But climbing the hill some 3,500 Sundays finally took their toll on John and by Christmas morning 1930, he was too weak to ring the bell and crank the old organ. He told a friend to ring the bell but not touch his beloved organ. It was silent on a Sunday for the first time in more than eighty years.

John Page Squire died six weeks later, on January 25, 1931, sixty-nine years after he had begun work at his beloved church. After the funeral service, John was buried in the family plot in the churchyard where his parents already lay. At the vestry meeting held on January 27, 1931, a small leaflet dedicated to John Squire was inserted into the minutes, and the following year, November 27, 1932, a brass tablet was unveiled on the north wall in his memory.

In 1875 a new work bee was called to dismantle the old rectory in preparation to build a new one. Lumber was carefully piled and sorted, while bricks from the old chimney were cleaned and neatly piled to be used later. The ladies gathered to raise money for the building fund by holding a bazaar, and further materials were donated by neighbours and friends.

The churchyard got its share of attention, as well. Volunteers again donated their time and efforts. A team and mower cut the grass in open areas, while owners of the family plots cut their grasses and planted flowers. In June 1827 an afternoon bee was called to clear away unwanted growth and dismantle an old driving shed. The women used fruits, flowers, leaves, and grasses from the churchyard to decorate the church and altar.

Sunday school picnics had started in 1840 to celebrate the end of the Sunday school year. Picnics were usually held on the Saturday nearest June 24 (St. John's Day) on

Whitton's Grove, south of the church. The first large festival was held on July 24, 1842, with rewards given (usually religious books) for good conduct and attendance. Rev. Alexander Sanson had crafted the awards himself. The children gathered around tables laden with dainties and plum puddings prepared by the ladies of the church. When attendance at the church became too much, the picnic moved to the property behind the church, flowing onto the lawns of van Nostrand's Green Gates and the adjoining Marsh estates. With the coming of the radial railway, families from St. John's also travelled to Centre Island or Bond Lake for picnics.

Over the years Sunday school picnics came to include tugs-of-war, races, and, for older children, target shooting with bows and arrows, and rifle shoots. There were penny tosses and demonstrations of a sewing machine. In June 1938 an electric shocking machine was added. Children would pull various handles, not knowing which would ring a bell and which would give an electric shock.

There were also musical entertainments and exhibits by the church and neighbours. Music was usually provided by the band of Col. van Nostrand's Third York Militia Regiment. Men, women, and the older children would dress in historical costumes. Women hulled strawberries, donated by Thomas Mercer, and served them with the baked goods they had made. Bazaars were held on the Saturday closest to June 24 each year, to raise funds for church additions and renovations. The ladies supplied baked goods, while the men lent personal items for display — coins, an 1815 Dutch Bible, weapons from the van Nostrand family, and farm implements and tools from the Harrisons. There was even a candlestick with a bullet hole in it, from the battle of the Plains of Abraham and capture of Quebec in 1759.

Church picnics and barbecues are still popular in 2015. Sexton Mark Anderson and Damien Benedict, barbecuing to help raise funds for the Sandy Bay, Jamaica, outreach program.

Fathers and children helped out, too. Paul, Tom, Frank, and Betty Boultbee were usually dressed in appropriate costume. In fact, the men's group — organized in fall 1930 to bring in speakers and help with repairs in and around the church — was very active in planning and running the Sunday school picnics and other entertainments. Eric Boultbee worked during the annual picnics, while Rev. George Trew organized musical entertainments to raise money for St. John's. Garden parties were also held in nearby estates to raise money for the church — Katherine Boultbee held many events in her home in the valley. They also held Christmas bazaars — first in the rectory, then in the parish hall.

As the congregation matured, the informal work bees of the past gave way to organized groups that often carried over from generation to generation. A Bible group had been working from as early as 1843, when the new church was built. The St. John's branch of the Diocesan Women's Auxiliary was organized in October 1889, the meetings set for Saturday or Sunday afternoons, with Mrs. Henry Bath Osler as convenor. Mrs. Osler had been Harriet Parsons, the daughter of William Parsons of Thornhill, and had married Henry shortly after Rev. Osler's ordination in 1844. By the time they came to St. John's, their family had grown up and Henry and Harriet could devote all their time to the church. Their daughter Emma Osler was the organist from 1887 to 1905, until the family moved down to St. Clement's Church in Davisville. The Auxiliary's first fundraising efforts were directed to picnics.

In 1928 the Afternoon Women's Guild was organized and, with the Auxiliary, could always be counted on to raise funds needed for building additions and renovating and upgrading the church interior. Women of the parish decorated the church for special occasions and Sunday services, as well as sewing and embroidering cushions for the pews and linens for the altar. During the wars they rolled bandages and knit socks, mittens, and hats. These were turned over to the Canadian Red Cross Society, which raised money and provided care and knitted goods for those serving overseas. The North York branch of the Red Cross was

Facing: A tug-of-war is still popular at a Sunday school picnic. This battle took place in 2008 with Peter Martin in the key position.

founded in October 1914 — a month after the outbreak of the war — with Mrs. Charles (Marion) Catto of St. John's Church as its first president.

Later, Mrs. Catto and her many friends at St. John's helped the Canadian Red Cross to organize and carry out one of the largest festivals in the country to date — a flax festival held on the farm of William Wallace on Yonge Street at Newtonbrook. Linen (the cloth made of flax fibre) was used in the making of airplane wings, 150 yards of it for each wing. Linen was also used to make clothes, rugs, and twine. Bottles of linseed oil were also popular sellers at this event.

The flax festival was held during the week of August 10, 1918, to coincide with the flax harvest. The Ontario government had established flax fields in various areas of Toronto — the Wallace farm of seventy acres, thirty acres at Lawrence Park, and twenty-five acres at Armour Heights.

Girls from England staying at the nearby Willowdale School worked on the Wallace farm, while boys of the area (who, it was said, didn't work as fast as girls) were sent to smaller farms across southern Ontario. In addition, "Land Army" girls were brought from France, Belgium, and Great Britain to cut flax. They were met at Union Station by Mrs. William (Emma) Galbraith of the Red Cross Society. The festival lasted a week, with the Union Jack and the Canadian Red Cross flags flying high. Each day featured a special event. More than five thousand people came daily on the radial car to Stop 33 to see the various exhibits. To help with the festivities, there was Irish hospitality and good humour in the Great Pavilion, where waitresses wore costumes of various countries, such as the white stars and red-and-blue stripes that were meant to demonstrate American hospitality.

The Monday booth, staffed by Mrs. John (Jack) Nettie, featured cleaning supplies: Lux soap, Dutch Cleanser, and laundry soaps. The Tuesday booth, tended by Hilda Laing (of St. John's) and Aileen Lewis, exhibited first-aid supplies and demonstrated how to roll bandages and dress wounds. On Wednesday a group of women in Belgian costume sold fancy articles trimmed with Belgian lace. On Thursday and Friday, home-baked goods and drinks were sold and served by girls in appropriate costumes. Fresh fruits and vegetables came from local farms. A flower booth was staffed by Mrs. Joseph (Clara) Bales, a member of St. John's Church. Saturday and Sunday were days of food, celebration, and more fundraising. A booth featuring "useful" things for sale was tended by Miss Betty Boultbee, dressed as the children's character "Mrs. Wiggs of the Cabbage Patch." The highlight of the week was the aviation show, with planes soaring, performing loop-the-loops, and diving so low that they could almost touch the heads of the spectators. The festivities ended with a large Sunday dinner for volunteers.

The festival was a huge success, and the money raised was divided between the Canadian Red Cross Society and the Franco-British Aid Society. They decided to hold a reunion the following year. On the Wallace farm on August 18, 1919, Mrs. Nettie set out small tables with pink flowers. More than fifty veterans were honoured for their service in the war. In the afternoon there were games and races for the children, directed by Katherine Wallace who awarded prizes of twenty-five cents to a dollar. There were also ice cream booths and a lavish supper, with the food donated by neighbours and volunteers.

The North York branch of the Canadian Red Cross Society was active during both World Wars and after. Many ladies of St. John's served in various capacities. Mrs. Catto served as president until 1920, assisted by Mrs. Milton (Marian) Stong, Mrs. S. Cleland (May) Holley, Mrs. Arthur J. van Nostrand (Katherine), and Mrs. Lorne (Edith) Pierce. The branch met regularly in the rectory of Mrs. Richard (Ethel) Ashcroft, and Nora van Nostrand ran her fundraising Orchard Tea Garden for many years.

Perhaps because of their civic efforts, the ladies of St. John's had the privilege of meeting (and dancing with!) royalty on their visits to Canada and Toronto. In 1860 Queen Victoria sent her son Albert Edward (later King Edward VII) to represent her at the opening of Queen's Park. Prince Edward hosted two balls in Toronto — one for citizens and one for lawyers. At the lawyers' ball, Mrs. William Boultbee (Marion), who was active at St. John's, had the privilege of dancing with Prince Edward.

*Princess Anne leaves the church
with Canon O'Neil after
attending a service in 1974.*

During another royal visit in 1919, the charming Prince of Wales was so attracted to Nora van Nostrand Wedd — then the newlywed wife of Brigadier Basil Wedd — that he asked her to dance with him twice. He was impressed at the way she could dance the Charleston — a fast dance of the day. Later, even though they were the parents of two young children, the Wedds responded to the Prince's invitation to balls in Montreal. Eight years later, Prince Edward and his brother George were back in Toronto to dedicate the Princes' Gate at the Canadian National Exhibition. At a formal military dance held at Government House, Prince Edward danced with Nora, who introduced him and his brother to her sisters Louisa, Elsie, and Kathleen van Nostrand. He also danced with Nora at the York Club. They met in seven different countries in Europe, where Basil was posted with the Massey-Harris Company. It is said that Edward danced with Nora more than twenty-five times.

St. John's last brush with royalty was in 1974 when Princess Anne and her husband Mark Phillips attended the morning service and met with the Reverend O'Neil and his wife as well as other members of the congregation.

CHAPTER EIGHTEEN

The Artists of St. John's

Over the years, many artists have been involved with St. John's York Mills. Some have only had a passing acquaintance, while others have lived within earshot of the tower's bells. If you know where to look, you can find traces of their artwork all around the property, both inside and out. Foremost among these artists must be Charles William (C.W.) Jefferys.

C.W. JEFFERYS

C.W. Jefferys was a well-known painter, illustrator, historian, and educator who is best remembered for his accurate artistic depictions of events in Canada's history. He was born in 1869 in Rochester, Kent, England. The family later moved to Gad's Hill, England, where Charles Dickens was one of their neighbours. In the mid-1870s they moved to North America, living in Philadelphia, Pennsylvania, and Hamilton, Ontario, before moving to Toronto in 1881. C.W. enrolled in evening classes at the Ontario School of Art and Design in 1884 and by 1885 he was apprenticed to the Toronto Lithograph Company for a period of five years. The lithographers farmed him out to the *Globe* newspaper, where he learned all about sketching for newspapers. He continued his studies through the late 1890s and also did some illustrating for the *Toronto Telegram* newspaper. In 1889 he was hired by the *Globe* as a staff illustrator, and by 1890 he had begun studying Canadian history and sketching local historic locales.

In 1892 C.W. moved to New York City to work and study. He returned to Toronto for the summer but, by 1893, he had moved back to New York to live, study, and work at the *New York Herald*. He married Jean Adams in New York on December 29, 1894. The couple moved to Woodside, New Jersey, the following year. Their daughter Jeanette was born there in December 1895. Their son Charles Robert was born in 1898 but, sadly, he died in 1899, at only nineteen months old.

Tragedy visited the family again in 1900 when Jean Jefferys died, along with two sons. Sources are unclear as to the whether the brothers were stillborn or died shortly after birth, but details matter little. A heartbroken C.W. Jefferys returned to Toronto, before leaving to spend time in Quebec along the Richelieu River. He returned to Toronto for good in 1901, where he was appointed art director of Grip Limited — the famous graphic design firm that gave work to many of the struggling young artists who would go on to form the Group of Seven. C.W. was also assigned to cover that year's cross-country tour of the Duchess and Duke of Cornwall, later King George V.

C.W. Jefferys was elected a member of the Ontario School of Art and Design in 1902 and appointed to the board in 1904. He began sketching and painting in northern Ontario and made several return trips to the United States to attend art shows. He joined the editorial staff of the *Toronto Star* newspaper in 1905, and in 1907 he married Clara West at Keewatin Beach in Kenora. The couple honeymooned in western Canada before returning to Toronto, where they took rooms on Pembroke Street. In 1910 the couple rented a house at 4111 Yonge Street in Hogg's Hollow as a summer home. Their daughter Elizabeth (Betsy) was born there in 1912. Her sister Margaret was born in 1915, followed by sister Barbara in 1916. The family were finally able to buy the house in 1922. They would live there for nearly ninety years.

Behind the house was a small barn that served as C.W.'s studio. It was off-limits to his daughters, even to his wife Clara. In the evenings C.W. would join the family at the dining room table. He supervised his daughters while they did their homework, and drew sketches for future paintings and murals.

The house soon became a popular meeting place for other artists, including Walter Allward and his son Hugh. Sculptor Emanuel Hahn — a one-time studio assistant to Walter Allward and designer of the caribou head for the Canadian quarter — was a frequent visitor, as was Emanuel's wife. Other visitors were noted sculptor Elizabeth Wyn Wood, whose bas-relief sculptures still grace buildings at Ryerson University, and sculptor E.B. Cox. The guest list also included C.W.'s friends: Group of Seven members such as Lawren Harris, A.Y. Jackson, and J.E.H. MacDonald. (C.W. Jefferys was invited to join the group in 1920, the year it was formed, but he politely declined.) The guest list at the C.W. Jefferys house was rounded out by writers and publishers such as Lorne Pierce and Herbert Tyrell, who became active members of St. John's York Mills.

C.W. Jefferys kept busy drawing and painting for William Perkins Bull's books and John Ross Robertson's columns in the *Toronto Telegram.* And, when he had the time, C.W. was painting murals and drawing pictures of historic events. These pictures were published in the three volumes of *The Picture Gallery of Canadian History.* In 1952 one year after C.W. Jefferys died, more than one thousand of his historical drawings and paintings were acquired by the Imperial Oil Company of Canada. The collection was donated to the Public Archives of Canada by Imperial Oil on April 12, 1972. During Imperial's ownership, C.W.'s most famous works were arranged in five separate portfolios for distribution to researchers, educators, and librarians. Nearly half-a-million portfolios were distributed in fifteen years.

This statue of C.W. Jefferys, by Adrienne Alison, stands in a park at the corner of Mill Street and Donino Avenue in York Mills Valley.

When daughter Betsy married Dr. George Alexander Fee in 1941, they bought the house at 4111 Yonge Street. Charles William lived with them until his death

A sample of Jefferys historical work entitled "The Founding of Halifax."

on October 8, 1951. Betsy often said that she enjoyed watching marriage and funeral processions going up the hill to St. John's, especially in springtime when the road was "decorated" with apple blossoms. Betsy was active in the church and its history, helping Audrey Graham to catalogue and preserve items for the St. John's archives. A display case and storage cupboard, designed by Bruce Napier Simpson Jr. for his friend Charles Jefferys to display his paintings, sketchbooks, and other memorabilia, was donated to St. John's by Dr. and Mrs. Fee in 1964. It stood in the narthex for many years before the most recent renovation, and it is now brought out for special displays. Inspired by her father's interest in history, Betsy was a founding member of the North York Historical Society and served for many years on the society's management board.

In 1955 the C.W. Jefferys house was moved sixty feet back on its lot to facilitate the widening of Yonge Street. A new kitchen was added at this time and the studio/barn was demolished. More alterations were completed in the mid-1980s. On August 30, 1960, a historical plaque at 4111 Yonge Street was dedicated to Charles William Jefferys. In 2001 a statue of C.W. Jefferys, created by artist Adrienne Alison, was unveiled in York Mills Valley Park near the corner of Mill Street and Donino Avenue.

BRUCE NAPIER SIMPSON JR.

Bruce Napier Simpson Jr. (1925–1978) was a prominent Ontario architect who was interested in the restoration of many historic buildings in and around Toronto. He was the son of Bruce Napier Simpson Sr. and Florence Heustis of Hillside on Pinewood Avenue, near Bathurst and St. Clair. The family were active members of St. John's York Mills. While still a young boy, Bruce rode his bicycle and then his motorcycle around North York and York Township, exploring old houses and buildings.

After graduating from the University of Toronto in 1951 with a degree in architecture, Bruce set up his own company to assist in the restoration of old houses. He was soon recognized as an authority on old Canadian homes and churches, and helped with the development of Toronto's Black Creek Pioneer Village and Upper Canada Village near Morrisburg in eastern Ontario. Bruce was also a member of the York Pioneer Society and served on advisory boards of the North York Historical Society and St. John's York Mills. He also helped with the restoration of many houses around York Mills and Toronto, including the Scadding Cabin on the CNE grounds, the Joseph Shepard house on Burndale Avenue, the Gibson House Museum in Willowdale, the Lodge at St. John's, and Dundurn Castle in Hamilton. In 1974 he designed a farmhouse for Riverdale Park.

Mr. Simpson also saved a historic house at 14 Colborne Street in Thornhill, when he purchased the derelict 1861 house in 1974 and restored it to serve as his offices. In 1966 he oversaw the relocation and restoration of master builder John Edey's house, which was moved from its original location on Yonge Street in Thornhill to save it from demolition during the widening of Yonge. The restored house, originally constructed in 1845, now stands at 4 Leahill Drive in Thornhill.

In March 1964, while examining John Howard's Colborne Lodge in High Park for restoration, Bruce discovered some old files and papers in a shed behind the house. On further examination he also found plans for the current St. John's Church (completed in 1844) and designs for a Holy Table, pulpit, and reading desk that Howard had hoped to build for the then-new St. John's. These plans were put on display in the narthex case that had been donated by Dr. and Mrs. Fee.

Unfortunately, Bruce Napier Simpson died at the height of his career in a plane crash on June 23, 1978. He was en route to unveil a plaque at the L'Anse aux Meadows National Historic Site on the very tip of Newfoundland's Great Northern Peninsula — the place where Vikings established the first European settlement in North America more than one thousand years ago. Bruce's body was brought back for a private funeral service and burial at St. Peter's Church on Maple Lake in Haliburton, where he had spent many happy summers with his family. A memorial service was held later in Holy Trinity Church in Thornhill.

E.B. COX

Elford Bradley Cox, usually called E.B., was born in 1914 in Alberta. His family spent a short time farming there before moving to Bowmanville, Ontario, in 1921. His mother died when he was only thirteen. After E.B. graduated from high school, his father sent him off to the University of Toronto with "five dollars, a suitcase, and a wish of good luck," according to E.B.'s youngest daughter Kathy Sutton, who is a Member of the Order of Canada and an internationally renowned parachute champion.

E.B. Cox enrolled at the university's Victoria College and felt immediately at home in his new environment. He studied languages from 1934 to 1938 and was befriended by German professor and painter Barker Fairley, who introduced the young E.B. Cox to Group of Seven artists Fred Varley, Arthur Lismer, and A.Y. Jackson. E.B. had learned carving from his grandfather, who had spent much of his time whittling by the fireside. E.B. put himself through college by making and selling small wooden carvings of totem poles and bears. At one point, he even had a small display in one of the windows at Eaton's on College Street. He would later work in other media, such as metal, ceramics, bronze, granite, limestone, marble, and glass.

After graduation E.B. taught languages at Upper Canada College (UCC) before leaving to join the war effort, where he travelled to Europe to interrogate prisoners of war. Following the war he returned to teach at UCC. During the summers he would take groups of students on canoe trips down northern rivers. In later years he travelled north on sketching trips with other artists, including members of the Group of Seven. Members of the group thought so much of his skills that he was later called upon to carve epitaphs on their tombstones.

E.B. married Elizabeth (Betty) Campbell in 1948 and, realizing that he could make a living being a full-time sculptor, he quit his teaching job and devoted himself to his art. The couple bought a farm near Palgrave, Ontario, and the family soon expanded to include daughters Kathy and Sally. By the early 1950s, E.B. Cox was receiving commissions for sculptures in schools, libraries, and other public institutions, as well as selling smaller sculptures of bears — each one unique — to individual buyers. He soon became a pioneer in sculpting in stone with power tools — a practice that raised the eyebrows of purists but made it possible for him to do the work of several sculptors. He never took a penny in government grants and was always willing to mentor younger artists.

In 1954 the Cox family moved to a one-acre lot on farmland near Bayview Avenue and Finch Avenue in North York, where E.B. could have a larger studio.

Left: Seated Bear *by E.B. Cox in the front garden of St. John's*

Right: *Limestone sculpture of a lamb carrying the cross, located in the Memorial Chapel of St. John's*

He lived and carved there until 1983, when he moved to a house on Broadview Avenue with a stable and garage.

While on Finch Avenue East, E.B. Cox was carving one-of-a-kind bears in stone and other media that were selling widely. One of these sculptures, titled *Seated Bear,* can be found in the garden just outside of the front door of SJYM, donated to the church by friends and family of the artist. Other examples of E.B.'s work can be found inside the church. For St. John's in 1954, he created a sheep carrying a cross, and smaller significant sculptures representing aspects of the Christian faith. All were donated to St. John's Church, and hang today in the Memorial Chapel in the north transept.

Elford Bradley Cox died on July 29, 2003, and a private family service was held on August 9, 2003, followed by a memorial service a month later in *The Garden of the Greek Gods* near the Horticultural Building on the CNE grounds.

CHAPTER NINETEEN

Historical Street Names in the St. John's Neighbourhood

When the first little log church was completed in 1816, it was surrounded by forest. Gradually more settlers came and cleared more land for their houses and farms. Many of the early settlers in the area were British army officers, granted the deeds to their land by a grateful Crown. The names of many of these settlers live on in the street names we recognize today.

York Ridge Road, just south of the church property, was once only a cow path on the Marsh and van Nostrand properties that allowed cows to graze in the churchyard of St. John's. When York Ridge Road was opened to housing development in the 1940s, it was the only street in the area to boast two cul-de-sacs. It was advertised as a restful country scene that included old apple trees, graceful elms, rugged oaks, and dark picturesque evergreens. Roads were laid out so as to save the five-hundred-year old trees, while large homes and estates were built on the large lots. A few of the trees had to be cut down and the firewood was neatly piled and sold to local residents.

A view of York Mills Valley as it looked in 1908

York Mills Road had been known as Mercer Avenue until 1928, when it became known as the road to the Don River and the village of York Mills on Yonge Street. Thomas Mercer, an Irish United Empire Loyalist, had come to area in 1794 and received a land grant on the south side of the concession road, which is today York Mills Road. Members of the Mercer family were soon active in the local church and community.

It was also south of York Mills Road where, many years later, William Mulock Boultbee bought land from Daniel Brooke to build a large home that he called Brookfield. Unfortunately, he died just before the house was completed, but his wife Margaret and their nine children lived there and were active in St. John's Church in the 1920s, hosting picnics, garden parties, and fundraising events for the church.

Around St. John's, roads were named for members of the church or places in those people's pasts. One such person was the Rev. Dr. John Strachan who, before coming to Upper Canada, taught in a school near his home at Denino (Donino) in St. Andrews, Scotland. John Strachan came to York during the war of 1812 to serve at St. James Church.

Church Street was built in September 1850, through dense woods up the hill from Yonge Street to the "church on the hill." Stuart Avenue and Owen Boulevard were named for people who served at St. John's Church. The Breen and Fenn families were early settlers and members of the church. Mary Ann Fenn married the Rev. James Mitchell of neighbouring York Mills Baptist Church in 1848.

Colin F. Gordon's family, who gave their name to Gordon Road, lived in York Mills and were members of St. John's. William Lockhart Gordon of All Saints

Church and a founder of the Toronto Church School, lost two sons in the First World War — Capt. Matthew Gordon and Capt. Walter Leslie Lockhart Gordon.

Neighbour Finlay Munro (1905–84) built many houses in the York Mills-Bayview area during the Second World War, and was a well-known contractor in Toronto and Muskoka. He was credited with building the first modern Loblaws supermarket — although it is uncertain where that store was — and the Dixie Curling Rink in Mississauga in 1956, which is still an active curling club today. Munro Boulevard is named after his family.

When Yorkminster Heights was developed in the late 1940s, many of its roads were named for those who were active in early Upper Canada. It was advertised as greater Toronto's first planned subdivision, with spacious houses selling for $13,500 with landscaped back gardens and large lawns.

The route of Lord Seaton Road was laid out on van Nostrand family farmland in 1825. It was later named after Sir John Colborne, former lieutenant governor of

Hogg's Hollow in 1955 with St. John's in the distance on the hill

Upper Canada and military commander-in-chief of British North America, who was named the first Lord Seaton in recognition for his services to the Crown.

Aldershot Crescent owes its name to two different places. Aldershot, England, was known for its flour mills and breweries until 1854, when a military camp was established there and Aldershot became a major military centre with extensive barracks. Aldershot, Nova Scotia, was another military centre, created during the First World War.

Looking north into Hogg's Hollow in 1956 after the widening of Yonge Street. The Jolly Miller, today the Miller Tavern, can be seen at the bottom of the hill. The Hollow was named after the pioneer family named Hogg.

Danville Drive can trace the origins of its name to Jean Baptiste d'Anville (1697–1782), a French geographer. Oakley Place was named for the country estate of Leigh Manners McCarthy (1878–59), a St. John's parishioner who is buried in the churchyard. He built his estate in 1929 to overlook the Don Valley. For many years the thirty-room house was called the Cardinal's Palace. Cardinal James McGuigan, who was a close friend of the Rev. McCollum of St. John's, lived there for more than twenty-five years from 1947 until his death in 1974.

St. Andrews Golf Club, its course designed by Stanley Thompson, opened in the area in 1926 as one of Canada's first pay-as-you-play courses. Lower Links Road was the driveway from Old Yonge Street to Lindally — the former home of Duncan Cameron — which became the clubhouse. Until St. Andrew's closed, it hosted many championships, including the Canadian Open. When the land was subdivided in the early 1960s, streets such as Foursome Crescent were named for golfing terminology, while others were named after well-known Canadian golfers, such as Al Balding and Babe Didrikson.

CHAPTER TWENTY

Early Neighbours

Many of the first settlers in Upper Canada came after the American Revolution (1776–83) for the land grants that were being offered to British Loyalists. These United Empire Loyalists chose to settle north of the Town of York. Those who had served in the Napoleonic wars and the War of 1812 were called Late Loyalists and many settled where the West Don River crossed Yonge Street. Not all the Loyalists were members of the Church of England. Some went on to establish their own Baptist, Methodist, and Presbyterian congregations. But until they did, they all helped to build the first church in the area — St. John's — and attended its services until their own churches were built.

Before St. John's was built, devoted churchgoers such as Seneca Ketchum (1774–1850), one of the first settlers in North Toronto, had been going to St. James Church which was the only Anglican Church in York County. After Seneca tired of the six-mile walk in the rain, snow, and cold, he set out to establish his own church north of the town. It began as worship gatherings in his home; then, when the gatherings grew too large, Seneca suggested moving to the little log school-house built by Thomas Mercer in 1807. He persuaded the Rev. John Strachan to

Bishop John Strachan

come up once a month and send his divinity students or associate clergy on the other Sundays. Chaplains from the British garrison also helped out when needed.

SENECA KETCHUM

Seneca had come to Upper Canada in 1792 with uncles Joseph and James and other Loyalists, seeking a better and freer life. Seneca settled in York Mills around 1796, while his brothers eventually chose Scarborough for their homes. In 1822 Seneca bought fifteen acres on North Yonge Street and built a little log house to serve as a home and tannery shop.

With hard work he was soon able to buy a larger lot on the east side of Yonge Street, north of North Toronto. He built a shop and a larger house for his family; the driveway, now Blythwood Road, was bordered on both sides by orchards.

The shop included a small tannery, cobblery, and a "service centre" where Seneca would rent out a yoke of oxen, pasture land, or a horse or cow, or sell salmon from the Don River and venison. Seneca was also selling his goods to the government at Fort York. During the winter, Seneca would buy woollen cloth from the wives of neighbours and trade apples for their potatoes and butchered hogs.

Seneca's younger brothers, Jesse Jr. and Zebulon, were living with him for a time and the brothers hired a housekeeper, recently widowed Anne (Nancy) Love, whose husband had been killed in a shooting accident. Jesse soon fell in love with Anne, and so did Seneca. Rather than fighting a duel in which one could be killed, the brothers drew lots, with Jesse winning. Seneca instead married Ann Mercer, the daughter of neighbour Thomas Mercer.

In 1819, after St. John's was well established, Seneca sold his farm in Bedford Park and moved to Orangeville, where he and Ann attended and served six churches and two rectories in the area. Later, Seneca and Ann Ketchum moved back to the area, settling in Lawrence Park, where they lived until their deaths. Both are buried in the Mercer family plot in St. John's churchyard. At a Thanksgiving service held in October 1952, a window was installed by members of St. John's in memory of the faithful efforts of Seneca Ketchum and his family. His desk, displayed only on special occasions, is one of St. John's heritage pieces and can be viewed in the south wing on request.

JOSEPH SHEPARD

In 1816, Joseph and Catherine Shepard donated two-and-three- quarter acres of their land high on the hill above York Mills for a church and churchyard. The following year a meeting was held with interested neighbours, and a document for fundraising for a church was signed by Joseph Shepard, Seneca Ketchum, and John Willson. Other English Loyalists soon joined in to help: the van Nostrands, Mercers, Harrisons, and Humberstones.

After the little church was ready in the fall of 1816, the Shepards continued to prosper — and to serve the church well. Joseph Shepard built a water-powered saw and gristmill on the West Don River, north of Sheppard Avenue and east of Bathurst Street. The gristmill, operated by Thomas, was shipping flour to Montreal, while Michael's sawmill, in addition to cutting and selling lumber, cast bullets used in the Rebellion of 1837.

Joseph Shepard Sr. (1765–1837), a private in the Third York Militia, was injured at the Battle of York in 1813 and was granted a large pension. Later, sons Joseph II, Thomas, Michael, and Jacob were reformers, helping William Lyon Mackenzie King to reform the local government and participating in the Upper Canada Rebellion of 1837.

In fact, Shepard's farm was a staging area for those going south to Montgomery's Tavern at Eglinton. Catherine Shepard helped by tying strips of cloth around the men's arms to identify them as rebels.

The tombstone of Catherine and Joseph Shepard can be found in the St. John's churchyard.

JOHN WILLSON

John Willson and his family were some of the first builders and members of St. John's Church. Along with Seneca Ketchum and Joseph Shepard, John served as a building trustee for the church.

After the American Revolution, John Willson (1739–1829) and his young wife Rebecca Thixton travelled from Genesee, New York, aboard the *May Fleet* to New Brunswick. Then, on the invitation of Governor John Graves Simcoe, they came to York, where Willson leased the government mill on the Humber River. When he learned he couldn't buy that mill, John moved his family to the Don River, north of the Town of York. They travelled in an ox cart that John had made himself from lumber he cut at Fort York. The land John had bought (from Thomas Hill) and, where he built a gristmill, is south of Sheppard Avenue.

John and Rebecca had five sons: John II, Stillwell, William, Isaac, and Jonathan, who were all active in St. John's Church throughout their lives and were all buried in St. John's churchyard when they died. All five sons joined the York Militia, serving during the Battle of York in 1813. For their services, the family was given more land on Yonge Street.

THOMAS MERCER

Another Loyalist who came to York after the American Revolutionary War was Thomas Mercer (1744–1829) of Hillsborough, Ireland — the son of Lord Mercer, a nephew of William of Orange. Thomas had travelled overland from Philadelphia in a light wagon with a cow tied onto the back. He settled on a hundred acres of land north of the town, between today's Yonge Street and Bayview Avenue on the south side of York Mills road. He cleared the land for farming and built a house. In 1807, he sold some of the land to Seneca

Ketchum to build a school that could be used by the St. John's congregation on Sundays.

Thomas had acquired his land grant in trade for the wagon he arrived in and his promise to serve his new country and the church. In 1811 he served as elected foreman of a grand jury of twenty-one men, which included Samuel Heron and Thomas Humberstone, who were members of the Church of England. His sons continued as devout Anglicans who were happy to serve the church and contribute money and land as needed. Thomas Hamilton Mercer was a warden from 1872 until 1875, and during that time he opened his home for the strawberry festival and other fundraising events. When Canon Henry Bath Osler came to St. John's in 1874 and refused to live in the church rectory, the Mercers opened their home to the Osler family.

The Mercers were also members of the Queen's Own Rangers and some gave their lives for their country. Many years later in 1913, Lieutenant-Colonel Malcolm Smith Mercer saw action in England, France, and Switzerland. On June 2, 1916, Malcolm Mercer, by then a major-general, was killed by enemy fire while conducting a tour of inspection on the frontlines in France. Contributions by the Mercer family to St. John's are remembered in a window in the sanctuary.

CHRISTOPHER HARRISON

Like many neighbours and fellow members of St. John's Church, Christopher Harrison had moved his family to Nova Scotia during the American Revolution, before finally settling in Upper Canada on Yonge Street, north of York Mills. The Harrison family soon became active in the local Church of England, serving St. John's for many generations.

Son William Harrison (1784–1838), being a supporter of William Lyon Mackenzie King, was forced to flee to the United States after he was wounded during the Upper Canada Rebellion of December 1837. He died there in February 1838 from a combination of his wounds and the pneumonia he had contracted while fleeing across Lake Ontario in an open boat. William's son Joshua wanted his father to be buried in the family plot in the St. John's churchyard. So young Joshua — then only twenty-two years old — made the trek, dragging a sleigh across the border to bring his father home for burial. As he was a young rebel carrying a large wooden box (a coffin he had made), Joshua was stopped and questioned many times and forced to open the coffin for searches.

At the funeral neighbour John van Nostrand — himself a supporter of the government side during the Rebellion — reminded young Joshua that he was still a wanted man and that he would be well advised to go back to the United States and not return until it was safe. Joshua took the advice, not returning to York Mills until the rebels were pardoned several years later.

When Joshua returned home to York Mills, he had another duty to carry out for his father: to build a proper house for his mother Elizabeth and his ten younger siblings. The one-storey house he built of red and yellow bricks he acquired from a neighbour and timber and shingles from the forests on the farm, still stands at 111 Harrison Road in North York. In 1850 his brother Christopher inherited the house and added a second storey. The house remained in the Harrison family until 1943, when the land around it was sold for development.

Joshua was active in the church his whole life, and his wife Sarah was always helping in fundraising activities and church picnics. Members of the Harrison family are buried in the family plot, which used to feature a gigantic elm like the many elms that shaded the family farmhouse. In 1956 the churchyard elm succumbed to Dutch Elm disease.

THOMAS HUMBERSTONE

Another family who served St. John's Church for many years was the Humberstones, who came from Philadelphia in 1788. Samuel Humberstone (1744–1823), a potter, had come from Staffordshire, England, to set up his trade and raise his family in Philadelphia. But being loyal to the British Crown, he came to Montreal after the American Revolution, then went to Brockville and the Town of York. In York he was granted two hundred acres of land on Yonge Street. Samuel set up a pottery business and taught the craft to his eldest son Thomas (1776–1849).

As well as operating the family pottery business, Thomas served his new country and church. In 1800 he married Anna Harrison and was granted another two hundred acres on the east side of Yonge Street, north of York Mills. Thomas was elected overseer of highways and fence viewers, for which he also received five acres of cleared land with a house and barn at York Mills.

A true loyalist, Thomas served in the War of 1812 with the Third Regiment of the Incorporated Militia of York. While fighting at Queenston Heights, he saw General Brock mortally wounded and helped carry him off the battlefield; Brock's last words were "If I die, remember Humberstone, remember Humberstone." Later, Lieutenant Humberstone was himself captured while taking a group of American prisoners from Beaver Dams near Queenston to Fort Henry near Kingston for confinement. En route one of the prisoners was able to recapture Thomas and take the prisoners across the lake to freedom.

After he returned home after the war, Thomas was given a Crown grant on the west side of Yonge Street north of York Mills. It included a thirty-by-fifty-foot house and barn, with outhouses, a good well, and an orchard of two hundred apple trees. He made flowerpots for his neighbours and experimented with various pottery shapes and colours, such as Egyptian black and cobalt blue. But it was the cobalt blue that made his pottery famous. His pottery business prospered and he was able to add a huge fireplace in the house for cooking.

The tombstone of Thomas Humberstone in the churchyard at St. John's

Then in 1822 tragedy struck. An old fowling piece or shotgun had been found in a field and was being used as a fireplace poker. A few days later, the Humberstones' fifteen-year-old daughter Elizabeth was using the firearm poker when it exploded, killing her instantly.

Thomas died on October 17, 1849, and was buried in the family plot in St. John's churchyard, his tombstone inscribed with the following verse:

> Remember friends as you pass by,
> As you are now, so once was I;
> As I am now, soon you must be,
> Prepare for death and follow me.

After Thomas Sr. died, Thomas Jr. (1811–95) took over the business, making earthenware, pitchers, flower pots, bricks, and other articles. In spite of numerous fires, he expanded the business to Thornhill, Willowdale, and Newtonbrook. Then he turned it over to his son Simon Thomas Humberstone (1846–1915), who continued in the pottery business while engaged in municipal politics, serving as reeve of York Township from 1890 until 1895.

After Simon Thomas died on March 28, 1915, his son Thomas Allan (1887–1952) inherited the property. Just before the First World War, Thomas decided to close down the business. In 1912 a motorist discovered a fire in an outhouse on the Robinson farm, three hundred feet to the south; burning fragments were carried by high winds to the Humberstone buildings, which burned up completely, leaving only the kiln standing.

After five generations the Humberstone dynasty had ended, remembered only in a few pieces of antique pottery and in a nearby street name.

CORNELIUS VAN NOSTRAND

Cornelius van Nostrand brought his family to York Mills in 1805, buying a two-hundred-acre farm that stretched from Yonge Street to Bayview Avenue, halfway between York Mills Road and Sheppard Avenue East. Cornelius was a fifth-generation descendant of Jacob Jansen van Nordstrandt, who had sailed with his family from the Netherlands in 1638 to settle in Saratoga County, New York. Things went peacefully and well for the family for many generations, until the Revolutionary War erupted in 1775. Cornelius, who is credited with changing the spelling of the family's surname, fought with the British and was promoted to colonel. Surprisingly, the family stayed in the United States for twenty years after the British were defeated. It wasn't until the late 1790s that Cornelius cast his eyes northward and applied to the Crown for a land grant in Upper Canada. He was granted five hundred acres in Markham Township in 1799 and moved his family there from their home in Oyster Bay, Long Island, in the winter of 1799–1800. In 1805 the van Nostrands moved to York Mills.

As members of the Church of England, the van Nostrand family faithfully served the little church on the hill for many generations. Cornelius was on the first building committee. Due to ill health, he was confined to bed when the building commenced. But from his bedroom window he was able to watch the cornerstone laying on September 16, 1816. He died a year later. Afterward, his son Cornelius II (1796–1878) took over the mills and built a large house — Green Gates — on what would become Old Yonge Street. He served St. John's as churchwarden and treasurer of the fund set up to build the 1843 church. John van Nostrand led the choir from 1850 until 1854. His son Arthur Jabez van Nostrand (1861–1939) served the church as envelope secretary, and oversaw many renovations and additions from his nearby home. While the van Nostrand Cloister was built in 1939, Col. A. J. was constantly watching its progress from his bedroom window, but succumbed to an illness just before it finally opened on October 27, 1939. When a new parish hall was dedicated in November 1939, a memorial plaque was unveiled by Major Frederick Harold van Nostrand (1896–1975).

The family also opened Green Gates for church events, such as picnics, teas, dinners, and fundraising events. In 1934 their land was sold to the Suydam Realty Company. A year later, Green Gates was destroyed by a fire believed to have been started by transients. The family was living at the time in the smaller "Fairview," closer to the churchyard, and Green Gates was vacant until it too was burned down in 1935.

Today the van Nostrand burial plot, on the southwest side of the churchyard, is the resting place of seven generations of the van Nostrand family.

LIEUTENANT-COLONEL DUNCAN CAMERON

Many members of the Cameron family are buried in St. John's churchyard. Lt.-Col. Duncan Cameron had fought with the Cameron Highlanders — named after relative Sir Alan Cameron — in the low countries of Europe and during the Peninsular War between Spain and Britain. Lt.-Col. Cameron also served as guard of honour in the funerals of British soldiers Lord Horatio Nelson (1758–1805) and Sir John Moore (1761–1809). During the Battle of Waterloo, when he was one of only two officers left unwounded after the Battle of Toulouse, Duncan Cameron was made a Companion of the Bath for his service. In 1820 he retired from the army. He was granted land in York Mills for his services and, on the advice of his uncles and military friends, brought his family to Upper Canada in 1835 from Lochaber, Scotland.

After he acquired the property of Richard Gamble, Duncan built a lavish twenty-eight room mansion for his family, seven servants, and the abundance of furniture they had brought with them. He called his new home Lindally, after the family home in Scotland. The square red-brick house was surrounded by a large verandah and featured small-paned windows, two wine cellars, seven fireplaces, and very large rooms. Rooms on the ground floor had eleven-foot ceilings, and two heavy doors separated the living and dining rooms. A round, black oak banister led up to the second floor. Wood for the house was cut on the property. Outside there were spacious lawns with lavish gardens and shrubbery, tended by the seven servants. On his 190-acre farm, which extended east to Bayview Avenue, Duncan grew wheat and raised sheep and cattle. As soon as they were settled, Duncan, Katherine, and their nine children attended the little church that had been built on the hill overlooking the valley. Over the years they gave much time and money to support St. John's.

During the 1837 Rebellion, as a true Loyalist, Duncan Cameron was calling the rebels "evil-disposed people who just kept busy trying to agitate and poison the minds of people against the government." So, when William Lyon Mackenzie King was leading the rebels and trying to oust the government, Lt.-Col. Cameron stood firm in his conviction. In 1838 Duncan Cameron assumed command of the newly minted North York Militia, who held their drills on the flat fields behind Anderson's Tavern on Yonge Street.

During one cold wintery night in December 1837, the rebels were marching down Yonge Street and visited the van Nostrand store opposite the Cameron house. They stole any firearms and ammunition they could find, plus one fur hat — which they returned later. Then they turned toward the Cameron house.

At Lindally one of the servants told Mackenzie that Lt.-Col. Cameron was asleep and not to be disturbed. Then, when he was awakened anyway, Duncan Cameron said he had no firearms in the house, as they had all been shipped to Montreal for a Cameron clan gathering. During the palaver, his son Archibald — who was only nineteen — set off with a coachman down Yonge Street to warn the government authorities of the oncoming attack. They were taken prisoner near Montgomery's Tavern. When Governor Francis

Bond Head heard about it, he sent a company of 93rd Highlanders north to guard Lindally. Later, the rebels were taken prisoner and Archibald and the coachman were set free.

When Lt.-Col. Duncan Cameron died in October 1842, his funeral was held at St. John's. Twelve Highlanders of the 93rd Regiment, then stationed at Fort York, served as pallbearers. The colonel was buried under flat stones in the family plot. Cameron family members continued to serve St. John's. Archibald Cameron was a churchwarden from 1849 until 1851, while mother Katherine and her daughters embroidered cushions for the kneelers at each end of the Holy Table. As active members of the Young People's Association (founded in 1913), daughters Katherine, Sarah, Margaret, Barbara, and Caroline helped with the various bazaars and teas, usually held in the Lindally gardens.

Katherine Cameron lived in the house until she died. Archibald and his son Kenneth and other family members lived there until the farm was sold to Thomas Botham in 1870. Lindally served as the clubhouse for St. Andrew's Golf Club until it was demolished in the 1960s.

LOVE AND MARRIAGE

As St. John's York Mills was the centre of the community for young and old, entire families attended services and took part in activities in church and school. In many cases children grew up to marry and settle in the York Mills area, and were buried in St. John's churchyard. Many were loyalists who had immigrated to Upper Canada after the American Revolution and were granted land in the Home District (York County). Others came after the War of 1812, while their descendants served in both World Wars.

THE VALLIERES

One of the first pioneers in York Mills was Jean Baptiste Valliere — a trained blacksmith who had come with the French Royalists to settle in Oak Ridges in 1799. A year later the Vallieres move down to York Mills and established an inn where Yonge Street crossed the West Don River. Jean Baptiste died quite young, leaving his wife Marguerite to raise six children. She carried on operating the inn until after the War of 1812, when she moved to the Nottawasaga River. There she met Asher Mundy, the keeper of the Gin Rock Lighthouse on Mundy's Bay on Georgian Bay. Marguerite married Asher and continued supplying food and drink to soldiers from Lake Ontario to Fort Penetanguishene on Lake Huron. Many of the Vallieres chose to remain in York Mills, however, and they all supported St. John's Church.

The Vallieres soon became friends with neighbour John Pennock who operated the tollgate across Yonge Street. Beside the gate, he built a house for his family and raised chickens to earn some extra money. Pennock's eggs soon became so popular that people came from the city to buy them, attend a church service, and have a meal at Valliere's Inn. Many could then return to town without paying tolls.

THE PENNOCKS

Son John Pennock and daughter Charlotte Valliere met at Vallieres' Inn and were married in St. John's Church. Many Pennocks continued to live in the area and attend St. John's Church. In 1875 builder and carpenter Joseph Pennock won the contract to build a new rectory. He was also kept busy building bridges and improving roads around York Township.

The tollgate was operated by John Pennock until 1865, when the provincial government bought the tollgates from York County, then leased them to various operators taking the profits. Tollgates were finally abolished in 1864.

THE MARSH FAMILY

In 1828 William Marsh (1790–1874), his wife Susannah, and their four children came to York Mills from Kilmington, Somerset, England, settling near the wooden St. John's Anglican Church on land owned by Thomas Johnson. The land on Yonge Street reminded William, who was a great lover of nature, of his homeland's steep wooded hills.

As well as planting more seeds and cutting down trees, William worked at St. John's, improving its churchyard and donating more land to the church. While the Marsh family were on their way to Canada, a poor man had committed suicide, leading William to give him a proper burial in Canada. William planted a black walnut tree and built a fence around the gravesite. Just south of the burial ground, William Marsh sowed a row of apple seeds, these trees affectionately known as Marsh's seedlings, and their fruit was used by a local cider mill built by William Marsh.

After Susannah died in 1836, William married her half-sister Diana Lush and built a new home on the hill, which they named Clovercot for the many four-leafed clovers on the land. Clovercot was torn down in March 1966, and the bricks were taken to Black Creek Pioneer Village.

Like her new family, Diana was active at St. John's. Daughter Elizabeth was baptised in the new church on June 16, 1849, and in appreciation, William and Diana and their heirs were given "first class" pews.

In 1839 William Marsh granted an acre of land to the church that would extend the church grounds to the brow of the hill overlooking Yonge Street. When the wardens, of whom William was one, decided to build a larger more permanent church, William gave them an eight-foot roadway at the south side of the churchyard, which veered west down the steep hill to Yonge Street. But soon this new roadway was causing problems for the church, as Marsh and van Nostrand cows were continually grazing on the pathways. In 1846 a new road, which crossed the property of Moses Willson on the north side of the church, was laid out. This road was still steep but more passable by carriages, horses, and pedestrians. The original eight-foot road was kept as a pathway down to Yonge Street.

Once again, members of the St. John's family married each other as William's daughter Susan Mary married George Harrison.

THE MCKENZIE FAMILY

One of the most active and longest-serving families of St. John's was that of Philip McKenzie, who had moved down to York Township in the late 1880s. Philip and Sarah (Thompson) had been active in St. John's Church Jefferson at Oak Ridges, until they moved south to the Cummer farm on Yonge Street at Newtonbrook. At St. John's York Mills, Philip served as rector's warden from 1883 until 1897. As a farmer, cabinet-maker, and casket maker, Philip was kept busy at the church. After he died in 1901, son John McKenzie inherited the farm that extended to Bayview Avenue, and he, too, was a warden of the church, serving from 1904 until 1920.

John married Allie (Alice) Carson in 1902, the daughter of hotelkeeper Wallace Carson. Tragically, she died only a year later and John then married neighbour Eva May Hill, the daughter of neighbour and St. John's Church member Silas Hill. Eva was active in the church, donating and arranging flowers from her garden each Sunday for services.

One of the homes that John McKenzie and his wife built in 1913 on Parkview Avenue in Willowdale is today the headquarters of the Ontario Historical Society.

All four of John's daughters were married by St. John's rector the Rev. Arthur McCollum. Florence married Frank Herbert Brown, the son of Benjamin Brown, who operated a store at Sheppard Avenue and Yonge Street for thirty years. It was sold to brothers George and Bill Dempsey and became known as Dempsey's

Hardware. In 1996 the historic building, built by Joseph Shepard II in 1860, was moved to nearby Beecroft Road in Dempsey Park and is maintained by Toronto Parks and the North York Historical Society.

Ethel married Dr. Percival Plummer, while Jean married Robert Nicholson, and Gretchen married William Ward Jr. of Ward's Funeral Home of Weston. Philip married Gladys Foote of North Toronto, also in St. John's Church.

John McKenzie's brother, George Henry McKenzie, married neighbour Jennie Dunn and operated a wood and lumber business in Willowdale. They later moved to Woodbridge.

A typical Sunday at St. John's in 1955

THE FINAL WORD

The strands of the history of St. John's York Mills are tightly woven into the history of this area of Toronto, and the stories of its families form a tapestry reflective of the building of this country. Those of us who have helped collect and tell the stories in this book hope that an understanding of the rich history of St. John's York Mills will help shape the present and future actions of the parishioners and friends of the church, and give purpose to their welcome, their worship, and their continued outreach to the diverse community that surrounds them.

PART THREE

Photo Gallery 2016

Left: *Office staff of St. John's: Clockwise from the top left, Laura Peetoom, Catherine Bryant, (administrator), Jane Turcot (bookkeeper), Daphne Flint-Polo*

Below: *Technical team: Back row (left to right): Chris Shim, Mark Anderson, Peter Raynham, Victor Likhachov, James McNeish; Middle row (left to right): Sylvia Raynham; Front row (left to right): Tim Orser, Gillian Mitchell*

Former wardens of St. John's (1): Back row (left to right): Sylvia McConnell, John Davies, Michele Mcdonald, Paul Barry, Dunbar Russel, Venetia Cowie, Cliffe Nelles, Faye Roberts, Chris Prentice; Front row (left to right) Mary Nelles, Bruce Snell, Brenda Parkes, Forest Buckingham, Marcia Brooks

Former wardens of St. John's (2): Back row (left to right): Doug Ball, Maurice Bent, Bill Barnett, Peter MacPherson, Bob Girard; Front row (left to right): Wayne McLeod, Linda Grasley, Bev McLeod, Doug Hart, Carol Seare Hanlon, Win Herington, Bev Salmon

Men's Supper Club: Back row (left to right): Hugh Crosthwait, Jeff Cuthbert, Alan Cuthbert, Paul Heersink, Dunbar Russel, Peter Raynham, Ian Bowles, David Andrew White, Randal Orser, James Parrish, Bill Barnett, Hugh Moore; Middle row (left to right): Les Monita, Peter Martin, Peter Miller, Brian Hull, Tim Taylor, Chris Prentice, Justin Grenier, Rob Ellis, John Bower, Tony Abraham, Gavin Cheung, Doug Ball; Front row (left to right): Bob McClellan, Wayne Minett, Doug Hart, Ted Williams, James McNeish, Max Dionisio, Paul Warrington, Para Sathi; Absent: the Rev. Drew MacDonald

Lychgate Group: Back row (left to right): Yvonne McGregor, Sandy Russel, Carolyn Martin, Venetia Cowie, Liz Keddie, Ellen-Jean Dewberry; Middle row (left to right): Bev McLeod, Gillian Gillespie, Karen Barnett, Elizabeth White, Linda Grasley, Sylvia Raynham; Front row (left to right): Pamela Smith (chair), Carol Barney, Penny Potter, Virginia Holmes, Gail Moore

Welcome team: Back row (left to right): Vicki Parrish, Hugh Crosthwait, Venetia Cowie, Cliffe Nelles, Pat Smith, John Yarker; Front row (left to right): Bev McLeod, Shiam Sathi, Gail Moore (leader), Mary Nelles, Sylvia McConnell, Connie Hunt Hamson, Wendy Aspinall

Choir: Back row (left to right): Bernadette Gorman, Blake Woodside, Dave Finneran, Emma Burns; Front row (left to right): Anne Curtis, Nancy Shim, Patrick Dewell (director), Marg Colman, Pat Stephenson; Absent: Diana Bucur, Jan Gardiner-Williams, Justin Grenier, Dani Loach, Jo Millar, Elizabeth White

Worship Band: Clockwise from top left, Ambrose Swanston, Carol Redstone, Patrick Dewell, Monika Burany, Rob Ellis (leader), Brian Hull, Tim Orser

Chimers: Back row (left to right): Charlotte Quinn, Carolyn Martin (program director), Catherine Orser (helper); Middle row (left to right): Nicolas Martino, Amber-Lynn Burke, Alex Quinn, Zack MacDonald, Quincy Charles, Janet Benedict (leader); Front row (left to right): Trent Benedict, Abby Oliver, Merek Benedict, Alicia Goodman

Rockin' Ringers: Back row (left to right): Stephanie Brander (helper), Carolyn Martin (director), Carolyn Parkes (helper); Middle row (left to right): Zack Goodman, Annie Likhachova, Briar Benedict, Thomas MacDonald, Grace Oliver, Daniel Mitchell, Charlotte Polo; Front row (left to right): Maya Charles, Sean Martin, Charlotte Bent, Hudson Bent

Brass ringers: Back row (left to right): John McNeish, Nagaty Banayoty, Carolyn Parkes, Kevin Maksym; Middle row (left to right): Catherine Orser, Maryanne McNeish, Monica Banayoty, Daniel Mitchell, Kathryn Maksym; Front row (left to right): Janet Benedict, Carolyn Martin (director), Stephanie Brander

Ingram Ringers: Back row (left to right): Pat Burford, Susan Mole, DJ Downie, Susan Johnson, Diana Kennedy; Middle row (left to right): Millie Raulfs, Lian Omar, Tracy Lewis, Yvonne Gettins, Stephanie Brander, Victoria Panos; Front row (left to right): Ginny McMullen, Carolyn Martin (director), Elizabeth White; Absent: Jo Millar

APPENDIX

WARDENS 1960–2016: CHURCHWARDENS

1960–1969

H.C. Crowder
J.A.M. Belshaw
H.P. Herrington
John D. Frewer
Allan C. Tully

Edmund C. Bovey
Charles W. Fenton
William J. Hemmerick
Alexander E. Curry
James E. MacNelly

1970–1979

Alexander E. Curry
James E. MacNelly
A. Edgar Wadham
F. Donald Rosebrugh
Norman W. Bethune
L. William Lake

Peter C. MacPherson
William F. Saynor
Albert M. Fischer
William C. Coles
Douglas F.S. Coate
J. Donald Cambridge

1980–1989

Douglas F.S. Coate

J. Donald Cambridge

William H. Adams

R.J. Anderson

Paul O. Barry

Ronald W. Chisholm

Forest M. Buckingham

Cliffe Nelles

Winifred Herington

H. Dunbar Russel

Robert D. Finlayson

William Michael Ogden

1990–1999

Robert D. Finlayson

William Michael Ogden

William E. Barnett

William F. Saynor

Douglas F. Ball

Linda Grasley

Wayne McLeod

Beverly Lewis

Peter F.M. Jones

Bruce Snell

Carol Seare

Christopher A. Millar

2000–2011

Christopher A. Millar

Mary Pember

Mary Nelles

Randy Smith

Eleanor Pask

Douglas Hart

Robert Girard

Marsha Brooks

Christopher Prentice

Stephen Bent

John Davies

Michele Mcdonald

Beverly Salmon

Beverly McLeod

Peter Singer

Dunbar Russel

Venetia Cowie

Brenda Parkes

2012-2016

John Bruce	Yau Man Siew
Blake Woodside	James Parrish
Steve Bickley	Max Dionisio
Faye Roberts	Hugh Moore
Sylvia McConnell	Suzanne Sutherland
Maurice Bent	Tony Martino

ASSISTANTS IN MINISTRY THROUGH THE DECADES

In the 1960s

Ron Davidson	Ken Maxted
Brian Gamble	Bob Leckey

In the 1970s

Archdeacon Terence Crosthwait	David Mulholland
David Flint	Bria Pearson
Tim Foley	Margery Pezzack
Bruce Fraser	Glenn Simm
David Luck	Tom Traynor
Lawrence McErlean	

In the 1980s

David Flint	Dr. Bruce Williams
Margery Pezzack	Sally Armour-Wotton
Bruce Fraser	Catherine Bryant
Phelan Scanlon	

In the 1990s

Mark Genge	Shirley Coles
Margery Pezzack	Kathy Waugh
Bruce Fraser	Frank Lee
Mathias Der	Carol Langley
Bruce Williams	Jack Adams

In the 2000s and 2010s

Patrick White	Simon Chambers
Mary Lewis	Sally Armour-Wotton
Pat Blythe	Carolyn Martin
Shirley Coles	Boni Strang
Bruce Williams	Stephen Monk
Catherine Keating	Monique Ingalls
Anne Crosthwait	Chantal Sathi

ORGANISTS AND CHOIRMASTERS THROUGH THE YEARS

1844–1850:	Daniel Grigg (Gregg) Hewitt
1850–1871:	John van Nostrand Jr.
1854:	Thomas Nightingale
1856:	William Henry
1856–1861:	James and Margaret Toulmin
1861–1864:	Jane van Nostrand, daughter of John van Nostrand
1861–1864:	Jane Finch
1864–1867:	Mary Ann Wilkinson
1867–1873:	John Morley

1870–1919:	Blanche Squire, daughter of John Squire
1887–1905:	Emma Osler, daughter of Canon Henry Bath Osler
1905:	Mrs. Eva Heslop
1905–1912:	May Wiltshire
1908:	Violet Hall
1909–1912 :	Mrs. Young
1917–1922:	Isabel Ashcroft, daughter of Rev. Richard Ashcroft
1922–1928:	Sybil Pawley
1928:	Cleland Holley
1928–1933:	C. Strickland Thompson
1930–1963:	Whitney Cameron, retired December 22, 1963
1963–2001:	Maurice White
2001–2011:	Robin Davis
2011–present:	Patrick Dewell

(Overlapping dates are most likely due to the fact the positions of organist and choirmaster were sometimes held by two different people. Gaps may indicate the temporary absence of official directors or mistakes in record keeping.)

SOME HYMNS IN THE BARREL ORGAN

Barrel One
Manchester
Creation
London New
Old Hundred
Peckham
Morning Hymn

Hark the Herald
Saint Anne's
Helmsley
Sheldon
Advent Hymn
Oxford

Barrel Two
Martins Lace
Evening Hymn
Devises
Luther's Hymn
Abingdon
Carey's
Abridge
Burford
Irish

BIBLIOGRAPHIES

BIBLIOGRAPHY FOR PART ONE

Articles, Booklets, Handouts, Newsletters

The Link, SJYM newsletter; Winter 2014–15, Spring 2015, Fall 2015, Winter 2015–16.

Our Life in the Parish (A History) Toronto. Compiled by Daphne M. Dittman, 1991.

Books

Adamson, Anthony, and Marion MacCrae. *Hallowed Walls: Church Architecture in Upper Canada.* Toronto: Clarke Irwin and Co. Ltd., 1975.

Christie, Norm. *For King & Empire: The Canadians at Vimy, April 1917.* Ottawa: CEF Books, 2002.

Graham, M. Audrey. *150 Years at St. John's, York Mills.* Toronto: General Publishing Co. Ltd., 1966.

Hart, Patricia W. *Pioneering in North York : A History of the Borough.* Toronto: General Publishing Co. Ltd., 1968.

Hayes, Geoffrey, Andrew Iarocci, and Mike Bechthold, eds. *Vimy Ridge: A Canadian Reassessment.* Waterloo, ON: Laurier Centre for Military Strategic and Disarmament Studies and Wilfrid Laurier University Press, 2007.

Kennedy, Scott. *Willowdale: Yesterday's Farms, Today's Legacy.* Toronto: Dundurn Press, 2013.

McConnell, Sylvia, ed. *Renewal 2014 Commemorative Book.* Toronto: St. John's York Mills, 2014.

Newspapers

Black, Debra. "Old Soldier recalls past glory," *Toronto Star,* April 1, 2005.

Byers, Mary, and Maynard McBurney. "Group of Seven Convened in the Parlour," *Globe and Mail,* December 13, 1984.

"Grand Old Sexton Tolls Last Bell," *Toronto Telegram*, January 26, 1931.

Polanyi, John, and Sue Polanyi. "Lives Lived," *Globe and Mail,* January 8, 1997.

Will, Joanne. "Churches and the parking lot collection plate," *Globe and Mail,* March 5, 2015.

BIBLIOGRAPHY FOR PART TWO

Books

Adam, G. Mercer. *Toronto Old and New: A Memorial Volume.* Toronto: Coles, 1972.

Andre, John. *Infant Toronto as Simcoe's Folly.* Toronto: Centennial Press, 1971.

Arthur, Eric. *Toronto: No Mean City.* Toronto: University of Toronto Press, 1964.

Bull, William Perkins. *From Strachan to Owen.* Toronto: Perkins Bull Foundation, 1938.

Commemorative Biographical Record of the County of York Ontario. Toronto: J.H. Beers & Co., 1907.

Eglinton-Pears Park Walk. Toronto: North Toronto Historical Society, 1980.

Fahey, Curtis. *In His Name: The Anglican Experience in Upper Canada 1791–1854.* Ottawa: Carleton University Press, 1991.

Filey, Mike. *Mount Pleasant Cemetery: An Illustrated Guide.* Toronto: Firefly Books, 1990.

Firth, Edith G. *The Town of York, A Collection of Documents of Early Toronto, 1793–1815.* Toronto: The Champlain Society for the Government of Ontario, University of Toronto Press, 1962.

Fitzgerald, Doris M. *Thornhill 1793–1863: The History of an Ontario Village.* Thornhill, ON, 1964.

Flynn, Kevin. *The Stained Glass Windows of St. John's Anglican Church, York Mills, 1816–1976.* Toronto: St. John's Church, 1976.

Friendly Church on the Hill: St. John's Church, York Mills. Toronto: Sampson-Matthews Ltd., 1938.

Graham, M. Audrey. *150 Years at St. John's, York Mills.* Toronto: General Publishing, 1966.

———. *Historic St. John's York Mills, 1826–1843.* Toronto: Audrey Graham, 1943.

Guillet, Edwin C. *Pioneer Life in the County of York.* Toronto: Hess-Trade Typesetting Company, 1946.

Guthrie, Ann E. *Don Valley Legacy: A Pioneer History.* Erin, ON: Boston Mills Press, 1986.

Hart, Patricia. *Pioneering in North York: A History of the Borough.* Toronto: General Publishing, 1968.

Hathaway, E. J. *Jesse Ketchum and His Times.* Toronto: McClelland & Stewart, 1929.

Hayes, Derek. *Historical Atlas of Toronto.* Vancouver: Douglas & McIntyre, 2009.

Henderson, J.H. *John Strachan, 1778–1867.* Toronto: University of Toronto Press, 1969.

History of Toronto and County of York, Ontario. Toronto: C. Blackett Robinson, 1885.

Hopkins, Jeanne. *The Henry Farm, Oriole: An Early Settlement of North York.* Willowdale, ON: Henry Farm Community Interest Association, 1987.

———. *Jackson's Point: Ontario's First Cottage Country*. Erin, ON: Boston Mills Press, 1993.

———. *St. George's Anglican Church and Cemetery*. North York, ON: Jeanne Hopkins, 1990.

———. *York Mills Heights: Looking Back*. York Mills, ON: York Mills Heights Association, 1998.

MacIntosh, Robert M. *Earliest Toronto*. Renfrew, ON: General Store Publishing, 2006.

Myers, Jay. *Remember When: A Collection of Articles About the History of North York, 1976–1979*. Don Mills, ON: Don Mills Mirror, 1979.

Pearson, William H. *Recollections and Records*. Toronto: W. Briggs, 1914.

Ritchie, Delores. *St. John's Church, York Mills: A Brief Narrative and Tour Guide*. Rev. ed. North York, ON: Heritage Group, 1984.

Ritchie, Don. *North Toronto*. Toronto: Stoddart, 1992.

Robertson, John Ross. *Robertson's Landmarks of Toronto*. Belleville, ON: Mika, 1974.

Saywell, John T. *Canada Past and Present*, Rev. ed. Toronto: Clarke Irwin, 1981.

Scadding, Henry. *Toronto of Old*. Toronto: University of Toronto, Press, 1966.

Smith, William Lee. *The Pioneers of Old Ontario*. Toronto: George N. Morang, 1923.

Somerville, Patricia, and Catherine MacFarlane, eds. *A History of Vaughan Township Churches*. Maple, ON: Vaughan Township Historical Society, 1984.

St. John's Anglican Church Cemetery (York Mills), North York, Ontario. Toronto: Ontario Genealogical Society, 1997.

Newspapers

Globe and Mail, 1844–2014.

Hilliard, Harold. *Toronto Star*, 1981–1987.

Hopkins, Jeanne. "Looking Back." *Bayview Post*, 1989–2005.

Hopkins, Jeanne. "Looking Back." *North Toronto Post*, 1991–2005.

Hopkins, Jeanne. "Looking Back." *Thornhill Post*, 1990–1995.

Toronto Star, Pages of the Past, 1894–2014.

PHOTO CREDITS

The photos in this book were supplied for the most part by the parishioners or clergy of St. John's York Mills and from the St. John's Archives (SJYM Archives). Many photos are not attributed. The majority of parishioners' photos were supplied by Martin Block, Paul Heersink, Brian Hull, and Sylvia McConnell. Photos in the concluding Photo Gallery were taken by IPC Canada Photo Service Inc. If you know the provenance of any historical photos not credited, we would appreciate your letting the editor know.

OTHER PHOTOS

Page 13	Bishop's Office, Diocese of Toronto.
Page 17	IPC Canada Photo Service Inc.
Page 30	SJYM Archives, PH029.
Page 31	SJYM Archives.
Page 33	Left: SJYM Archives, PHO68.4.
	Right: SJYM Archives, AL02.1.
Page 35	SJYM Archives PHO592.1a.
Page 36	SJYM Archives.
Page 37	SJYM Archives.
Page 40	Left: SJYM Archives, PH1037.8.
	Right: SJYM Archives, PH1053.4.
Page 41	SJYM Archives, 1051.5.
Page 42	SJYM Archives.
Page 43	SJYM Archives, PH035.22.
Page 45	SJYM Archives, PH541.2.
Page 47	SJYM Archives, PH1026.6.
Page 51	SJYM Archives, PH052.2K.
Page 52 and 53	SJYM Archives, PH1029.5, PH1029.12, PH1029.18.

Page 60   SJYM Archives, PH502.1q.

Page 61   SJYM Archives, PH502.2.

Page 64   SJYM Archives, PH1001.3.

Page 66 and 67 SJYM Archives.

Page 82   SJYM Archives, PH1001.1 and PH1003.

Page 104   SJYM Archives, PH052.4.

Page 105   SJYM Archives, PH052.1.

Page 112   SJYM Archives, PH1029.15.

Page 114   Left: SJYM Archives, AL02.2.

            Right: SJYM Archives.

Page 143   IPC Canada Photo Service Inc.

Page 146   Left: IPC Canada Photo Service Inc.

Page 156   SJYM Archives, PH1047.4.

Page 160   IPC Canada Photo Service Inc.

Page 184   Infinitely More by Linda van der Beek.

Page 191   Rob Ellis by Monika Burany.

Page 209   Top left: SJYM Archives, PH1010.

            Top right: SJYM Archives, PH1025.

            Bottom: SJYM Archives, PH1034.

Page 213   Left: SJYM Archives, PH1018.6.

Page 214   Left: SJYM Archives, 1011.1.

            Right: Lychgate Group Archives.

Page 215   All photos: Lychgate Group Archives.

Pages 216–26 Chapter Eight: all photos of the Vimy Ridge Memorial by the Reverend Drew MacDonald.

Page 231   Photo by Ted Chirnside, 1955, Toronto Public Library TC77A.

Page 234   Supplied by Infinitely More.

Page 237   Left: SJYM Archives, PH021.

            Right: SJYM Archives, PH068.4.

Page 240   IPC Canada Photo Service Inc.

Page 255   IPC Canada Photo Service Inc.

Page 262   Archives of Ontario Ref.#S-17267.

Page 263   Left: North York Historical Society.

Page 267   SJYM Archives, PH508.

Page 269   Right: SJYM Archives, PH542.

Page 270 — Toronto Public Library JRR3579.

Page 273 — Left: Toronto Public Library, E4-33T, T10765.

Page 274 — SJYM Archives, PH021.

Page 276 — North York Archives, 1998-001 Goodwin Family Fonds, circa 1908.

Page 277 — Left: SJYM Archives, PH051.

Right: Toronto Public Library JRR3581.

Page 279 — Bottom: Toronto Public Library S1-3656A.

Page 280 — Top left: SJYM Archives.

Bottom left: SJYM Archives.

Page 281 — Bottom left: SJYM Archives.

Page 288 — SJYM Archives PH1026.1.

Page 292 — Collection of the Art Gallery of Ontario, Estate of C.W. Jefferys.

Page 298 — City of Toronto Archives, SC244-7128.

Page 299 — Photo by Ted Chirnside, 1955, Toronto Public Library, TC 20B.

Page 300 — Photo by Ted Chirnside, 1956, Toronto Public Library, TC 121.

Page 303 — Photo supplied by Jeanne Hopkins.

Page 308 — Photo supplied by Jeanne Hopkins collection.

Page 316 — SJYM Archives, Ashely & Crippen.

Page 318 — Toronto Public Library S 1-3643B.

INDEX

Page numbers in *italics* mark the locations of photographs.

A

Abraham, Tony, *322*
Adam, Judith, 47
Adams, Jean, 290
Advisory Council, 89
Albert Edward, Prince, 287, 288
Albino, Laura, 177
Aldershot Crescent, 300
Alison, Adrienne, *292*, 293
Allward, Hugh, 224–25, 291
Allward, Walter Seymour, 216–19, 220,
    223, *224*, 225, *226*, 291
Allward family, *226*
Alpha program, 126
Anderson, Mark, *166*, 167, 240, *249*, *283*,
    320
Anderson, Norma, *160*
angel window niches, *246*
Anglican Conference Center, *65*
Anglican Life, 73
Anglican traditions, 124, 127–28, 206–07
Anne, Princess, 46, *47*, *288*

Archbold, George, 270 71
Armour, James, 230
Arsenault, Judy, *215*
Arthur C. McCollum Wing, 32, *237*
Ashcroft, Richard, 28, 42–43
Aspinall, Wendy, *146*, *323*
Aurora weekends, 65–66, *67*

B

Bailey, Isabelle, 48–49
Bakker, Michael, *196*
Ball, Carol, *142*
Ball, Doug, *321*, *322*
Banayoty, Monica, *326*
Banayoty, Nagaty, *326*
banners, 64, 84
baptismal font, 48–49, 156, *167*
Barber, Patti, *196*
Barley, Catherine, 63
Barnabas ministry, 153, 156, 158–59, *160*,
    253
Barnett, Bill, *142*, *321*, *322*

Barnett, Karen, *215, 322*
Barnett, William, 73
Barney, Carol, *215, 322*
Barney, Sharon, *215*, 240
Barney, Vern, *213*
Barry, Paul, *321*
Bartlett, Thomas H. M., 28
Bawden, Anne, 50, *213*
Bawden, David, 88
Beck, Adam, 148
Bedford-Jones, Michael, 92, 99
Benedict, Briar, *325*
Benedict, Damien, *252*, 253, *256, 283*
Benedict, Janet, *325, 326*
Benedict, Merek, *325*
Benedict, Trent, *325*
Bent, Charlotte, *325*
Bent, Hudson, *325*
Bent, Maurice, *31*, 137, 239, *240, 321*
Bent, Pat, *31*
Bent, Stephen, 106
Bethune, Archdeacon, 129
bibles, *271*
Bickley, Robin, *170*
Bickley, Steve, 130, 135, 239
Blackwell, Douglas, 117
Block, Martin, *53, 256*
Blyth, Pat, 63
bottle drives, *209*
Boultbee, Elizabeth M., 147
Boultbee family, 285, 287
Bovey, Edmund, 236
Bower, John, *322*

Bowles, Ian, *256, 322*
Boyd, Doug, 166
Brander, Stephanie, *325, 326*
Brandon, Laura, 220
Brass Ringers, 197, *198*, 201, *326*
Break Forth, 182
Brooks, Marcia, *321*
Brophy, Margaret, *209*
Brown, Arthur, 73, 74, 75, 81
Brown, George, 275
Bruce, John, 135, *136, 170*, 239
Bryant, Catherine, 55, *67, 116*, 137, 239, *240, 320*
Buck, Derek, 236
Buckingham, Cheryl, 199
Buckingham, Forest, *321*
"Building For The Future" campaign, *90*, 91–92
building SJYM, 274–75
Buranyi, Monika, *193, 324*
Burford, Jay, 66, *211, 225*
Burford, Pat, *326*
Burgess, Olga, 170
burial plots, 92–93, *113*, 153, 165, *224, 226*, 232, 259–60, 282, *303*, 304, 306–07, *308*, 310
Burke, Amber-Lynn, *325*
Burns, Emma, 205–06, *324*
Burr, Rowland, 229, *231*
Burton, Anthony, 152
Butler, Alice, 84
Butler, William, 84

C
Cambridge, Don, 46
Cambridge, Martha, 46
Cambridge Cremation Plot, 46
Cameron, Archibald, 312
Cameron, Duncan, 310–12
Cameron, Katherine, 279, 312
Canadian Federation of Independent
    Business (CFIB), 54, 134
Carrington, Russ, *160*
Catto, Marion, 286
Centre for Excellence in Christian
    Education (CECE), 158
Chambers, Simon, *87*, 96–97
Charles, Maya, *325*
Charles, Quincy, *325*
Cherry, Warren, *198*
Cheung, Gavin, *322*
children's chapel, 97
children's programming, 65–66, 68, *94*,
    96–98, 97, 145, 146, 158
chimes group, 187–88, 194–95, *204*, *325*
choirs, 205, *324*
Christie, Joseph, 276
church bell, 275
church income, 82, *169*
Church of England, historical overview,
    266–67
church organs, 168, *190*, 207, 210, *280*,
    332
churchyard, *164*, 165
Churchyard Sustaining Fund, 50, 195
Colborne, Elizabeth, 271

Colborne, John, 271
Coles, Bill, 51, 62
Coles, Shirley, 61, 63
Collins, Henry, 280
Colman, Marg, *324*
Comer, Constance Louise (Connie), 233,
    235, 242
Comer House, 233, *234*, 235
commemorative plaques, *82*, 83, 156, *211*,
    226, 282, 293, 310
Communications Board of the Diocese of
    Toronto, 88
Compass Groups, 126, *144*, 145, 253–54,
    255
Contemplative Fire, *143*
Cook, Sam, 43
cornerstones, *33*, 83, *237*, 255, 270, 278,
    279
Costinak, Derwyn, *182*
Coulman, John, 68
Cowie, Jennifer, *215*
Cowie, Venetia, *146*, *170*, *215*, *321*, *322*,
    323
Cox, E.B., 49, 291, 294–95, *296*
Crosthwait, Anne, 63, *132*, 139–40, *143*,
    144, *145*, 146, 147, *182*, *243*, *251*, *256*
Crosthwait, Hugh, 143, 145, *146*, *322*, *323*
culture, 16, 25–26, *25–27*, 51–52, 126, 169
Cummer, Jacob, 265–66
Cunningham, Margaret, *160*
Curtis, Anne, *144*, *215*, *324*
Cuthbert, Alan, *322*
Cuthbert, Jeff, *322*

C.W. Jefferys House, 227, *228*, 229–30, *231*, 290–91, 293

D
Danville Drive, 300
Davidson, Ronald, 83
Davies, John, *321*
Davis, Marshall, 236
Davis, Robin, 87, 116, *176*, *177*, 178, 201, 204
Davis, Ruth, *114*
Davis, Sally, 116
deacons
    defined, 154
    See also individual deacons
declining numbers, 52, 73, 80, 117, 125, 150, 162, 211
    See also parish lists
Denney, Gwen, *97*, *178*
Dennis, Bill, *85*, 137, *142*, *162*, 163–64, *165*, *166*, *167*, 168–69, *170*, 172, *173*, 239, *243*
Der, Matthias, 76–77
Dewberry, Bill, *213*
Dewberry, Ellen-Jean, *215*, *322*
Dewell, Patrick, 178, *182*, *184*, 185–87, *188*, *189*, 204–06, 206, 242–44, *249*, *324*
Dionisio, Max, *256*, *322*
Dixie, Ann, *146*
Dobias, Carolyn, 122, *123*, *130*, 137, 239, 240
Downie, D.J., *326*

drama productions, *85*, 101, *114*, *115*, *116*, 158, 177, 179
drama programs, 95, 113, *114*

E
Easter, *143*
Eckert, Elizabeth, 66
Ellis, Rob, 188–90, *191*, *192*, *193*, 194, 204–05, *322*, *324*
Englebright, Bill, 44
Evans, Kenneth, 149

F
Family Compact church, 127–28, 267
Fee, Alexander, 230, 291
Fee, Elizabeth, 230, 231–32, 290–91, 292
Festival Handbells Choir, 195, *196*, 197
Finlay, Terence, 83
Finlayson, Robert, 55, 73, 75 , 76
Finneran, Dave, *192*, 205–06, *324*
fire, 271–72
First World War, 110, 138, *139*, 216–17, 219–20, 221, 298–99
Fisher, Albert, 51
flax festivals, 286–87
Flemming, Gerald, *127*, 180–81, *182*, 183, *184*, *234*
Flint, David, *55*, *65*, 68, 83, 115
Flint, Joanne, 66, *195*, 205
Flint, Sarah, 195, *196*, 199
Flint-Polo, Daphne, *320*
Flynn, Barbara Alice, 84
Flynn, Kevin, 48

footpaths, 132, *133*, 134, *273*

Fraser, Bruce, 55

Fraser, Corrie, 73

Fraser, Heather, 195, *196*

Frewer, John, 83, 84

Frewer, Joyce, 84

fundraising, 89–92, 130, *178*, 210, *213*, *215*, 282

Furlong, Lianne, *198*

Fussell, Andrew, 166

G

Gage, William, 248

Gale, G.A., 52

Galilee, Dorothy, 195

Garnsworthy, Lewis S., 15, 28, *30*, *31*, 32–34, *35*, 36, 38–39, 42, *43*, 44, 62, 106, *237*

Garnsworthy Room, 14, 237, 245, *246*, *255*

Genge, Mark, 76–77, 234

George, Prince, 288

Gettins, Yvonne, *326*

Gillespie, Gillian, *215*, *322*

Girard, Bob, 137, 239, *321*

Goodman, Alicia, *325*

Goodman, Zack, *325*

Goodwin House, 229–30

Gordon, Andy, 68

Gordon, Craig, 195, *196*

Gore, Francis, 255, 270

Gorman, Bernadette, *324*

Graham, Audrey, (*150 Years at St. John's, York*

Mills), 15–16, 211, 230, 232, 259, 292

Grasley, Linda, *52*, 73, *165*, *215*, *321*, *322*

Grasley, Michael, 195, *196*

Gravely, Steven, 68

Graydon, Ruth Orr, 114

Grenier, Justin, *322*

Griffith, Irene, 248

Griffith, William M., 248

H

Hahn, Emanuel, 291

Hamson, Connie Hunt, 122, *116*, *215*, *323*

handbell choirs, 50, 52, 88, *93*, 95, 177, 187–88, 194–95, *196*, 197, *198*, 200–05, *325*, *326*

   See also Brass Ringers; chimes group; Ingram Ringers; Rockin' Ringers

Hanlon, Carol S., *321*

Hansen, Dean, 244

Harrington, Aleksandra, *160*

Harrison, Christopher, 306–07

Harrison, Elizabeth, *269*, 279

Harrison, Joshua, 306–07

Harrison, William, *269*, 306

Hart, Doug, *321*, *322*

Heersink, Paul, *244*, 245, *256*, *322*

Helbig, Avril, 199

Helen and Hollis Initiative Fund, 101

Henderson, Donald S., 56, 76

Hendrick, Alison, *115*

Herington, Winifred, 73, *75*, 78, *321*

Heron, Samuel, 262, 278, 305

Hewitt, Daniel G., 276

Hills, William, 38, 58
Hiltz, Fred, 120
Hiscock, Allison L., 85, *87*, 101
Hiscock, Helen, 74–75, *76*, 84, *97*, *99*
Hiscock, Hollis, 28, 63, *64*, *69*, 70–75, *76*,
    77–81, *82*, *85*, *88*, 91–96, *97*, *98*, *99*,
    100–03, *105*, 106, 157, *214*
Hodge, Thomas P., 28, 104
Hogg, James, 262–63
Hogg's Hollow, 53, 86, 132, 227–28, 229,
    262, *299*, *300*
Holley, Mrs. S. Cleland (May), 287
Holmes, Virginia, *322*
Howard, John G., 128–29, 272, 275
Hull, Brian, *192*, *214*, *322*, *324*
Hull, Jennifer, *256*
Humberstone, Thomas, 307, *308*, 309
Hunt, Heidi, 195, *196*, 199

I
Infinitely More, *127*, 181, *182*, 183, *184*,
    234
Ingalls, Monique, *180*, 181, 204
Ingram, Shirley, 50, 194–95, 205
Ingram Ringers, 50, 194–95, 197, 201, *326*

J
Jefferys, Charles. W., 230, 289–90, *291*, 292
Jefferys, Elizabeth, 290–91
Jefferys, Jeanette, 290
Johnson, Colin, *247*, 255
Johnson, Susan, *326*
Jones, Sheila, *198*

Jukes, Matthew, *198*

K
Kaye, William R., 134
Kayes, Helen, 170, 273
Keating, Catherine, 100, *157*, *158*, *159*,
    160, *251*, *256*
Keating, John, 160
Keddie, Liz, *160*, *215*, *322*
Kennedy, Diana, 202, *326*
Ketchum, Jesse, 172, 302
Ketchum, Seneca, 255, *269*, 301–03
Kjollesdal, Heidi, 195, *196*, 198–99

L
Laing, Krena, 48
land agreements, 53–54, 132–36, 242
Lang, Joanne, *160*
Langley, Carol, 63, *87*
Langtry, John, 28
Lastman, Mel, *82*, 83, 134–35
Lawson, Mrs. Ray, *209*
lay parishioners, 79, 88
Lee, Doug, *160*
Lee, Frank, 234
Lee, Jennifer, *198*
Lee, Olivia, 84, 86, *160*
Leeder, Mary A., *281*
Lewis, Beverly J., 84
Lewis, Donald M., 151–52
Lewis, Mary, 63
Lewis, Tracy, *326*
Likhachov, Tanya, *146*

Likhachov, Victor, *320*

Likhachova, Annie, *325*

Lindally, 278, *279*, 300, 311

Lister, Scott, *64*

Little Trinity, 149

Lord Seaton Rd., 299–300

Lower Links Rd., 300

Lowry, Donovan, 233

Lychgate Group, 208, *211*, 212, *213*, *214*, *215*, 254, *322*

Lynn, Allison, *127*, 180–81, *182*, 183, *184*, *234*

M

Macaulay, Allan, 28, 270–71

McAuliffe, Shawna, *198*

MacCallum, Beth, 38

McClellan, Bob, *322*

McCollum, Arthur C., 28, 30, *33*, 42–43, 106, 210, 230, 280

McCollum, Olive, *114*

McConnell, Sylvia, 18–19, 137, *146*, *215*, 239–40, 244, *321*, *323*

MacDonald, Drew, 14–16, 28, *56*, 108, *117*, 118–22, *123*, 124–29, *130*, 131, *132*, *137*, 141, *142*, *182*, 217, 224, *225*, 239, *251*, 252, *256*

Mcdonald, Michele, *252*, *321*

MacDonald, Thomas, *325*

MacDonald, Zack, *325*

McDougald, Bud, 47

McDougald, Maude, 47

McDougall, Josephine, *160*

McFarlane, Al, 62

McGill, Ann, 267

McGlashan, Andrew III, 229, 230

McGregor, Yvonne, *160*, *215*, 240, *322*

McGuigan, James, 300

McKenzie family, 315–17

McLeod, Bev, 102, *146*, *160*, *321*, *322*, *323*

McLeod, Wayne, *321*

McMullen, Ginny, *326*

McNeish, James, *182*, *320*, *322*

McNeish, John, *326*

McNeish, Maryanne, *326*

MacPherson, Peter, 60, *321*

Maksym, Kathryn, *326*

Maksym, Kevin, *326*

Marsh, Dinah, 273

Marsh, William, 104, 134, 172–73, 229, 273, 314–15

Marsh family, 314–15

Martin, Carolyn, 66, *67*, 87, *179*, 187–88, 194–95, *199*, *200*, 203, *204*, 205, *249*, *322*, *325*, *326*

Martin, Daniel, 203

Martin, Pamela, *198*, 200

Martin, Peter, 203, *284*, *322*

Martin, Sean, *200*, *325*

Martino, Nicolas, *325*

Martino, Tony, *256*

Mason, Peter, 120

Mathews, Charles S., 28, *267*

Matthews, Victoria, 234

Men's Supper Club, 146, 214, 254, *255*, *322*

Mercer, Ann, 279

Mercer, Thomas, 283, 305

Merrall, Greg, 166

Methodist Church, 265–66

Miller, Peter, *159*, *322*

Minett, Wayne, *322*

ministry, 13–14, 131–32, 158–59

Mitchele, Richard, 28

Mitchell, Daniel, *325*, *326*

Mitchell, Gillian, *146*, *320*

Mole, Susan, *326*

Monita, Les, *322*

Monk, Stephen, *116*

Moore, Gail, *146*, *215*, *322*, *323*

Moore, Hugh, *256*, *322*

Moore, Peter, *198*

Moss, Tay, 158

Music On The Hill, 86

music programs, 174, 180–81, 185, 186, 188–90, 192, 206
   See also handbell choirs; *individual music directors*

MusicFest, 87, 183, 201–02, 203, *204*

N

Nee, Jess, *182*

Nelles, Cliffe, *144*, *146*, *321*, *323*

Nelles, Daniel, *198*

Nelles, Mary, 91, *144*, *146*, *321*, *323*

Neville, Helen, 101

newsletters, 43, 153, 158, 165

North York Historical Society, 231–32, 292

North York Red Cross, 285–87

O

Oakley Place, 300

Obata, Sue, 56, 246

Ogden, Evie, 50

Ogden, Michael, 55, 73, 76

Okwuosa, Ify, *160*

Old Rectory, 50, *51*, 103–04, *105*, 106, *107*, 108, *109*, 122, *301*

Olde Lantern Café, 213, *214*

Oliver, Abby, *325*

Oliver, Fiona, *198*

Oliver, Grace, *325*

Oliver, Peter, *213*

Omar, Lian, *326*

150 Years at St. John's, York Mills (Audrey Graham), 15, 17, 211, 230, 259

150th Anniversary, 32–33, 174, 236

160th Anniversary, 48, 212

175th anniversary, *64*, *82*, 83–84, 94

O'Neil, James F., 28, 34, *37*, 38–39, *40*, *41*, *42*, *43*, 44, *45*, 46, *47*, 48–50, 52, 54, *55*, *56*, 57–59, 83, 95, 106, *112*, 233, *288*

O'Neil, Jean, 38–40, *42*, 51

O'Neil Choir, 198

Ontario Guild Handbell Festival, 203

Ontario Heritage Act, 108–09, 232

ordinations, 34, *35*, 36, 38, 52, 60, 62–63, 69–70, 157, *160*, 253, *254*

Orser, Catherine, *325*, *326*

Orser, Charlotte, 202

Orser, Randal, *322*

Orser, Tim, 202, *320*, *324*

Osler, Henry B., 28, 104, 230, 305
Osler, Henry B., Mrs, 285
Otter, David, *198*
"Our Faith-Our Hope" campaign, 130, 242, 244
outreach programs, 84–85, 87–88, 95–96, 252–53

P
Packer, James, *150*
Palm, Doug, 195, *196*
Palm, William, 73, *75*
Pankhurst, D., Mrs, *32*
Panos, Victoria, *326*
Papst, Elizabeth, 276
Papst, Henry G., 275, 276
parish lists, 43–44, 52, 73, 80–81, 90, 94, 125–26, 237–38
Parker, David, *238*, 239
Parkes, Brenda, 202, *321*
Parkes, Carolyn, *325, 326*
parking lots, 171
Parr, Steve, *182*
Parrish, James, *256, 322*
Parrish, Vicki, *146, 323*
Passiontide and Gospel Concerts, 87
Passport to Easter, 86
Patterson, Grace, 91
Pease, Edward, 276
Peers, Michael, *64*
Peetoom, Laura, 205–06, *320*
Pennock family, 313–14
Peters, Arthur, 121

Peters, Ernie, 163
Pezzack, Margery, 34, *35*, 36, 50, 52, 55, *60, 61*, 62–63, *64*, 76, 92, 153
Phillips, Mark, 46
picnics, *40, 101, 209*, 282, *283, 284*, 285
Pierce, Edith, 287
Pierce, Fred, 38–39
Pierce, Lorne, 291
Plain Talk, 31
Polo, Charlotte, *325*
Poole, Philip, 68
Potter, Penny, 50, *52*, 61, 153, *322*
Prentice, Bill, 88
Prentice, Chris, 106, *321, 322*

Q
Que and Pew, 87, *87, 156, 179*, 180
Quinn, Alex, *325*
Quinn, Charlotte, *325*

R
"Ramble in a Country Churchyard," 212
Raulfs, Millie, *326*
Raynham, Peter, *244, 256, 281, 320, 322*
Raynham, Sylvia, *160, 215, 244, 320, 322*
Redstone, Carol, *192, 324*
refugees, 159, 233, 252
Renewal 2014 Commemorative Book, 153, *244*
renovations, 48–49, 92, 106, 129–30, 132, *136*, 137, 156, *167*, 168–69, 235–37, *238*, 239, *241, 243*, 248, 276, *277*
repurposed furniture, 244, *245*
Ring in Christmas cd, 177, 201–02

Robarts, Thomas T., 28
Roberts, Faye, 130, *321*
Robertson, John, 38, 148
Robinson, Frances, *149*
Robinson, Harry, 118, 121, 124, 129–30, *147*, 148, *149*, *150*, 151–52
Robinson, Jaye, 135, 153
Robinson, John R., 147–48
Robinson, Mary, 152–53
Robinson, Shirley, 50
Robinson, Stony, 153
Robinson, Thomas, 152–53
Rochefort, William C., 273–74
Rockin' Ringers, *200*, 201, *325*
Ross, Alexandra, 195, *196*
Ross, Marshall, 195, *196*
Roth, David, 177
Russel, Dunbar, 73, 135, *321*, *322*
Russel, Sandy, *322*

S
saddlebag preachers, 265–66
St. Andrews Golf Course, 300
St. George's Anglican Church, 39
St. James, 131, 134, 266–69, 271–72
St. John's Chorale, 177
St. John's grand piano, 242, 244, 248, *249*
St. John's Norway Anglican Church, 34, 38
St. John's Shaughnessy, 118, 121, 124, 130, 149, 152
St. John's York Mills (SJYM)
    historical overview, 259–60, 264, 269–71

in pictures, *24*, *29*, *36*, *128*, *133*, *136*, *237*, *238*, *245*, *256*, *262*, *270*, *274*, *275*, *276*, *277*, *281*, *316*, *318*
St. Leonard's, 254
St. Mary's Anglican Church, 39, 42
St. Nicholas Anglican Church, 36
St. Paul's Anglican Church (Halifax), 34, 120–21
St. Thomas' Church (Newfoundland), *72*, 75, 93
Salmon, Beverley, *160*, *321*
Sandars, Richard, 28
Sandy Bay school project, *252*
Sanson, Alexander L., 28, 273, 275
Sathi, Chantal, *145*
Sathi, Charlene, *192*
Sathi, Para, *256*, *322*
Sathi, Shiam, *146*, *215*, *323*
Saunders, Mardi, *215*
Saynor, Bill, 48, 55, 60, 62, 73
Scadding, Henry, 268
Scanlon, Phelan, 55, 68, 83
Scott, Ted, 80–81
Second World War, 47–48, 57–58, 111, 138–39, 216–17
service broadcasts, 36, 46
services
    in the basement, 241, *242*
    Blessing of the Animals, *97*
    Christmas, 95
    Gathering, *127*, 182, *182*, 234
    Gospel Vespers, 87, 180
    Holy Week, 94

introduction of, 84

opening, 275–76

rededication, *138*, *157*, *247*

Remembrance Day, 86, *87*

Sacred Table, 140, 250

thanksgiving, 83, 101–02, 255–56

The Open Door, 140, 250

times, 88, 117, 125, 140, 170, 250

Sexton, Harold, 59

Shearer, Barbara, *142*

Shepard, Catherine, 127, 269, 278, 279, *303*, 304

Shepard, Joseph, 127, 269, 278, *303*

Sheppard, Paul, 274

Shim, Chris, *320*

Shim, Nancy, *324*

Shone, Jamie, *198*

Shone, Susan, 202

Silent Movie Nights, 98

silver objects, 166

Simpson, Henry, 218

Simpson, Bruce Napier, Jr., 51, 171–72, 292, 293–94

Sing and Ring, 203–05

Sirianni, Giovanna, *256*

Sisters of St. John the Divine, 46

Smith, James B. (*The Apprenticeship Series*), 144

Smith, Jonny, *182*

Smith, Pamela, *142*, 215, *322*

Smith, Pat, *146*, *323*

Smith, Randy, 90

Snell, Bruce, *213*, *321*

Snell, John, sketch of SJYM, *29*

Spooktacular costume fundraiser, *178*

Squire, Blanche, 281

Squire, John P., 162, 229, *280*, *281*, 282

stained glass windows, 48, 56, 246

Stanley, Susan, 82

Stephenson, Pat, *324*

Stephenson, Tracy, 195, *196*

Stewart, Heather, 56

Stewart, Ian, 56

Stong, Marian, 287

Stott, John R.W., 149, *150*, 153

Strachan, John, 83, 104, 122, 124, 237, 255, 267, 269, 270–71, 273, 275, 298

Strading, Leslie E., *237*

Strang, Boni, 178, *179*, 202, 204, *211*

Strong, John, 280

Stuart, George O., 268, 269

Sunday school, *61*

Sutherland, Suzanne, *256*

Syrian refugee crisis, 252

T

Taylor, E.P., 32, 47–48

Taylor, Tim, *160*, *251*, 252, *253*, *254*, *256*, *322*

The Book of Alternative Services, 78–79, 117

The Book of Common Prayer, 117, 124

The Family Portrait, 116

"The Forum", 140

The Founding of Halifax (C.W. Jefferys), *292*

"The House Where Prophets Speak", 183

The Old Soldier (Walter Allward), 218, *219*

things we didn't have, 26–27

This is... episode, 203

Thompson, E.G., *32*

Thompson, Walter, 128

Thornton, Diane, *160*

Tisdall, Diana, 248–49

Tonight, Everywhere Is Bethlehem cd, 183

Trew, Archibald L. G., 28, 285

Tryanor, Tom, 234

Tully, Alan, 236

Tunnell, Arthur, 229–30

Turcot, Jane, *320*

Tuttle, John, 187

Tutu, Desmond, *98*

200th Anniversary, 162, 176, 183, 214, 254–55

2016 Doors Open Toronto, *170*

Tyrell, Herbert, 291

V

Valliere family, 313

van Nostrand, Arthur J., 110, 310

van Nostrand, Cornelius, 110, 309

van Nostrand, Cornelius II, 273–74, 309–10

van Nostrand, Elsie, 288

van Nostrand, Innes, 173

van Nostrand, John, 229, 306, 310

van Nostrand, Katherine, 287

van Nostrand, Kathleen, 288

van Nostrand, Louisa, 288

van Nostrand, Mary, 279

van Nostrand, Nora. *See* Wedd, Nora

van Nostrand, Peter, 173

Vancouver (BC), *196*

vestry meetings, 82, 89, 106, *135*, *136*, 138, 171–72, *247*

Vimy Ridge memorial, *139*, 216, *217*, 219, *220*, *221*, *222*, *223*, 224–25

Visitation and Response Programs, 44, 54, 80, 130

W

Walker, Jane, *53*

Walker, Kelly, 66

Warrington, Paul, *142*, *322*

Way, Guggi, *160*

Way, Keith, *160*

Way, Kevin, *198*

Way, Steven, 195, *196*

Webbe, Henry C., 28

Wedd, Basil, 111, 288

Wedd, Nora, 110–11, *112*, *113*, 170, 287–88

Wedd, William, 111

weddings, *31*, 52, *53*

Welcome Back Sunday, *142*

welcome ministry, 131–32, *146*

West, Clara, 290–91

White, David A., *322*

White, Elizabeth, *322*, *326*

White, Jane, *160*, *215*

White, Maurice, 55, 68, 84, 174–76, 178, 204

White, Patrick, 157, 234

Williams, Bruce, 55, *66*, 100–101, *154*, *155*, *156*, 244

Williams, Jan G., 155, 202, 244

Williams, Ted, *322*

Willson, Margaret, 279

Wilson, Bill, 84

Wilson, John, 304

Wilson, Marg, 84

Winter, Kim, *196*

Wismath, Peter, *196*, *198*, 199

women's groups, 55, 208, *209*, 210–11,
     213, 285
     See also Lychgate Group

women's retreats, *146*

Wood, Elizabeth Wyn, 291

Woodside, Blake, *136*, 239, *324*

Woodside, Don, *115*

Woodside, Fraser, *115*

Worship Band, *182*, 189, *192*, 234, *324*

Wotton, Sally Armour, 55, *66*, 95, *115*,
     116, 200

Y

yachts, 59–60

Yarker, John, *146*, *323*

Yonge Street, *88*, 132–33, 134, 228–29,
     230, *231*, 261–62, 272

York Mills Baptist Church manse, *263*

York Mills Centre, *87*

York Mills community, 13, 53, 60–61,
     261–64, 268

York Mills Rd., 263, 298

York Mills Valley, 263, *298*

York Ridge Rd., 297

York-Trillium, 53

Yorkminster Heights, 299

Yu, Patrick, 13–14, 122, 137, 158, *160*

ABOUT THE AUTHORS

SCOTT KENNEDY

Scott grew up on land that was once part of the St. John's York Mills clergy reserve. As a teen, he attended dances in the auditorium at St. John's York Mills.

He was born to Royal Canadian Navy veteran Peter Raymond Kennedy and Barbara Elizabeth Kennedy (née Thompson), who worked as a "bomb girl" at Research Enterprises in Leaside during WWII. The bungalow that the young couple built in 1949 in York Mills stayed in the family for more than sixty-five years.

Scott pursued a career in music, performing all over North America and in Toronto venues as varied as Massey Hall and the Gerrard Tavern. He joined his father's children's-wear business in the late 1970s and worked there until the company was sold in 1994. Scott continued to work as a musician. He has served as a director on the boards of the Toronto Vegetarian Association and Animal Alliance of Canada.

Through it all, Scott has been compiling stories and photographs from the rural edge of Toronto that he knew as a child. His first book, *Willowdale: Yesterday's*

Farms, Today's Legacy, was published by Dundurn Press in 2013. The next book in his series on the farms of North York, titled *Don Mills: From Forests and Farms to Forces of Change*, was published in 2016.

Scott and his partner Anne Livingston live with two rescued cats — and all the wildlife the backyard can handle — in a Heritage Conservation district they helped create in the Beaches.

JEANNE HOPKINS

Jeanne Hopkins has spent most of her life in the historic Henry Farm community of North York — an area bounded by Don Mills, Sheppard Avenue, and the 401. Her first career was as a teacher and she later worked at the North York Public Library for twenty-seven years. Her specialty was the Canadiana department with a focus on the history of North York. Her responsibilities included the organization of the historical files and responding to patrons' requests for information on the past.

Jeanne has been writing constantly for many years — articles for radio stations, as well as the *Bayview Post* and the *Town Crier* newspapers in Thornhill and Richmond Hill. She has published five books on local history: about Henry Farm, Oriole; York Mills Heights; Jackson's Point (where she lived for five years); and Bayview Village.

Jeanne is a member of the North York and North Toronto Historical Societies, the York Pioneer and Historical Society, and the Society for the Preservation of Historic Thornhill. She is now retired, but still lives in the area and continues to write. Her current project is a book about the John McKenzie House in Willowdale — the headquarters of the Ontario Historical Society.